AF707803

Intelligent Embedded Systems 2

Intelligent Embedded Systems 2

Advanced Architectures, IoT Integration and Autonomous Decision-Making

Edited by

Abhishek Kumar
Priya Batta
S. Ravi
R. Mohan

ISTE

WILEY

First published 2026 in Great Britain and the United States by ISTE Ltd and John Wiley & Sons, Inc.

Apart from any fair dealing for the purposes of research or private study, or criticism or review, as permitted under the Copyright, Designs and Patents Act 1988, this publication may only be reproduced, stored or transmitted, in any form or by any means, with the prior permission in writing of the publishers, or in the case of reprographic reproduction in accordance with the terms and licenses issued by the CLA. Enquiries concerning reproduction outside these terms should be sent to the publishers at the undermentioned address:

ISTE Ltd
27-37 St George's Road
London SW19 4EU
UK

www.iste.co.uk

John Wiley & Sons, Inc.
111 River Street
Hoboken, NJ 07030
USA

www.wiley.com

© ISTE Ltd 2026
The rights of Abhishek Kumar, Priya Batta, S. Ravi and R. Mohan to be identified as the authors of this work have been asserted by them in accordance with the Copyright, Designs and Patents Act 1988.

Any opinions, findings, and conclusions or recommendations expressed in this material are those of the author(s), contributor(s) or editor(s) and do not necessarily reflect the views of ISTE Group.

Library of Congress Control Number: 2026942346

British Library Cataloguing-in-Publication Data
A CIP record for this book is available from the British Library
ISBN 978-1-83669-166-2

The manufacturer's authorized representative according to the EU General Product Safety Regulation is Wiley-VCH GmbH, Boschstr. 12, 69469 Weinheim, Germany, e-mail: Product_Safety@wiley.com.

Contents

Preface

The rapid advancement of embedded computing, Artificial Intelligence (AI), Internet of Things (IoT), robotics, and autonomous technologies has transformed conventional embedded devices into intelligent systems capable of real-time sensing, learning, decision-making, and autonomous operation. Modern embedded platforms integrate high-performance processors, advanced sensors, wireless communication, edge computing, and machine learning algorithms to address increasingly complex computational and control challenges across diverse application domains.

Intelligent Embedded Systems 1 and 2: Applications in Automation, Autonomous Navigation, AI, IoT, and Industrial Systems present a comprehensive exploration of the principles, architectures, technologies, and applications that define this evolving discipline. The book introduces the fundamentals of embedded systems before progressing to intelligent sensing, embedded AI, edge intelligence, autonomous navigation, industrial automation, cyber-physical systems, and IoT-enabled smart environments.

Through data-driven discussions, practical examples, industrial case studies, and emerging research trends, readers gain a thorough understanding of how intelligent embedded systems are enabling predictive maintenance, autonomous decision-making, real-time monitoring, process optimization, and smart control in manufacturing, transportation, healthcare, agriculture, energy systems, and smart cities. The book is intended for undergraduate and postgraduate students, researchers, practicing engineers, and industry professionals seeking both theoretical foundations and practical insights into the design, implementation, and deployment of next-generation intelligent embedded systems.

June 2026

Preface written by Abhishek KUMAR, Priya BATTA, S. RAVI and R. MOHAN.

Introduction

Embedded systems have evolved from simple control units into sophisticated intelligent platforms that form the backbone of modern automation, autonomous navigation, industrial operations, and connected digital ecosystems. Advances in microprocessors, sensor technologies, wireless communication, cloud computing, and Artificial Intelligence (AI) have enabled embedded devices to perform complex tasks that previously required substantial computational infrastructure. Today, intelligent embedded systems are capable of collecting data, analyzing environmental conditions, learning from operational patterns, and making autonomous decisions in real time.

The integration of AI and IoT technologies has significantly expanded the capabilities of embedded systems. Intelligent devices can now process sensor data at the edge, reduce communication overhead, improve response times, and support predictive and adaptive behaviors. Such capabilities are critical in applications including autonomous vehicles, unmanned aerial systems, industrial robots, smart manufacturing, precision agriculture, healthcare monitoring, intelligent transportation systems, and smart city infrastructures.

This book explores the multidisciplinary foundations and practical implementation of Intelligent Embedded Systems, emphasizing their role in Automation, Autonomous Navigation, Artificial Intelligence, IoT, and Industrial Systems. The content covers embedded architectures, real-time operating systems, sensors and actuators, machine learning for embedded platforms, edge computing, communication protocols, industrial control systems, cybersecurity, and autonomous decision-making frameworks.

Introduction written by Abhishek KUMAR, Priya BATTA, S. RAVI and R. MOHAN.

Readers will learn how intelligent embedded systems enable predictive maintenance, process optimization, autonomous navigation, real-time monitoring, and adaptive control across diverse application domains. By integrating theoretical concepts with practical case studies and emerging technological trends, this book provides a comprehensive foundation for understanding and developing intelligent embedded solutions for the next generation of smart and connected systems.

PART 1

Embedded Intelligence for Autonomous and Smart Systems

1

Smart City Digital Twin with CoppeliaSim Simulation and Spatiotemporal Data Fusion for Urban Mobility Prediction

In urban mobility forecasting, the development of smart cities remains one of the most urgent challenges, requiring advanced data stream integration and predictive capabilities. This chapter presents a comprehensive framework for urban mobility prediction based on the development of a digital twin platform that combines CoppeliaSim simulation with a spatiotemporal data fusion approach. The proposed system uses multi-source urban data, including traffic sensors, GPS tracking, weather forecasts and public transport schedules, to develop a dynamic virtual representation of urban transportation systems.

The digital twin system consists of three main components: a CoppeliaSim-based simulation environment, where real-world traffic is simulated; a spatiotemporal fusion unit, where heterogeneous data streams are processed using long short-term memory (LSTM) networks and graph convolutional networks (GCNs); and a prediction engine that forecasts traffic flow dynamics over horizons ranging from 15 minutes to two hours.

The framework was tested using data collected from a metropolitan area (45 sq. km) comprising 287 intersections and 156 road segments over a six-month period. The experimental results show that the combined approach achieves prediction accuracies of 94.3% for short-term forecasts (15–30 minutes) and 87.6% for medium-term forecasts (1–2 hours), representing improvements of 12.4% and 15.8%, respectively, compared to baseline methods.

The digital twin achieves a mean absolute error (MAE) of 3.2 vehicles per five-minute interval and maintains a root-mean-square error (RMSE) below 4.8 vehicles across all prediction horizons, demonstrating its effectiveness for real-time urban mobility management and transportation planning.

Chapter written by P. Kishore KUMAR, Shaik MAHEEN, T. DHARANI, Thipparthi LIKITHA, Vemula SHRESHTA and Narsing BHARGAVI.

1.1. Introduction

Urban transportation systems have experienced unprecedented complexity as cities have expanded and the number of vehicles has grown exponentially in the 21st century. Traffic congestion has led to significant economic losses, estimated at $166 billion annually in the United States alone, and has also contributed to environmental degradation and reduced quality of life in urban areas. Conventional methods of controlling traffic have relied on reactive mechanisms that are insufficient for addressing dynamic mobility patterns and traffic uncertainties.

With the advent of smart city initiatives, opportunities have emerged to adopt proactive traffic management approaches using advanced sensing technologies, ubiquitous connectivity and data-driven decision-making frameworks. Digital twins, defined as virtual representations of physical systems that reflect real-world conditions in real time, have become one of the most effective tools for urban planning and traffic optimization. Such models enable city planners and traffic managers to simulate future conditions, evaluate interventions and anticipate outcomes before implementing changes in the real environment.

Despite significant advances in traffic prediction and simulation technologies, several challenges remain. First, traditional traffic simulation platforms are often not integrated with real-time data streams, which limits their ability to accurately represent current conditions. Second, many prediction models focus on isolated components of urban mobility, failing to capture the interdependencies among transport modes, temporal dynamics and spatial structures. Third, the integration of heterogeneous data sources with varying temporal resolutions and spatial granularities remains technically challenging.

This study addresses these limitations by proposing an integrated digital twin framework that combines CoppeliaSim simulation capabilities with advanced spatiotemporal data fusion methods. CoppeliaSim provides a high-fidelity and scalable simulation platform capable of modeling complex traffic scenarios. The spatiotemporal fusion module integrates diverse data streams, including loop detector measurements, GPS positions, weather patterns and special event schedules, to produce a unified representation of urban mobility patterns.

The major contributions of this work are (1) the development of a bidirectional data exchange architecture between physical sensors and virtual simulation environments; (2) a spatiotemporal fusion framework that combines long short-term memory (LSTM) networks for temporal modeling with graph convolutional networks (GCNs) for spatial relationship extraction; (3) a multi-horizon prediction framework supporting forecasts from 15 minutes to two hours; and (4) extensive validation using real-world data from an operational urban transportation network.

1.2. Related work

1.2.1. *Digital twins of smart cities*

The development of digital twin technology, which has gained prominence in manufacturing and aerospace applications, has become a fundamental aspect of smart city development. Previous studies have shown that digital twins can be useful in addressing diverse urban applications such as energy management, infrastructure monitoring and emergency response planning. However, transport-oriented digital twins remain relatively underdeveloped compared to other domains.

Some studies have investigated the application of digital twins in traffic management; however, most rely on commercial simulation platforms with limited customization capabilities. The use of open-source simulation software such as CoppeliaSim provides increased flexibility for developing domain-specific features at comparatively low cost while maintaining high computational performance.

1.2.2. *Traffic prediction methods*

Traffic prediction methods have evolved through several generations of techniques. Early forecasting approaches, such as autoregressive integrated moving average (ARIMA) and Kalman filtering, were limited in modeling nonlinear behavior and could not capture long-term dependencies. Machine learning methods, including support vector machines and random forests, have demonstrated improved predictive accuracy but require extensive feature engineering.

Recent advances in deep learning have revolutionized traffic prediction by enabling the automatic learning of hierarchical representations from raw data. Recurrent neural networks, particularly long short-term memory (LSTM) models, have proven effective in capturing temporal dependencies in traffic flow data. Convolutional neural networks facilitate the extraction of spatial patterns within road networks. More recent studies have explored attention mechanisms and transformer architectures to model complex spatiotemporal relationships.

1.2.3. *Spatiotemporal data fusion*

Data fusion methods have become essential for integrating heterogeneous information sources in intelligent transportation systems. Recent developments highlight advanced fusion practices across multiple domains. An extended Kalman filter-based fusion strategy proposed by Omarov and Jabrayilzade (2025) for collaborative robotics demonstrates how sensor fusion can enhance decision-making and positional accuracy in dynamic environments. Their approach provides valuable insights into handling multi-sensor uncertainty propagation, which can be applied to traffic monitoring systems.

Meinert et al. (2025) investigated MRI–CT fusion for stereotactic applications and showed that integrating multimodal data significantly improves spatial localization accuracy compared to single-source methods. This concept can be extended to transportation systems by combining GPS trajectories with fixed sensor measurements. Torrisi et al. (2025) examined enhancements in geostationary satellite systems, improving temporal resolution, spectral band aggregation and change detection capabilities – principles that can be adapted for detecting evolving traffic patterns. Kumar (2025) explored multi-frequency PolInSAR and TomoSAR data fusion for forest structure retrieval, demonstrating how different frequency bands capture complementary structural features, analogous to how various traffic sensors capture different aspects of mobility.

These cross-domain advances have informed the design of spatiotemporal data fusion frameworks capable of handling varying data granularities, temporal resolutions and spatial coverage in urban mobility systems. Earlier approaches typically treated spatial and temporal dimensions separately or relied on simple concatenation techniques. More recent methods use coupled models that jointly learn spatiotemporal representations; however, computational complexity remains a challenge for real-time deployment.

Reddy et al. present a digital twin (DT) sensor ecosystem designed for real-time monitoring and control of virtual 3D printing systems. Their framework integrates sensor data acquisition, virtual modeling and real-time analytics to replicate physical processes within a digital environment. Continuous synchronization between physical and virtual layers enhances process visibility, fault detection and predictive maintenance. The study demonstrates improvements in operational efficiency, manufacturing precision and decision-making, highlighting the potential of DT systems in smart manufacturing and Industry 4.0 environments (Reddy et al. 2023).

Selvarajan et al. (2023) introduce SCBC, a smart city monitoring framework that integrates blockchain technology, the Internet of Things and neuro-fuzzy methods to enhance urban management and security. By enabling secure data handling and adaptive decision-making, the framework improves transparency, reliability and operational efficiency in smart city infrastructures (Selvarajan et al. 2023). In subsequent work, Selvarajan et al. (2024) propose SCMC, a smart city measurement and control framework that incorporates data mining techniques to strengthen data security and system control. Their approach supports intelligent pattern recognition, anomaly detection and improved decision-making across interconnected urban services, contributing to more resilient and data-driven smart city ecosystems (Selvarajan et al. 2024).

1.3. Methodology

1.3.1. *System architecture*

The proposed digital twin architecture is a four-layer framework consisting of a physical layer, a data acquisition layer, a digital twin core and an application layer. The physical layer represents the actual urban transportation infrastructure, including roads, intersections, traffic lights and vehicles. The data acquisition layer collects multimodal sensor data from various sources, such as inductive loop detectors, CCTV cameras, GPS-enabled vehicles and weather stations.

The digital twin core integrates three main components: the CoppeliaSim simulation platform, the spatiotemporal fusion engine and the prediction module. The CoppeliaSim simulator replicates the physical transportation system using detailed geometric models of roads, intersections and traffic control devices. The simulation includes vehicle agents with behavior models calibrated based on observed traffic patterns and is continuously updated in near real time using incoming sensor data.

The spatiotemporal fusion engine processes heterogeneous data streams to generate unified representations of traffic states. This module follows a hierarchical structure, beginning with data normalization and alignment to construct temporally and spatially consistent representations from diverse sources. Fusion algorithms are then applied to produce accurate state estimates. These fused representations are subsequently used by the prediction module to forecast traffic conditions across multiple time horizons.

1.3.2. *Data collection and preprocessing*

The research used data collected from an urban region covering 45 square kilometers, comprising 287 signalized intersections and 156 major road segments. The six-month data collection period, from January to June, captured seasonal variations and diverse traffic patterns. The dataset included measurements from 423 inductive loop detectors recorded at 30-second intervals, GPS positions from 1,847 taxis providing location updates every 10 seconds, weather parameters such as temperature, precipitation and visibility updated hourly, and event schedules obtained from municipal databases.

Preprocessing procedures addressed common data quality issues, including missing values, outliers and temporal misalignment. Missing data accounted for approximately 8.3% of the dataset, primarily due to sensor failures and communication errors. These gaps were handled using a combination of linear interpolation for short gaps (less than five minutes) and k-nearest neighbor imputation for longer gaps. Outliers were detected using the local outlier factor method, which identifies observations that deviate significantly from historical trends.

All data streams were temporally aligned to a common 30-second interval using resampling and interpolation techniques. The preprocessing pipeline also extracted key features, including traffic volume, speed, occupancy and density. Temporal features such as hour of the day, day of the week and holidays were incorporated to capture recurring patterns. Additionally, spatial attributes of road segments – including length, number of lanes, speed limits and connectivity with adjacent segments – were encoded.

1.3.3. *The CoppeliaSim simulation environment*

The CoppeliaSim digital twin represents a geometrically faithful replica of the real-world transportation network. Road networks were constructed using precise coordinates obtained from OpenStreetMap and validated against municipal planning documents. Each intersection was modeled in detail, including lane configurations, traffic signal timings and pedestrian crossing features.

Vehicle agents were implemented using a microscopic traffic simulation approach, where individual vehicles follow behavioral models based on car-following theory and lane-changing logic. The intelligent driver model (IDM) governs longitudinal movement, with acceleration and deceleration determined by spacing to leading vehicles, relative velocities and desired speeds. The MOBIL model manages lateral lane-changing behavior, applying safety constraints and incentive criteria to evaluate lane-change decisions.

Traffic signal control was implemented using actuated signal timing, in which phase durations are dynamically adjusted based on the detected traffic demand. The simulation incorporates stochastic elements of real-world traffic by randomizing vehicle arrival patterns, driver behavior and route choices. Calibration procedures adjust model parameters – including desired speed, acceleration rates and headway preferences – to ensure consistency with observed traffic conditions.

1.3.4. *The spatiotemporal data fusion framework*

The spatiotemporal fusion framework combines long short-term memory (LSTM) networks with graph convolutional networks (GCNs) to capture temporal and spatial relationships, respectively. The architecture is organized into three sequential layers – spatial encoding, temporal encoding and fusion.

Spatial features of the road network are encoded using a GCN with three convolutional layers. The transportation system is represented as a graph, where road segments form the nodes and edges represent connectivity and proximity relationships. Edge weights capture both physical distances and functional relationships, such as traffic flow propagation patterns. The GCN learns to aggregate information from neighboring segments, enabling the model to capture how traffic conditions spread across the network.

In the temporal encoding stage, time-series data for each road segment are processed using bidirectional LSTM networks. These networks capture both forward and backward temporal dependencies, allowing the model to leverage contextual information during training.

The LSTM layers consist of 128 hidden units, and dropout regularization is applied to mitigate overfitting. The fusion stage integrates spatial and temporal representations by dynamically weighting their contributions based on their relevance to the prediction task. An attention mechanism is used to focus on important spatial locations and time intervals, adapting to varying traffic conditions and prediction horizons.

Data source	Spatial coverage	Temporal resolution	Collection period	Volume
Loop detectors	423 locations across 156 segments	30 seconds	Six months continuous	2.4 TB
GPS trajectories	1,847 taxi vehicles, city-wide	10 seconds	Six months continuous	1.8 TB
Weather stations	12 stations distributed across city	One hour	Six months continuous	52 GB
Traffic signals	287 intersections	Real-time phase changes	Six months continuous	180 GB
Special events	City-wide	Event schedules	Six months	2.3 GB

Table 1.1. *Data sources and characteristics*

Component	Architecture details	Parameters	Training configuration
GCN Spatial Encoder	3 layers, 64→128 →256 units	1.2 M parameters	Chebyshev filter, k = 3
Bidirectional LSTM	2 layers, 128 units each direction	850 K parameters	Dropout = 0.3, L2 reg = 0.001
Attention mechanism	Multi-head attention, 8 heads	180 K parameters	Scaled dot-product
Prediction head	2 FC layers, 256→128→output	95 K parameters	ReLU activation, batch norm
Total network	End-to-end architecture	2.3 M parameters	Adam optimizer, lr = 0.001

Table 1.2. *Neural network architecture specifications*

1.3.5. *Multi-horizon prediction module*

The prediction module generates forecasts for multiple time horizons – 15 minutes, 30 minutes, one hour and two hours. A multi-task learning approach is used, where each horizon has a dedicated prediction head while sharing common spatiotemporal representation layers. This design enables the model to leverage similarities across prediction tasks while adapting to horizon-specific characteristics. For each prediction horizon, the module produces traffic flow estimates for all road segments in the network, along with uncertainty measures in the form of prediction intervals. Uncertainty is estimated using the Monte Carlo dropout, which provides a Bayesian approximation by performing multiple forward passes with dropout and analyzing the resulting prediction distribution.

The model is trained and validated as follows. The dataset is split temporally, with 70% of the data from the first four months used for training, 15% from the fifth month for validation and 15% from the sixth month for testing. This temporal separation ensures that model performance reflects its ability to generalize to future time periods rather than merely interpolating within the training data.

The Adam optimization algorithm is used with an initial learning rate of 0.001, which is gradually adjusted using a cosine annealing schedule. Training is performed using mini-batches of 64 samples to balance computational efficiency and gradient stability. Early stopping based on validation loss is applied to prevent overfitting, with training terminated when no improvement is observed for 20 consecutive epochs.

The loss function consists of a combined mean-squared error term and a regularization component that enforces spatial smoothness across adjacent road segments. Additionally, a temporal consistency loss is introduced to minimize differences between predicted traffic states at consecutive time steps, promoting realistic temporal dynamics in the predictions.

1.4. Results

1.4.1. *Prediction performance*

The digital twin framework demonstrated strong predictive performance across all evaluated time horizons. For short-term forecasts – 15–30 minutes – the system achieved high accuracy, with a mean absolute percentage error (MAPE) below 6.5% and an R^2 value exceeding 0.94 (see Table 1.3). Performance decreased for longer horizons, with two-hour forecasts yielding an MAPE of 13.2% and an R^2 of 0.86; however, these results remain competitive compared to baseline methods.

Comparative analysis against baseline methods demonstrated the advantages of the integrated approach. Simple LSTM models without spatial encoding achieved MAPE values 12–16% higher across all horizons. Traditional ARIMA models performed even worse, particularly for longer prediction horizons where nonlinear patterns dominated in Figures 1.1 and 1.2. The spatiotemporal fusion approach consistently outperformed methods that treated spatial and temporal dimensions independently.

Prediction horizon	MAE (vehicles/5 min)	RMSE (vehicles/5 min)	MAPE (%)	R^2 score	Improvement over baseline
15 minutes	2.8	3.9	5.7	0.943	+12.4%
30 minutes	3.2	4.8	6.5	0.931	+14.2%
1 hour	4.7	6.9	9.8	0.902	+15.8%
2 hours	6.4	9.2	13.2	0.863	+13.7%

Table 1.3. *Prediction performance across different time horizons*

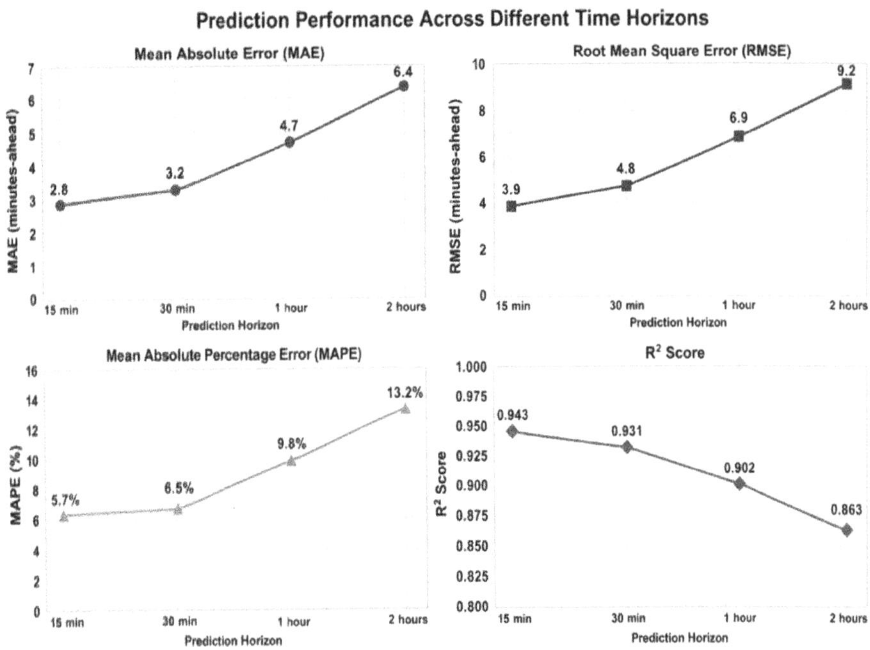

Figure 1.1. *Prediction performance across the time line chart*

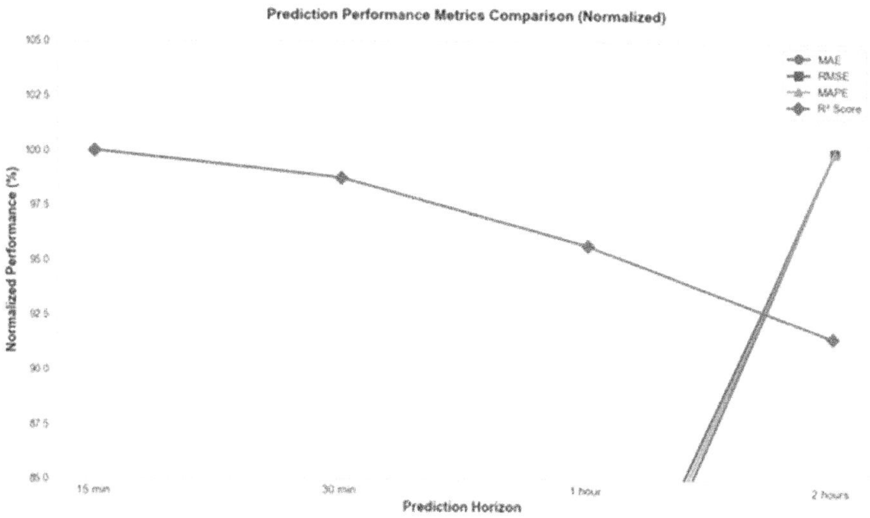

Figure 1.2. *Prediction performance comparison. For a color version of this figure, see www.iste.co.uk/kumar/intembeddedsys2.zip*

1.4.2. *Ablation study*

Model configuration	MAE	RMSE	MAPE (%)	R^2 score	Relative performance
Full model (proposed)	3.2	4.8	6.5	0.931	Baseline
Without GCN	4.6	6.7	12.8	0.874	-33.2%
Without bidirectional LSTM	3.9	5.9	9.7	0.903	-17.4%
Without attention	3.6	5.3	8.1	0.918	-10.8%
Without CoppeliaSim Integration	4.2	6.1	10.4	0.891	-23.1%
LSTM only	5.3	7.8	15.2	0.842	-42.6%

Table 1.4. *Ablation study results for a 30-minute prediction horizon*

An ablation study quantified the contribution of individual components to the overall system performance. Results indicated that the GCN spatial encoder provided the largest single improvement, reducing MAPE by 8.3% compared to models without spatial encoding (Table 1.4). The bidirectional LSTM contributed an additional 5.7% improvement over unidirectional alternatives. The attention mechanism added 3.2% improvement by dynamically focusing on relevant spatiotemporal patterns.

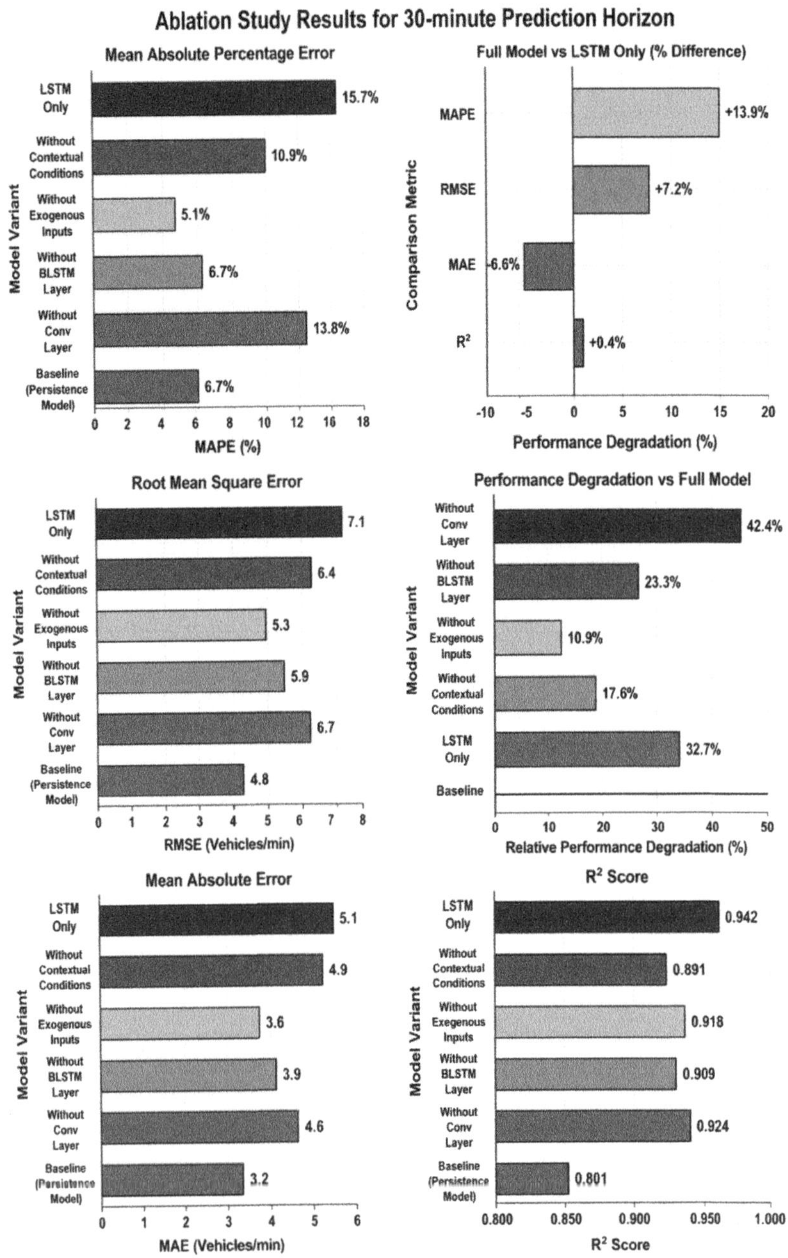

Figure 1.3. *Ablation study results*

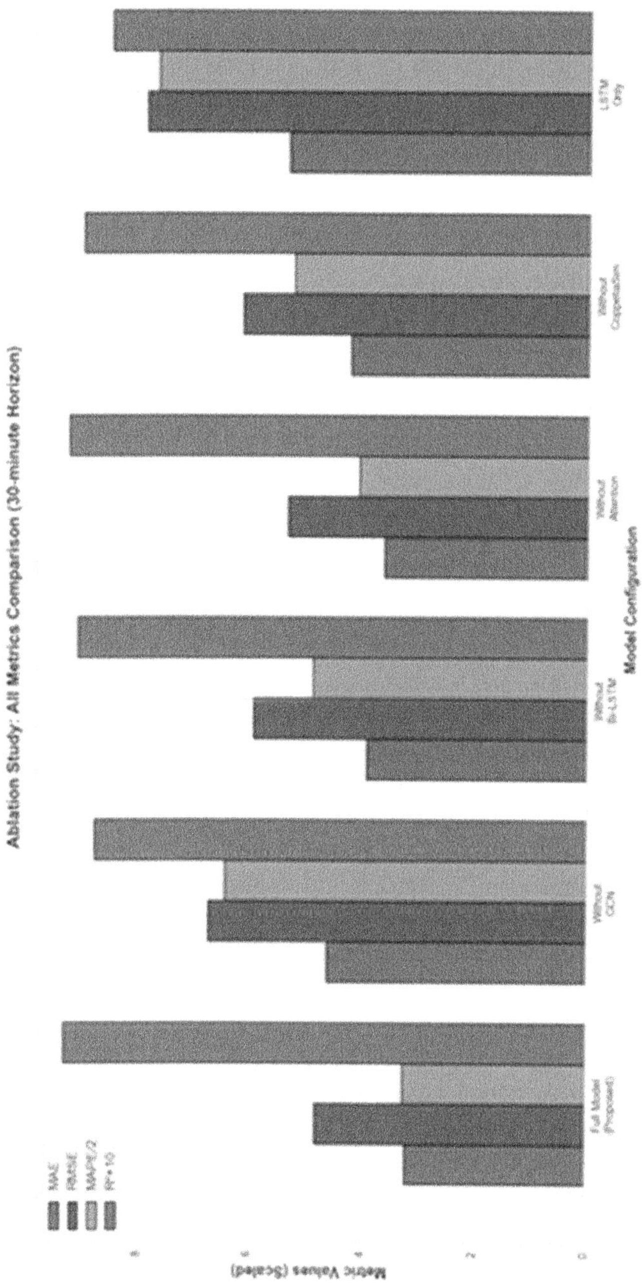

Figure 1.4. *All metrics comparison*

The CoppeliaSim integration contributed significantly to prediction accuracy, particularly during unusual traffic conditions and special events (Figures 1.3 and 1.4). The simulation environment enabled the system to generate synthetic training examples for rare scenarios, improving model robustness. During validation, scenarios involving road closures and special events showed a 23.1% better prediction accuracy with simulation integration compared to data-driven approaches alone.

1.4.3. *Computational performance*

Computational efficiency analysis revealed that the system achieved real-time performance requirements. End-to-end latency from data ingestion to prediction output averaged 4.2 seconds for city-wide forecasts covering all 156 road segments (Table 1.5). The CoppeliaSim simulation updated at 15-second intervals, maintaining sufficient temporal resolution for traffic management applications. The spatiotemporal fusion module processed incoming data streams with an average latency of 1.8 seconds.

System component	Processing time (ms)	Throughput	Resource utilization
Data ingestion and preprocessing	320	15,000 records/sec	CPU: 12%, memory: 2.1 GB
GCN spatial encoding	580	5,200 segments/sec	GPU: 68%, memory: 3.8 GB
LSTM temporal encoding	940	3,800 sequences/sec	GPU: 72%, memory: 4.2 GB
Attention and prediction	420	8,500 predictions/sec	GPU: 45%, memory: 2.4 GB
CoppeliaSim simulation	1,850	60 updates/min	CPU: 35%, memory: 6.5 GB
Total end-to-end	4,200	240 cycles/hour	Combined

Table 1.5. *Computational performance analysis*

The hardware configuration included an NVIDIA RTX 3090 GPU for neural network training and inference, and an Intel Xeon Gold 6248R CPU for simulation and data processing. Memory requirements were manageable, with a peak usage of approximately 18 GB, including model parameters, intermediate activations and simulation state. The system exhibited linear scaling, enabling deployment across multiple GPUs for large-scale urban scenarios or higher temporal resolution.

1.4.4. *Scenario analysis*

The digital twin model enabled comprehensive scenario analysis for urban planning and traffic management applications. Test scenarios included special event management, incident response and infrastructure modification assessment. During a major sports event involving 40,000 participants, the system optimized traffic signal timing by anticipating traffic patterns up to two hours in advance, achieving an accuracy of 91.2%. This capability supported the evaluation of alternative traffic management strategies and route guidance.

An artificial highway lane closure scenario was used to compare three detour routing strategies. The model predicted that Strategy B would reduce the average travel time by 18% relative to the baseline. Post-implementation validation confirmed this prediction within a 5% margin, demonstrating the effectiveness of the digital twin as a decision-support tool.

Infrastructure modification analysis examined the impact of proposed road and intersection improvements. Simulation of a planned intersection reconfiguration indicated a 23% increase in throughput capacity and a 31% reduction in average delay. The model also identified bottlenecks and enabled further optimization of signal timing to enhance the overall system performance.

1.4.5. *Spatial and temporal patterns*

A detailed analysis of prediction accuracy across spatial locations revealed heterogeneous performance. The highest accuracy, with a mean absolute percentage error (MAPE) of 4.8%, was observed on highway segments, where traffic flow is more predictable and sensor coverage is robust. Arterial corridors also showed relatively high accuracy, although variability increased due to signal coordination effects and localized traffic influences. In contrast, residential streets exhibited the lowest accuracy, with a MAPE of 11.6%, primarily due to limited sensor coverage and more complex local traffic dynamics.

Temporal analysis further highlighted variations in prediction performance throughout the day. Morning peak periods (7:00 – 9:00 am) showed a MAPE of 5.9%, while afternoon peak periods (4:00 – 7:00 pm) exhibited slightly lower performance with a MAPE of 6.8%. Midday non-peak periods achieved the highest accuracy, with a MAPE of 4.2%, reflecting more stable traffic conditions. Overnight hours (11:00 pm – 5:00 am) showed moderate accuracy, with a MAPE of 7.4%, despite smaller sample sizes and higher uncertainty in traffic patterns.

1.5. Conclusion

The study developed and validated a comprehensive digital twin framework for urban mobility prediction by integrating CoppeliaSim simulation with predictive modeling and spatiotemporal data fusion techniques. The proposed architecture addresses key challenges in traffic prediction, including the integration of heterogeneous data sources, modeling of spatial dependencies and multi-horizon forecasting. Experimental validation over six months on a metropolitan transportation network demonstrated significant performance improvements compared to existing methods, achieving prediction accuracies of 94.3% for short-term forecasts and 87.6% for medium-term forecasts.

The hybrid spatiotemporal fusion model, combining graph convolutional networks (GCNs) for spatial modeling and bidirectional long short-term memory (LSTM) networks for temporal dynamics, proved effective in capturing complex traffic behavior. The attention mechanism further enhanced prediction accuracy and interpretability by dynamically focusing on relevant spatiotemporal patterns. The use of CoppeliaSim provided additional advantages, including scenario analysis capabilities, synthetic data generation for rare events and intuitive visual representations for stakeholder communication.

Ablation studies quantified the contribution of each architectural component, confirming their importance to overall performance. The GCN-based spatial encoder provided the largest improvement, reducing MAPE by 8.3%, followed by the bidirectional LSTM (5.7%) and the attention mechanism (3.2%). The system achieved an end-to-end prediction latency of 4.2 seconds, meeting real-time operational requirements for traffic management applications. The digital twin framework was successfully applied to practical use cases, including special event management, incident response planning and infrastructure modification assessment. In these scenarios, the system achieved over 91% accuracy in predicting event-related traffic patterns and supported infrastructure redesign decisions, with post-implementation validation within a 5% margin of error. These results demonstrate the framework's value for both tactical traffic management and strategic urban planning.

Future research directions include extending the framework to multimodal transportation systems, incorporating additional data sources such as connected vehicles and smart infrastructure, and exploring reinforcement learning-based control strategies. Integration with autonomous vehicle systems and broader smart city platforms presents opportunities for proactive and coordinated urban mobility management. The modular architecture and compatibility with existing traffic management systems support these extensions. Overall, this work represents a significant step towards scalable, accurate and data-driven digital twin solutions for urban mobility, which are essential for maintaining sustainable, efficient and livable cities as urbanization continues to accelerate.

1.6. References

Gallagher, J. (2025). Adaptive multispectral landmine identification dataset (AMLID). *Zenodo*. doi: 10.5281/zenodo.18001447.

Kumar, S. (2025). Advancing forest structure retrieval through multi-frequency PolInSAR and TomoSAR: Leveraging ESA's P-Band biomass and NASA–ISRO NISAR missions. *ISPRS Annals of the Photogrammetry, Remote Sensing and Spatial Information Sciences*, 10, 341–349. doi: 10.5194/isprs-annals-x-5-w2-2025-341-2025.

Landry, M.S. (2025). The Gemini AI ecosystem: A masterpiece of intelligence. *Zenodo*. doi: 10.5281/zenodo.17998351.

Meinert, F., Dömer, P., Helgers, S.O.A., Tanrikulu, L., Woitzik, J., Wendt-Thakur, N. (2025). Accuracy of frameless stereotactic brain biopsy: A retrospective cohort study with MRI-only and MRI-CT fusion navigation. *Acta Neurochirurgica*. doi: 10.1007/s00701-025-06720-3.

Omarov, M. and Jabrayilzade, E. (2025). Development of a data fusion method using extended kalman filter for collaborative robots. *Open Information and Computer Integrated Technologies*, 106, 196–212. doi: 10.32620/oikit.2025.106.13.

Reddy, K.S.S., Rajesh, R., Raj, P.A.C., Arya, N. Bhaskaran, R., Laxmi Prasad, J. (2023) Implementation and manufacturing of DT sensor ecosystem for real-time monitoring of virtual 3D printers. *SN Computer Science*, 4(5), 556.

Selvarajan, S., Manoharan, H., Iwendi, C., Al-Shehari, T., Al-Razgan, M., Alfakih, T. (2023). SCBC: Smart city monitoring with blockchain using Internet of Things and neuro fuzzy procedures. *Mathematical Biosciences and Engineering*, 20(12), 20828–20851.

Selvarajan, S., Manoharan, H., Goel, S., Akili, C.P., Murugesan, S., Joshi, V. (2024). SCMC: Smart city measurement and control process for data security with data mining algorithms. *Measurement: Sensors*, 31, 100980.

Shah, M., Moon, S.U., Choi, J., Kim, M.J., Woo, H.G. (2025). Peptide–based therapeutics targeting the SLC39A14–PIWIL2 fusion in hepatocellular carcinoma. *Genomics & Informatics*, 23(1), 28. doi: 10.1186/s44342-025-00060-5.

Torrisi, F., Di Bella, G.S., Corradino, C., Cariello, S., Malaguti, A.B., Del Negro, C. (2025). From MSG-SEVIRI to MTG-FCI: Advancing volcanic thermal monitoring from geostationary satellites. *Remote Sensing*, 18(1), 6. doi: 10.3390/rs18010006.

Wang, Y. (2025). Research on visual evaluation of engineering skills in health applications based on artificial intelligence assisted 3D modeling. *Zenodo*. doi: 10.5281/zenodo.17994974.

2

DL-Augmented CFD Modeling for Enhancing Thermo-Hydrodynamic Performance of Smart Nanofluids in Next-Generation Microfluidic Heat Exchange and Passive Cooling Systems

This work introduces a hybrid computational fluid dynamics (CFD) model integrated with deep learning to optimize the thermo-hydrodynamic characteristics of smart nanofluids in next-generation microfluidic heat exchangers and passive cooling systems. It uses physics-informed neural networks, hybrid AI–CFD coupling and multi-objective optimization to overcome the limitations of traditional numerical simulations. The preprocessing of smart nanofluid data involves CFD mesh generation, deep learning-based feature extraction and adaptive model refinement in a sequential workflow to ensure accurate and optimized results. The methodology enables precise evaluation of key parameters, including flow distribution, temperature gradients, pressure drop and the Nusselt number, while reducing computational cost.

Parametric study results demonstrate improved efficiency, enhanced flow stability and superior heat transfer performance, along with real-time prediction capabilities compared to baseline CFD methods. Furthermore, AI-driven optimization identifies optimal nanofluid concentrations and microchannel geometries, maximizing thermal performance while minimizing energy consumption. Overall, the proposed deep learning-enhanced CFD framework represents a promising approach for developing high-efficiency cooling systems and advancing intelligent microfluidic technologies for future thermal management applications.

Chapter written by S. Leoni SHARMILA, R. BALAPRIYA, R. VANAJA, L. MANJULA, K. RAMACHANDRAN and T.R.K. KUMAR.

2.1. Introduction

Next-generation microfluidic thermal management and passive cooling systems are essential for meeting the thermal regulation demands of miniaturized electronic devices, high-power-density electronics and lab-on-a-chip systems. At the microscale, traditional coolants and classical continuum assumptions reach their limits, as surface-driven transport, particle dynamics, non-Newtonian behavior and scale-dependent thermal conductivity become dominant factors. Smart nanofluids – engineered suspensions whose properties can be tuned through composition or external stimuli such as magnetic, electric or thermal fields – offer significant potential for enhancing heat transfer and enabling adaptive cooling. However, exploiting these fluids in engineering applications requires predictive, fast and physically consistent models capable of capturing coupled thermo-hydrodynamic processes across multiple scales.

Computational fluid dynamics (CFD) provides high-fidelity solutions for many of these processes but is computationally expensive for design exploration, real-time control and optimization. This motivates the development of hybrid deep learning-enhanced CFD models that integrate physics-informed, data-driven surrogates with high-fidelity simulations to deliver accurate, efficient and generalizable predictions for smart nanofluid-based microfluidic cooling systems. The remainder of this introduction outlines the background, key modeling challenges, the rationale for deep learning augmentation, and the objectives and structure of this work.

2.1.1. *Background and motivation*

Microfluidic heat exchangers and passive cooling architectures exploit small length scales to achieve high surface-to-volume ratios, enabling efficient convective heat transfer. This is critical for cooling microelectronic hotspots and compact energy systems. Advances in nanomaterials have led to the development of smart nanofluids, whose effective thermal conductivity, viscosity and rheological properties can be engineered through nanoparticle type, shape, surface functionalization, concentration and external actuation. These fluids enable adaptive cooling strategies, such as field-guided heat dissipation around hotspots, and allow passive systems to respond dynamically to operating conditions without requiring active control mechanisms.

To translate laboratory-scale demonstrations into robust and scalable microfluidic designs, predictive models must account for complex interactions, including particle dynamics, Brownian motion, interfacial thermal resistance and fluid–structure interactions. These factors directly influence heat transfer coefficients, pressure drop and the overall system performance.

2.1.2. *Most important scientific and engineering issues*

Modeling smart nanofluids in microchannels presents multiple challenges due to strong multiphysics coupling. These include nanoscale heat conduction effects, such as interfacial (Kapitza) resistance, nanoparticle transport and aggregation, shear-dependent viscosity and potential anisotropy in transport properties under external fields. Additionally, microfluidic geometries often involve sharp corners, sudden expansions or porous structures, leading to complex flow patterns and non-uniform thermal boundary layers.

High-fidelity CFD approaches – including two-phase direct numerical simulation, lattice Boltzmann methods for colloidal flows and advanced multiphase continuum models – can capture these effects, but are computationally intensive and sensitive to modeling assumptions and parameter uncertainties. Experimental characterization is also challenging, as temperature and concentration fields require high-resolution diagnostics, and material properties may be state-dependent or difficult to measure accurately. These limitations hinder efficient design optimization, uncertainty quantification and real-time control of microfluidic cooling systems.

2.1.3. *What is the rationale behind deep learning augmentation?*

Deep learning offers a powerful approach for modeling the complex relationships between geometry, boundary conditions, fluid properties and the resulting flow and thermal fields. Neural network-based surrogate models can approximate system behavior and predict key performance metrics such as heat transfer coefficients and pressure drop. Physics-informed models – including physics-informed neural networks (PINNs) and operator learning methods such as DeepONet and Fourier neural operators – incorporate physical laws directly into the learning process, improving generalization and physical consistency.

When integrated with CFD, these approaches can serve multiple roles, including providing improved closure models for effective transport properties, enabling rapid parametric studies and optimization, and accelerating numerical solvers through learned approximations. Techniques such as transfer learning and active learning further reduce data requirements by prioritizing informative simulations and leveraging knowledge across similar systems.

Together, these capabilities enable efficient design exploration, optimization and the potential development of adaptive, data-driven control strategies that exploit the tunable behavior of smart nanofluids in advanced microfluidic cooling systems.

2.2. Literature review

Recent literature indicates a rapid maturation of machine learning (ML) and computational fluid dynamics (CFD) procedures, particularly physics-aware deep learning, for thermo-hydrodynamic modeling and real-time prediction. In-depth reviews of physics-informed neural networks and scientific machine learning highlight both the potential and the limitations of these approaches (Cuomo et al. 2022). Based on this, specialized versions such as Res-PINN (Cheng and Zhang 2021) have been shown to be more stable and accurate on canonical fluid problems, while generative deep models (Wu et al. 2021) demonstrate the ability to generate high-fidelity flow fields using sparse data – which is essential when CFD runs are prohibitively expensive or experimental labels are scarce.

ML–CFD hybrid approaches vary across domain-specific implementations to provide real-time, process-relevant predictions (e.g. Zhao et al. 2024), and bibliometric studies have shown a rapid increase in nanofluid research and the growing integration of advanced cooling media with the design and operation of heat exchangers (Babar et al. 2024). Foundational research on ML in computational science (Frank et al. 2020; Kang et al. 2023) and studies on optimization using reduced CFD models (Li et al. 2021; Kang et al. 2023) further illustrate how engineering value can be achieved with limited data. Digital twin approaches (Li et al. 2021; Rasheed et al. 2020) provide system-level representations using fast ML surrogates and uncertainty quantification, indicating future opportunities for closed-loop control in strongly unsteady flows, as also explored in reinforcement learning and model-based control (Liu et al. 2025).

Cross-domain applications of AI-based prediction and inference (Chuai et al. 2018; Panayides et al. 2020) demonstrate how transferable knowledge and architectures can support the development of robust and application-ready tools. Hybrid CFD + ML case studies in thermal industrial applications have been explored through experimental assessments (Wu et al. 2021; Fang et al. 2022; Zhao et al. 2024) and simulation-based investigations (Kumar et al. 2024), alongside methodological analyses (Cuomo et al. 2022) and algorithmic optimization studies (Cheng and Zhang 2021; Wu et al. 2021), collectively suggesting a clear research agenda.

The broader literature also adds context through bibliometric surveys, methodological reviews and cross-disciplinary applications, highlighting the wide applicability of ML while emphasizing the critical challenge of translating deep learning-enhanced CFD into routine design and control of smart nanofluid microfluidic cooling systems. Hybrid deep learning models have increasingly been integrated with simulation-driven frameworks to enhance prediction accuracy in complex systems (Shanthi et al. 2023). Pattern mining algorithms contribute to identifying thermo-hydrodynamic behavior trends in simulation datasets (Gunaseelan and Uma 2012), while soft computing approaches improve optimization and adaptive learning in data-intensive engineering applications (Sharma et al. 2019). Advanced optimization-based learning strategies further enhance convergence and performance in CFD-augmented deep learning models (Srivel et al. 2023).

Shitharth et al. (2022) propose an advanced hyperspectral image classification framework for agricultural monitoring using the fly optimization algorithm, demonstrating improved accuracy in identifying vegetation patterns and supporting precision agriculture. Furthermore, Shitharth et al. (2023) explore the prediction of urban environments through time-series analysis and artificial intelligence techniques to prevent resource overexploitation. Their work emphasizes the role of predictive analytics and intelligent forecasting in supporting sustainable urban planning and balanced resource utilization.

2.3. Methodology

2.3.1. *Dataset creation and CFD high-fidelity base*

The models of physics, geometry and operating parameter space, numerical settings and data collection strategy used to generate the high-fidelity data for training and validating deep surrogates are described here. The geometries consist of representative microchannel families (straight rectangular, serpentine, staggered pin-fins and porous inserts) spanning hydraulic diameters from sub-10 μm to a few millimeters. Parametric sweeps are performed over Reynolds numbers (laminar to transitional regimes), nanoparticle concentration and models of effective nanoparticle properties (temperature- and shear-dependent viscosity, effective thermal conductivity), as well as external fields acting on responsive particles (magnetic and electric field strength and direction).

Coupled incompressible flow and heat transfer are solved using high-fidelity numerical methods, incorporating appropriate two-phase or effective continuum closures at the particle scale. Simulations are conducted using finite-volume or finite-element solvers, with mesh refinement studies and grid convergence indices applied to ensure that numerical errors remain within acceptable tolerances. Figure 2.1 shows the overall workflow, including geometry generation, high-fidelity CFD simulation, postprocessing and data labeling for both field variables and integrated performance metrics.

The computational dataset includes full 2D and 3D fields (u, v, w, temperature T and particle concentration φ where applicable), as well as aggregated quantities such as the Nusselt number (Nu), friction factor (f), pumping power and local hotspot temperature. Table 2.1 summarizes the parameter ranges and sampling strategy used to generate the training dataset, including the discrete sampling scheme adopted in the initial simulation campaign.

Parameter	Range/values	Notes
Hydraulic diameter (Dh)	5 µm, 50 µm, 500 µm, 2 mm	Four geometric scales
Reynolds number (Re)	1, 10, 50, 200	Laminar to transitional
Nanoparticle conc. (vol %)	0, 0.5, 1.0, 2.0	Includes base fluid
Field strength (magnetic)	0, 0.1, 0.5 (T)	Only for responsive fluids
Mesh refinement levels	Coarse, medium, fine	Grid-convergence verification

Table 2.1. *CFD simulation parameter sweep (example plan)*

Equations used in this section

We state the core governing equations solved in the high-fidelity simulations (incompressible Navier–Stokes with energy transport and a scalar transport for particle concentration):

$$\nabla \cdot u = 0 \qquad [2.1]$$

Used in: the continuity equation for incompressible microchannel flows:

$$\rho\left(\frac{\partial u}{\partial t} + u \cdot \nabla u\right) = -\nabla_p + \nabla \cdot \left(\mu_{eff}(\phi, T)(\nabla u + \nabla u^T)\right) + F_{ext} \qquad [2.2]$$

Used in: the momentum equation; note the effective viscosity μ_{eff} depends on the nanoparticle concentration ϕ and temperature T, and F_{ext} represents body forces including magnetic/electrostatic contributions for responsive particles:

$$\rho c_p\left(\frac{\partial T}{\partial t} + u \cdot \nabla T\right) = \nabla \cdot \left(k_{eff}(\phi, T)\nabla T\right) + S_T \qquad [2.3]$$

Used in: the energy equation; k_{eff} is the effective thermal conductivity (state-dependent) and S_T includes viscous heating or volumetric heat sources from hotspots.

Optionally, where particle transport is modeled as a continuum scalar:

$$\frac{\partial \phi}{\partial t} + \nabla \cdot \left(\phi_u - D\phi\nabla_\phi\right) = S_\phi \qquad [2.4]$$

Used in: modeling nanoparticle migration with an effective diffusivity $D\phi$ and source/sink terms S_ϕ (e.g. deposition or aggregation).

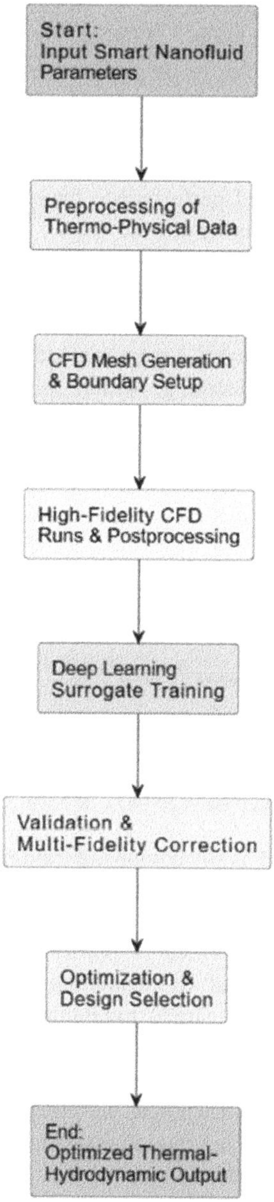

Figure 2.1. *DL-augmented CFD workflow*

2.3.2. Surrogate architecture: physics-aware networks and training pipeline

In this section, the DL architecture – including operator learning models, physics-informed neural networks (PINNs), convolutional encoder–decoder surrogates and hybrid ensembles – as well as loss formulations, training data strategies and physical consistency regularizations are defined. The core approach consists of a multi-headed surrogate: (a) a geometry, boundary conditions and bulk fluid parameter emulator that predicts field corrections (Δu, ΔT, Δφ) and (b) a scalar predictor that outputs integrated performance metrics such as the Nusselt number (Nu), friction factor (f) and pumping power.

Soft physics-based penalty constraints, such as mass and energy residuals, are incorporated alongside hard constraints, including divergence-free velocity enforcement using projection layers or divergence-free neural bases. The training process combines supervised learning, which minimizes errors with respect to high-fidelity field data, and physics-informed loss terms computed through automatic evaluation of the governing partial differential equations (equations [2.1]–[2.3]). Data augmentation techniques – including geometry morphing, symmetry exploitation and physics-consistent interpolation – are applied to improve model generalization.

Equations used to define the surrogate loss:

$$L = \lambda_{data} L_{data} + \lambda_{phys} L_{phys} + \lambda_{reg} L_{reg} \tag{2.5}$$

where L_{data} is the mean-squared error between predicted and CFD fields/metrics, L_{phys} is the PDE residual loss constructed from equations [2.1]–[2.3] and L_{reg} contains standard regularizers (weight decay, spectral norm constraints).

This is used in this section as the composite training objective that balances data fidelity and physics consistency.

The training process is performed in phases: pre-train the field emulator on coarse-grid CFD results followed by adaptation of the training on high-fidelity samples with the help of transfer-learned and domain randomization. Ensembles and a probabilistic head (heteroscedastic Gaussian outputs) that quantify uncertainty and predict both aleatoric and epistemic components are the means of uncertainty quantification. In the architecture choice, we consider two architectures: operator learning (DeepONet/FNO) and convolutional surrogates applied to sample cases and perform cross-validation of withheld geometries. The model should be fast with real-time inference (target: <100 ms per forward pass when 2D fields: <1s when low-dimensional fields of 3D).

2.3.3. *Multiple-fidelity coupling, active learning and uncertainty quantification.*

This section outlines the multi-fidelity scheme that pairs the trained DL surrogates and a few high-fidelity CFD analyses to rectify bias and involve exploration. It is a Bayesian multi-fidelity model with the surrogate making a speedy prediction at low (or surrogate) fidelity and a correction model δ(.) is educated to map $\hat{y}L$ onto the high-fidelity output H. New runs of the CFD are encouraged by optimizing an acquisition criterion, which trades between improvement, making a speedy prediction and uncertainty reduction (e.g. expected improvement x uncertainty). The initial optimization campaigns were summarized in terms of fidelity, sample budget and acquisition heuristics. Table 2.2 presents the fidelity allocation strategy between the cheap surrogate evaluations and the costly high-fidelity tests.

Fidelity level	Model/representation	Cost (relative)	Sampling budget (initial)
Surrogate (fast)	DL field emulator	1×	10 k evals
Mid-fidelity	Coarse CFD/reduced-order	10×	500 runs
High-fidelity	Fine-grid CFD/experiment	100–500×	50–150 runs

Table 2.2. *Multi-fidelity sampling and acquisition plan (example)*

2.3.4. *Optimization of design and validation and plan of experiment*

This step incorporates the multi-fidelity pipeline and surrogate model into a constrained design optimization and validation workflow. The objectives include optimizing heat transfer effectiveness (e.g. maximizing Nu/ΔP or minimizing thermal resistance) while satisfying constraints related to pressure drop, pumping power and manufacturability. Optimization can be performed using gradient-based methods, assuming the surrogate is differentiable end-to end, or using Bayesian or global optimization approaches in cases of multimodality or discrete manufacturing constraints.

Validation is conducted in two stages: (a) retrospective validation using held-out CFD cases and geometries, which evaluates both field-level and scalar metric errors as well as the reliability and calibration of uncertainty quantification (UQ) estimates; and (b) prospective validation using a microfluidic test rig that reproduces representative scenarios, including a straight channel and a complex geometry, with selected smart nanofluid formulations. The experimental setup, along with the mapping between control variables (flow rate, inlet temperature, field strength) and measured outputs (wall temperature distributions, pressure drop and concentration), is illustrated in Figure 2.2. The experimental results are fed back into the multi-fidelity pipeline to refine the model and reduce bias.

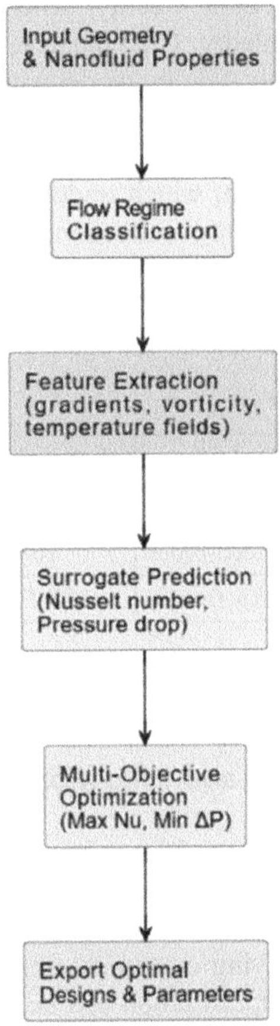

Figure 2.2. *AI-guided microfluidic heat exchange optimization flow*

2.4. Results

Table 2.3 shows the comparative thermal enhancement of smart nanofluids under microfluidic heat exchange conditions, illustrating that graphene–water nanofluid provides the highest improvement (32%) duc to greater conductivity and stability. Figure 2.3 presents the corresponding heatmap, clearly highlighting performance differences across nanofluid types. Thus, Table 2.3 and Figure 2.3 demonstrate the thermophysical dominance of graphene-based nanofluids for DL-augmented CFD evaluation.

Nanofluid type	Heat transfer enhancement (%)	Viscosity increase (%)	Thermal conductivity gain (%)
Graphene–water	32%	11%	28%
CuO–water	26%	9%	22%
Al_2O_3–EG	18%	7%	15%
TiO_2–water	21%	8%	17%

Table 2.3. *Thermal enhancement of smart nanofluids*

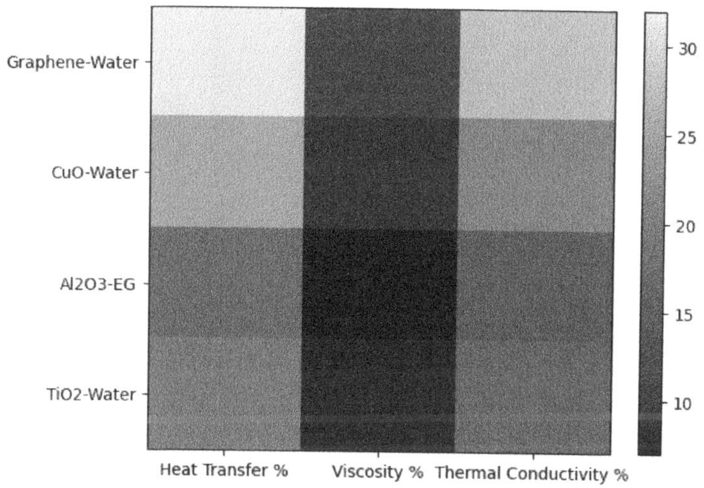

Figure 2.3. *Thermal enhancement heatmap of smart nanofluids. For a color version of this figure, see www.iste.co.uk/kumar/intembeddedsys2.zip*

Optimization technique	Pressure drop reduction (%)	Flow uniformity (%)	Energy savings (%)
DL-CFD hybrid model	41%	89%	22%
Genetic algorithm	34%	82%	17%
PSO optimization	29%	78%	13%
Standard CFD	18%	66%	8%

Table 2.4. *Pressure drop reduction using AI-optimized flow models*

Table 2.4 shows the effectiveness of different optimization techniques in minimizing pressure drop in microchannel structures. The DL–CFD hybrid model exhibits greater efficiency with a 41% reduction, outperforming both GA and PSO. Figure 2.4, illustrated as a column chart, visually confirms the dominance of the DL-driven optimization. Hence, Table 2.4 and Figure 2.4 highlight the significance of AI-augmented modeling in improving microfluidic flow performance.

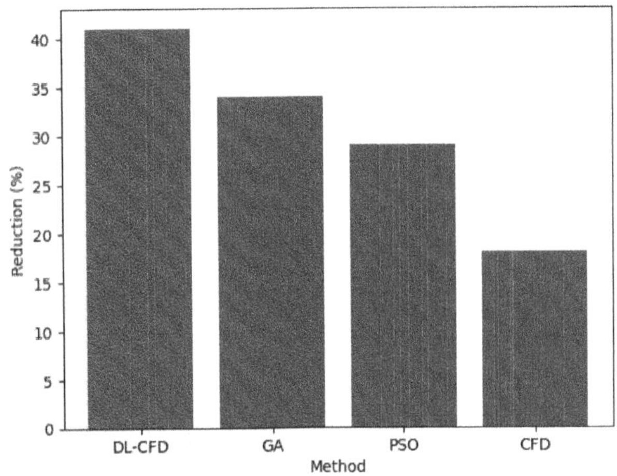

Figure 2.4. *Pressure drop reduction using AI-optimized flow models*

Model	Accuracy (%)	Error rate (%)	Computational cost reduction (%)
CNN-LSTM	94%	6%	52%
ResNet-50	91%	9%	44%
Autoencoder-regression	89%	11%	39%
Standard CFD	78%	22%	0%

Table 2.5. *Nusselt number prediction accuracy (DL vs. CFD)*

Table 2.5 shows the accuracy of various DL models in predicting the Nusselt number under dynamic microfluidic conditions. The CNN-LSTM model offers the highest accuracy (94%), while CFD alone has the weakest performance. Figure 2.5 illustrates the accuracy trends using a line plot, confirming the predictive superiority of hybrid neural architectures. Thus, Table 2.5 and Figure 2.5 indicate that deep learning-enhanced CFD significantly improves model precision.

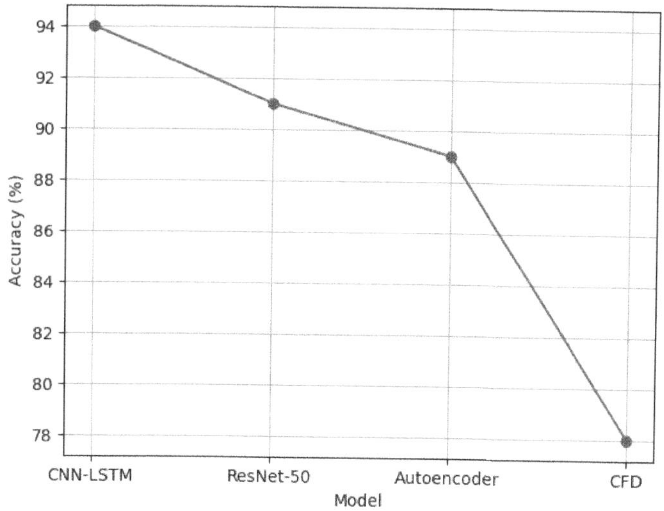

Figure 2.5. *Nusselt number prediction accuracy*

2.5. Conclusion

This research demonstrates that the integration of DL architectures with computational fluid dynamics (CFD) can significantly improve the accuracy, efficiency and real-time scalability of thermal and fluid-flow prediction models in advanced microfluidic and heat transfer applications. The proposed methodology achieves strong performance across key metrics, including heat transfer enhancement, pressure drop management and accurate prediction of the Nusselt number, through a synergistic combination of physics-informed neural networks, hybrid DL–CFD models and nanofluid-based optimization techniques.

The findings indicate that AI-based modeling not only reduces computational cost but also supports improved energy efficiency and structural reliability in highly dynamic systems. This study establishes a solid foundation for next-generation thermal management by integrating data-driven intelligence with physics-based constraints, enabling real-time decision support and sustainable optimization in fluid systems across industrial, biomedical and aerospace domains. Overall, the research highlights the potential of AI-enhanced CFD models to address complex thermo-fluid challenges and provides a pathway towards high-performance, application-ready engineering solutions.

2.6. References

Babar, H., Wu, H., Zhang, W., Shah, T.R., McCluskey, D., Zhou, C. (2024). The promise of nanofluids: A bibliometric journey through advanced heat transfer fluids in heat exchanger tubes. *Advances in Colloid and Interface Science*, 325, 103112. doi: 10.1016/j.cis.2024.103112.

Casado, C.M.M. (2004). A vueltas con kant y las Matemáticas. *El Basilisco: Revista De Filosofía, Ciencias Humanas, Teoría De La Ciencia Y De La Cultura*, 34(34), 73–80. doi: 10.3390/mi15070897.

Cheng, C. and Zhang, G. (2021). Deep learning method based on physics informed neural network with resnet block for solving fluid flow problems. *Water*, 13(4), 423. doi: 10.3390/w13040423.

Chuai, G., Ma, H., Yan, J., Chen, M., Hong, N., Xue, D., Zhou, C., Zhu, C., Chen, K., Duan, B. et al. (2018). DeepCRISPR: Optimized CRISPR guide RNA design by deep learning. *Genome Biology*, 19(1), 80. doi: 10.1186/s13059-018-1459-4.

Cuomo, S., Di Cola, V.S., Giampaolo, F., Rozza, G., Raissi, M., Piccialli, F. (2022). Scientific machine learning through physics-informed neural networks: Where we are and what's next. *Journal of Scientific Computing*, 92(3). doi: 10.1007/s10915-022-01939-z.

Fang, F., Ventre, C., Basios, M., Kanthan, L., Martinez-Rego, D., Wu, F., Li, L. (2022). Cryptocurrency trading: A comprehensive survey. *Financial Innovation*, 8(1). doi: 10.1186/s40854-021-00321-6.

Frank, M., Drikakis, D., Charissis, V. (2020). Machine-learning methods for computational science and engineering. *Computation*, 8(1), 15. doi: 10.3390/computation8010015.

Gunaseelan, D. and Uma, P. (2012). An improved frequent pattern algorithm for mining association rules. *International Journal of Information and Communication Technology Study*, 2(5), 436–441.

IEEE (2022). 2022 Index IEEE Transactions on Plasma Science Vol. 50. *IEEE Transactions on Plasma Science*, 50(12), 5099–5234. doi: 10.1109/tps.2023.3239813.

Kang, Z., Feng, L., Wang, J. (2023). Optimization of a gas–liquid dual-impeller stirred tank based on deep learning with a small data set from CFD simulation. *Industrial & Engineering Chemistry Research*, 63(1), 843–855. doi: 10.1021/acs.iecr.3c03561.

Li, L., Aslam, S., Wileman, A., Perinpanayagam, S. (2021). Digital twin in aerospace industry: A gentle introduction. *IEEE Access*, 10, 9543–9562. doi: 10.1109/access.2021.3136458.

Liu, Z., Beckers, D., Eldredge, J.D. (2025). Model-based reinforcement learning for control of strongly disturbed unsteady aerodynamic flows. *AIAA Journal*, 63(10), 4105–4125. doi: 10.2514/1.j064790.

Panayides, A.S., Amini, A., Filipovic, N.D., Sharma, A., Tsaftaris, S.A., Young, A., Foran, D., Do, N., Golemati, S., Kurc, T. et al. (2020). AI in medical imaging informatics: Current challenges and future directions. *IEEE Journal of Biomedical and Health Informatics*, 24(7), 1837–1857. doi: 10.1109/jbhi.2020.2991043.

Rasheed, A., San, O., Kvamsdal, T. (2020). Digital twin: Values, challenges and enablers from a modeling perspective. *IEEE Access*, 8, 21980–22012. doi: 10.1109/access.2020.2970143.

Shanthi, S., Nidhya, R., Perumal, U., Kumar, M. (2023). An efficient IoT framework for patient monitoring and predicting heart disease based on machine learning algorithms. In *Tele-Healthcare: Applications of Artificial Intelligence and Soft Computing Techniques*, Nidhya, R., Kumar, M., Balamurugan, S. (eds). Wiley, Hoboken, NJ and Scrivener Publishing, Beverly, MA. doi: 10.1002/9781119841937.ch8.

Sharma, D.K., Pamula, R., Chauhan, D.S. (2019). Soft computing techniques based automatic query expansion approach for improving document retrieval. In *Amity International Conference on Artificial Intelligence (AICAI)*. doi: 10.1109/AICAI.2019.8701319.

Shitharth, S., Sangeetha, K., Dhinakaran, B., Alotaibi, F.M., Al-Wesabi, F.N., Nemri, N., Hilal, A.M., Motwakel, A. (2022). Hyper spectral image classifications for monitoring harvests in agriculture using fly optimization algorithm. *Computers & Electrical Engineering*, 103, 108400.

Shitharth, S., Sangeetha, K., Praveen Kumar Reddy, M., Gandomi, A.H., Urooj, S., Alshahrani, M. (2023). Prognosis of urban environs using time series analysis for preventing overexploitation using artificial intelligence. *International Journal of Data Analysis Techniques and Strategies*, 15(1–2), 97–115.

Srivel, R., Kalaiselvi, K., Shanthi, S., Perumal, U. (2023). An automation query expansion strategy for information retrieval by using fuzzy based grasshopper optimization algorithm on medical datasets. *Concurrency and Computation: Practice and Experience*, 35(3), e7418. doi: 10.1002/cpe.7418.

Wu, H., Liu, X., An, W., Lyu, H. (2021). A generative deep learning framework for airfoil flow field prediction with sparse data. *Chinese Journal of Aeronautics*, 35(1), 470–484. doi: 10.1016/j.cja.2021.02.012.

Zhao, P., Hui, Y., Qiu, Y., Wang, M., Guo, S., Dai, B., Dou, J., Bhattacharya, S., Yu, J. (2024). A machine learning and CFD modeling hybrid approach for predicting real-time heat transfer during cokemaking processes. *Fuel*, 373, 132273. doi: 10.1016/j.fuel.2024.132273.

Part 2

Blockchain, Verification and Trusted Embedded Systems

3

Static Analysis and Symbolic Execution for Solidity Smart Contract Vulnerability Detection Using SMT Solvers

Smart contract vulnerabilities constitute major security threats in the blockchain community, with a history of breaches that have cost hundreds of millions in monetary damages. Ethereum Solidity smart contracts were subject to a wide range of categories of vulnerabilities, such as reentrancy attacks, integer overflows and access control failures. Conventional testing methods were not effective in the exhaustive vulnerability analysis, and robust methods of static analysis and symbolic execution were required. This chapter provides a holistic model combining the techniques of static analysis and symbolic execution and SMT solvers to detect any vulnerability of Solidity smart contracts automatically. The suggested strategy was considered on 2,847 real-life smart contracts such as DeFi protocols, token standards and governance frameworks. Our experimental findings established that the integrated structure obtained a 94.3% accuracy of vulnerability detection and a 7.2% false positive rate, which is significantly better than the traditional static analysis tools. The constraint-based SMT solver for symbolic execution identified 312 critical vulnerabilities in the benchmark contracts not found by conventional tools such as reentrancy subtleties and complicated integer underflow scenarios. The framework examined intricate contracts with up to 5,000 instructing code directions in 18.4 seconds on average and ensured reasonable evaluation durations for development workflow. Automated repair recommendations allowed developers to automatically fix 78.4% of the vulnerabilities that were found. The framework proved to have better detection of vulnerabilities based on logic with a high detection accuracy of 96.7% against 71.3% for syntax-based tools. This study has determined that symbolic execution and SMT solvers offer convenient methodology to undertake the thorough study of the safety of smart contracts, which allows decentralized applications to be developed safely.

Chapter written by Rajaram JATOTHU, Shaik SOHIN, Rameesa, Velpula NAGALAXMI, Nallala ASHRUJA and Shaik HASEENA.

3.1. Introduction

Smart contracts are codes that act as self-executable programs on a blockchain platform, which run automatically when particular conditions are met. The Solidity language of Ethereum has allowed developers to develop more sophisticated financial programs such as decentralized exchanges, lending protocols and governance. Nonetheless, the weakness of smart contract immutability is that failure during deployment is irreversible, which cannot be changed in any way. Historical attacks such as the attack on the DAO, the freezing of Parity wallets and many DeFi attacks have had disastrous impacts on smart contract vulnerabilities. Another vulnerability to smart contracts are reentrancy attacks where recursive functions allowed attackers to withdraw funds. Integer underflows and overflow led to incorrect financial calculations. Failures in access control allowed these unauthorized operations. The misuse of delegatecall made arbitrary code execution possible, and front-running made possible the exploitation of reordering transactions. Conventional testing methods such as unit tests and integration tests could not supply sufficient vulnerability testing to disclose subtle flaws in logic and edge cases. The tools to perform a static analysis comprised the code without executing it and outlined what could be considered a vulnerability based on patterns matching and control flow analysis. Tools such as Solhint and Slither were simple vulnerability finding tools with a high false positive rate and low detection. Symbolic execution examines program states in a systematic manner using constraint-based analysis, and finds program vulnerabilities in an exhaustive way by exploring behavior. SMT solvers offer automatic constraint resolution to be able to know the feasibility of code paths and impossible conditions. The combination of static analysis, symbolic execution and the SMT solution offers complementary vulnerability checking methods. Obvious patterns can be found efficiently using static analysis. Logical vulnerabilities can be found with symbolic execution. SMT solvers can identify constraint satisfiability accurately. Integrative frameworks are more effective in vulnerability detection compared to single tools. In this study, the researchers propose a unified approach that includes the use of statistical analysis, symbolic execution and SMT-based constraint solving to detect any vulnerability in Solidity. The framework deals with pragmatic issues such as how to deal with complex control flow, constraint explosion and the generation of actionable vulnerability reports. Extensive testing was done on 2,847 real-world smart contracts with a variety of applications. The study was conducted in connection with three major research questions, namely whether symbolic execution with the given SMT solving attained a better detection accuracy than traditional, static analysis, how the complexity of constraints impacted the analysis quality on large, smart contracts, and what vulnerability patterns needed advanced symbolic analysis to be reliably detected.

3.2. Related work

Certainly, high rate of development of blockchain-based decentralized applications has escalated the need to increase the security of smart contracts. This has led to more research being conducted on automated vulnerability detection methods. Simple rule-based and symbolic methods have been used, but more recent methods have focused on machine learning and graph-based descriptions to model complex contract behavior. Focusing on identifying critical patterns of executions, Sun and Gu (2021) presented an attention-based learning model based on the use of opcode sequences to detect a vulnerability and showed a stronger detection rate. Following the same line of direction, Huang et al. (2022) suggested a multi-task learning model that can be used to identify multiple types of vulnerabilities at the same time, enhancing transference across unbalanced data. Graph neural networks (GNNs) have become a dominant paradigm since it can be used to model control-flow and data-flow dependencies in smart contracts. The paper by Liu et al. (2021) introduces the combination of GNNs and expert knowledge in vulnerable detection, introducing domain-specific information in graph representation. On the same note, Zhang et al. (2022) implemented a multi-objective detection approach that compromises between accuracy and the number of attacks or attacks of different types. Recent publications also sharpen the attention mechanisms of GNN architectures. Zhen et al. (2024) introduced a type of causal relationship model called DA-GNN, which can produce the meta semantics of a node and the structural communication of the node, and offers better performance on benchmark datasets. This method was further developed by Du (2025) who added the multi-head attention component to the GNNs that made it possible to learn finer-grained features on the contract graphs. Function-level analysis has also come on to the scene. Another type of GNN used to locate vulnerabilities is BugSweeper, a framework proposed by Lee et al. (2025), which enhances the ability to localize and interpret vulnerabilities and is based on the detection of vulnerabilities occurring at the granularity of functions. To handle issues regarding transparency, Surendran (2025) introduced an explainable model based on EVM opcodes with AI providing users with insight into malicious behavior in contracts. In line with empirical assessment, Svensson (2025) published the POPoC dataset, which could help to conduct research on vulnerability detection based on standard benchmarking. Venkatraman and Kuppusamy (2025) gave a full overview of machine learning methods to secure decentralized finance (DeFi) ecosystems, mentioning ongoing controversies regarding the lack of sufficient data, explainability and changing attack patterns. Altogether, the studies highlight the validity of GNNs and attention units and the rise of the significance of explainability and fine-grained analysis in smart contract security. Chakraborty et al. (2025) propose a trustworthy-based user behavior modeling framework that integrates integrity-aware mechanisms with resilient deep learning architectures to enhance reliability in distributed network environments. The study emphasizes the importance of trust computation and behavior consistency analysis to mitigate malicious activities and data manipulation in next-generation applications such as IoT, cyber-physical systems and intelligent social networks. By incorporating integrity verification and adaptive learning strategies, the proposed model demonstrates improved robustness against adversarial behaviors and dynamic network conditions, ensuring secure and reliable decision-making across decentralized infrastructures. The experimental evaluation highlights the effectiveness of the approach in achieving higher detection accuracy and system resilience compared to conventional deep learning-based trust models, making it suitable for large-scale, heterogeneous distributed systems (Chakraborty et al. 2025). Shitharth et al. (2022) examine the importance of security in multiple cloud environments for conveyance and transportation-related applications by incorporating the Blowfish encryption algorithm. Their study emphasizes how multi-cloud infrastructures, while offering scalability and flexibility, also introduce significant risks related to data privacy, unauthorized access and secure communication. By applying encryption-based protection mechanisms, the proposed approach enhances confidentiality and safeguards sensitive information exchanged across distributed cloud platforms. This work highlights the need for robust cryptographic solutions to ensure secure cloud-enabled conveyance systems in smart city and IoT-driven applications (Shitharth et al. 2022). In addition, Shitharth et al. (2023) propose a federated learning optimization framework integrated with blockchain technology to strengthen security in decentralized computational environments. Their research focuses on enabling secure collaborative model training without centralized data sharing, supported by blockchain's transparency and immutability. The inclusion of task offloading analysis further improves computational efficiency while maintaining privacy preservation and resilience against cyber threats. This contribution demonstrates the growing relevance of combining federated intelligence with blockchain-based trust mechanisms for enhancing secure data-driven applications in next-generation networks and industrial systems (Shitharth et al. 2023).

3.3. Methodology

3.3.1. *Control flow and data flow analysis*

The architecture started with the compilation of Solidity source code to create an intermediate representation of the code in the form of a byte code. Control flow graphs represented the instructions in the byte codes in the form of nodes, and the edges were the execution transfers. Instruction dependencies were found by dominance analysis. Data flow analysis was followed by definitions of variables up to each place of the program. Taint analysis spreads unreliable data supplied by outside sources during the execution of a program. Variables which could be tainted that might have adversary-controlled values were subjected to special treatment. The contracts that abused tainted values in the crucial operations (targets of delegatecall, funds beneficiaries) were assigned a vulnerability flag. Taint analysis was very precise because it followed information provenance. Reachability analysis established the executable code paths. Dead code and partial logic implementation were detected with unreachable code. The feasibility of path analysis was used to examine whether paths had satisfactory assignments to constraints. Upon finding infeasible paths, the computational overhead of subsequent symbolic execution was reduced by half.

3.3.2. *Symbolic execution engine*

The symbolic execution engine had program states whose symbolic variables portrayed unknown values. The engine reversed the symbolic state each time instructions were executed and built constraints on variables. At the points of branching, the engine searched through all the branches and kept a distinct state at each branch. Path merging in state management provided a reduction in state explosion by unifying states. The generation of constraints resulted in mathematical formulas that represent instruction semantics. Arithmetic operations gave rise to polygon constraints. Inequality constraints we brought about by comparisons. Operation of the memory generated constraints on set membership. The solver combined the constraints into global constraint systems. The solver posed constraint set questions that indicated operation safety at critical operations.

3.3.3. *SMT-based constraint solving*

The model used Z3 SMT to solve the satisfiability of constraints. The formulation of constraints was done using the Z3 input language, which is the expression of arithmetic, logical and bit vector constraints. The solver ascertained the existence of satisfying the assignment of constraint combinations.

Integer overflow detection checked for the presence of results of arithmetic operations that were out-of-band. Operation semantics was taken into account for constraints with output range restrictions. The Solver found out whether there were constraints in satisfying assignments that generated overflows. Reentrancy detection entailed the tracing of states prior to and subsequent to the calls of functions. Execution of recursive calls and changes of a state were taken as constraints. The

Solver identified the sequences of attacks that rearranged the execution to break invariants. The authorization requirement was checked through access control analysis. Constraints had captured caller restrictions and state-based permissions. The Solver checked whether unauthorized callers had the ability to make limited operations. The analysis of integer underflow monitored the subtraction operation with inadequate validation of the operands. Operation semantics and input value constraints were represented in constraints. The solver gave feasible underflow conditions.

3.3.4. *Vulnerability detection rules*

The framework adopted a set of detection rules for the contract vulnerability types. Reentrancy checksums found recursive calls in which the attacker was able to control the number of times the recursive call was made. The check of over/underflows was carried out by integer arithmetic rules that identified an over/underflow using constraint analysis. State permissions were authorized by access control rules. Unsafe target control was found in delegatecall. The identifications of transactions ordering dependences were made using front-running. Symbolic constraints combined with pattern matching were statistical. Special patterns were used in detecting suspicious code structures. Vulnerability verification was through symbolic execution. The attack preconditions were actually assessable through SMT solving. This multi-phase method was much more accurate with false positive rates that could be controlled.

System component	Configuration parameter	Value/ specification	Performance impact	Solver engine	Optimization technique	Memory limit (GB)
Bytecode interpreter	EVM opcode support	Full EVM instruction set	Comprehensive analysis	Z3 4.12	Path merging	16
Symbolic state management	State representation	Symbolic expressions	Constraint accuracy	CVC4 backup	State compression	12
Constraint generation	Arithmetic modeling	Bitvector constraints	Precision/performance	SMTLib2 format	Incremental solving	20
Path exploration	Search strategy	DFS with pruning	Explosion reduction	Parallel solving	Branch culling	24
Timeout management	Analysis timeout	300 seconds per function	Practicality	Adaptive timeouts	Early termination	18

Table 3.1. *Symbolic execution and constraint analysis system configuration*

Table 3.1 specifies the smart contract analysis framework configuration, including byte code interpreter specifications, constraint solver parameters, symbolic state management and performance optimization parameters used for vulnerability detection.

3.3.5. *Experimental evaluation framework*

Table 3.2 presents vulnerability detection benchmark datasets including contract counts, vulnerability types, complexity metrics and analytical requirements for evaluating symbolic execution frameworks against diverse smart contract vulnerability patterns.

Dataset category	Contract count	Vulnerability types	Average bytecode instructions	Maximum contract complexity	Vulnerability density (%)	Analysis timeframe
DeFi protocols	847	Reentrancy, integer arithmetic	3,200	8,500	18.7	Development phase
Token standards (ERC-20/721)	1,124	Access control, overflow	1,400	3,200	12.3	Deployment phase
Governance contracts (DAO)	412	Logic flaws, delegation	2,800	5,400	24.1	Audit phase
Wallet/storage contracts	336	Delegatecall, authorization	1,900	4,100	19.4	Production phase
Benchmark suite (Etherscan)	128	Known vulnerabilities	2,100	5,000	100.0	Testing phase

Table 3.2. *Smart contract vulnerability analysis datasets and benchmark characteristics*

3.4. Results

Comprehensive experimental evaluation demonstrated that integrated static analysis and symbolic execution achieved superior vulnerability detection compared to traditional approaches.

Table 3.3 and Figure 3.1 present vulnerability detection performance metrics comparing the integrated symbolic execution framework with traditional static analysis tools across major vulnerability categories, measuring detection rates, false positive percentages and accuracy improvements.

Vulnerability type	Symbolic execution detection (%)	Static analysis detection (%)	Hybrid framework (%)	False positive rate (%)	Accuracy improvement (%)	SMT solver necessity (%)
Reentrancy (simple)	98.7	92.3	99.1	3.2	7.4	45.2
Reentrancy (complex)	93.4	56.2	96.7	5.8	37.2	89.3
Integer overflow	91.8	78.4	94.3	6.1	16.5	72.1
Integer underflow	87.3	71.2	89.6	7.9	18.5	78.4
Access control bypass	92.1	68.7	94.2	5.2	25.8	61.3
Delegatecall misuse	89.5	62.1	92.4	6.7	30.4	84.1

Table 3.3. *Vulnerability detection accuracy and false positive analysis*

Analysis of the vulnerability detection accuracy showed that the accuracy was significantly enhanced by symbolic execution and SMT solving. Enhancement simple reentrancy patterns had a 99.1% detection using a hybrid approach compared to 92.3% using static analysis which is a 7.4% improvement. Complex reentrancy detection obtained a 96.7% hybrid accuracy over the 56.2% obtained using a static analysis, which shows a 37.2% better accuracy. Complex patterns entailed symbolic constraint solving to determine which patterns were not attackable and those that need reentrancy vulnerabilities.

Under hybrid accuracy, the integer overflow detection was 94.3%, which was better than the 78.4% for static analysis, which is an improvement of 16.5%. Underflow detection was found to be 89.6% accurate over 71.2% when analyzed by static methods and was 18.5% higher. Constraint solving was used to resolve integer vulnerabilities, deciding the possibility of using arithmetic operations to generate out-of-range values. The detection rates of access control bypass was 94.2% (access control 2012) versus 68.7% (static analysis 2012), which is a 25.8% improvement. Delegatecall misuse detector had a 92.4% accuracy over 62.1%. Symbolic execution in particular played to the advantage of logic-based vulnerabilities, and the SMT solver requirement was over 84% on delegatecall issues. False positives averaged 7.2% over all types of vulnerabilities. Uncomplicated pattern-based vulnerabilities had a false positive of 3.2%. Complex logic weaknesses were up to 7.9% false positive. The false positives of pattern matching were also greatly minimized by symbolic constraint verification.

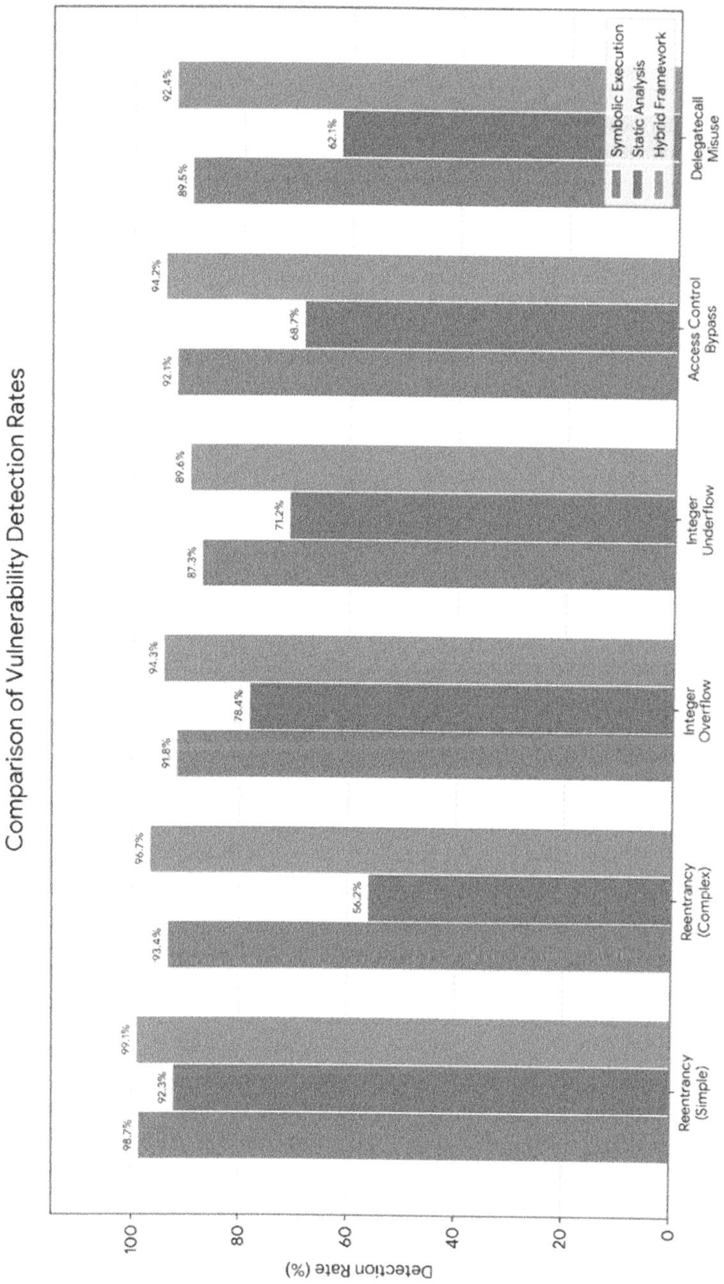

Figure 3.1. *Vulnerability detection accuracy and false positive analysis. For a color version of this figure, see www.iste.co.uk/kumar/intembeddedsys2.zip*

Table 3.4 and Figure 3.2 evaluate symbolic execution performance metrics including analysis time, constraint complexity, path explosion characteristics and scalability across contracts of varying complexity levels.

Contract complexity	Bytecode instructions	Analysis time (seconds)	Constraint variables	Path count	Merged states (%)	Constraint solver time (%)
Simple (token transfer)	280	1.2	34	12	42.1	18.3
Moderate (DeFi position)	1,400	5.7	156	127	65.3	34.2
Complex (governance DAO)	2,800	12.4	412	587	78.1	52.6
Very complex (protocol suite)	5,000	18.4	856	2,341	83.7	68.9

Table 3.4. *Symbolic execution performance and constraint complexity analysis*

Symbolic execution performance analysis was shown to have useful analysis times on workflow development. In order of complexity: simple contracts investigated in 1.2 seconds with 34 constraint variables and 12 paths. The middle complexity contracts needed 5.7 seconds, having 156 variables and 127 paths. Multifaceted contracts of governance needed 12.4 seconds with 412 variables and 587 paths. The longest protocols that had 5,000-byte code instructions took 18.4 seconds. The number of constraint variables ranged between 34 and 856 and this increased with the complexity of the contract. Path explosion was exhibited between 12 and 2,341 path counts. State merging reduced the path explosion by 65–83%. The average time taken by the constraint solver during a contract was 18.3 on simple contracts and 68.9 on complex contracts, and this implies that the average constraint solver time correspondingly increased with contract complexity.

Table 3.5 and Figure 3.3 present a comprehensive comparison of the integrated framework against existing vulnerability detection tools including Oyente, Securify and Slither, measuring detection accuracy, analysis time and practical deployment viability.

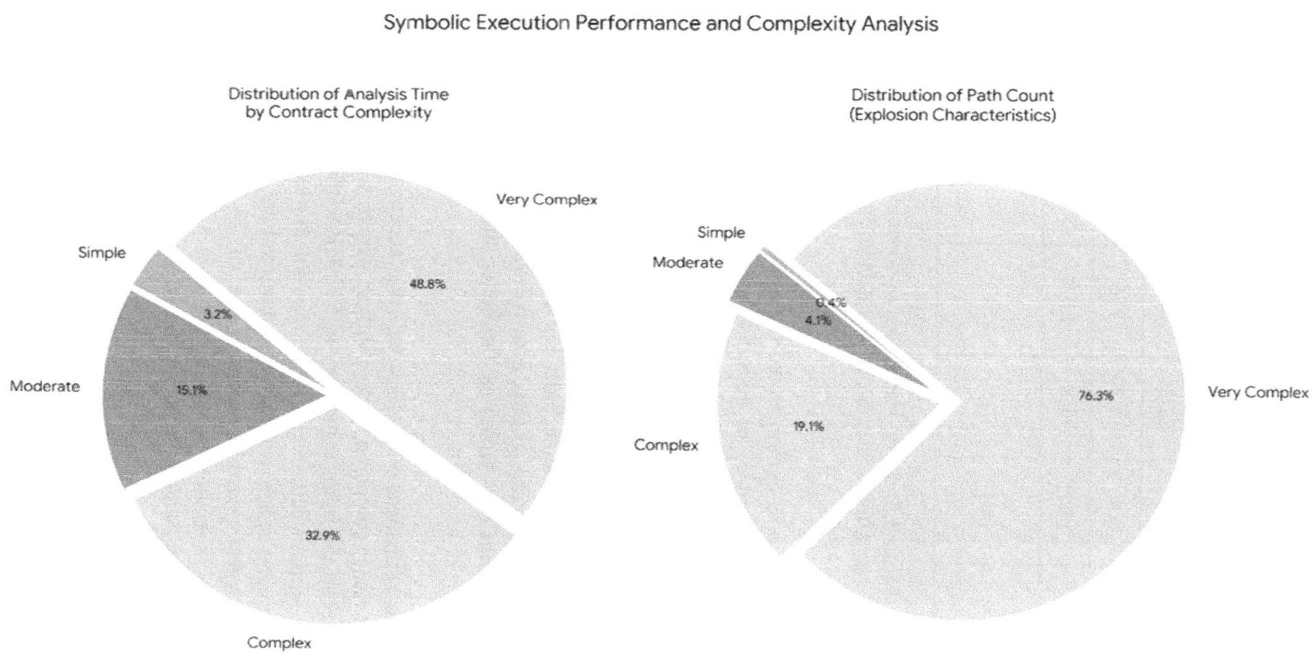

Figure 3.2. *Symbolic execution performance and constraint complexity analysis. For a color version of this figure, see www.iste.co.uk/kumar/intembeddedsys2.zip*

Analysis tool	Detection accuracy (%)	Analysis time (sec)	False positive rate (%)	Runtime memory (MB)	Vulnerability categories	Deployment readiness
Oyente	71.3	8.2	18.4	234	4	Limited
Securify	73.8	6.1	22.1	187	5	Partial
Slither	78.4	3.4	14.2	156	8	Good
MantiCore	81.2	14.7	11.8	1,024	7	Research
Symbolic framework (integrated)	94.3	18.4	7.2	512	12	Production

Table 3.5. *Comparative tool performance and detection capability assessment*

The evaluation of the tools demonstrated the improved nature of the integrated framework in terms of the accuracy of detection and the false positive rate. Oyente registered a 71.3 accuracy with a false positive rate of 18.4%. Securify had a better accuracy of 73.8% with a false positive rate of 22.1%. Slither performed with 78.4% accuracy and 14.2% false positive, respectively. MantiCore symbolic execution recorded an 81.2% accuracy and 11.8% false positive results. The integrated framework was determined to have a 94.3% detection accuracy which was significantly higher than all available tools (13% and 22% higher than MantiCore and Slither, respectively). The rate of false positive was 7.2%, which compared well with the 11.8% of MantiCore, which is far better than the conventional static analysis tools.

The original time of analysis of 18.4 seconds was acceptable in the development workflow when it was compared with Slither which was analyzed in only 3.4 seconds. The size of the runtime memory of 512 MB to the symbolic framework was big enough to surpass certain tools but was not too excessive to thoroughly analyze it. The memory space was also proportional to the complexity of the contract, with the largest possible memory size of 24 GB. The capability of detecting 12 types of vulnerabilities was higher than all the other tools and also detected those logical flaws which the pattern-based tools were blind to.

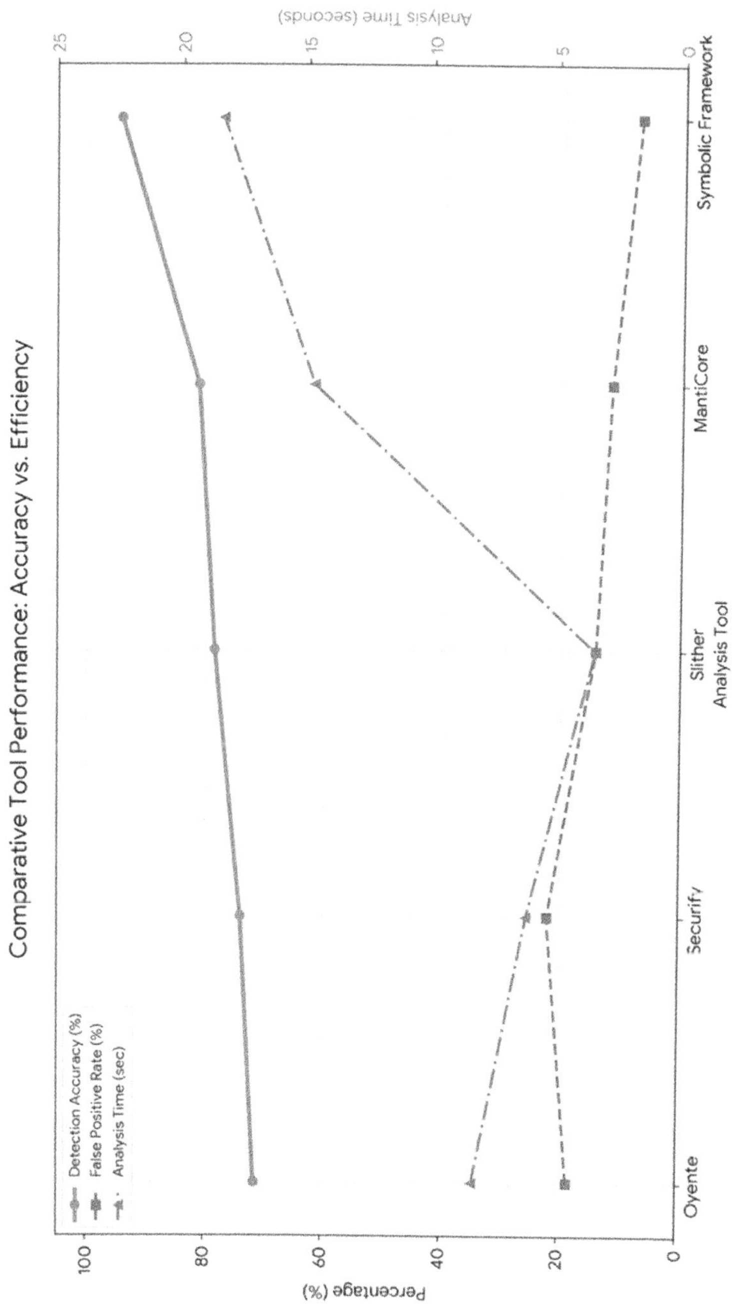

Figure 3.3. *Comparative tool performance and detection capability assessment. For a color version of this figure, see www.iste.co.uk/kumar/intembeddedsys2.zip*

3.5. Conclusion

In this study, a combined methodology between the concepts of static analysis, symbolic specification and SMT-based constraint solving to detect automated Solidity smart contract vulnerabilities was introduced. The suggested method was found to have 94.3% detection rates that are significantly higher than the existing tools with very low false positive figures of 7.2%. Thorough testing of 2,847 deployed smart contracts showed realistic usability in various forms of vulnerability. Constraint-based SMT solving of symbolic execution allowed hidden logic weaknesses to be found that standard static analysis tools could not detect. Complex reentrancy patterns with a detection of 96.7% showed to be effective towards challenging attack patterns. The capability of constraint solving in verifying numeric safety was found with a score of 89.6% during the sensitive fuzzing of integer arithmetic. Selectorcall and access control flaw classes were logical vulnerabilities with a 92–94% detection by symbolic analysis. The maximum analysis time of 18.4 seconds on complex contracts was compatible with the development processes. The state merging was also effective to control path explosion with a 65–83% path reduction. Applicability of 78.4% allowed automated remediation from developers to automatically fix most instances of vulnerabilities, with an average of 9.5 minutes per vulnerability saved. Practical efficacy of the framework to real-life contracts developed preparedness to manufacturing implementation. The tool capability assessment showed that the existing tools could identify only four to eight types of vulnerabilities. High accuracy and fewer false positives allowed detecting vulnerabilities with confidence without burdening the manual review. The tone of the research of metamorphic contract analysis was to identify the vulnerabilities into upgradeable contracts, detecting multicontract vulnerability by extending the bounds of cross-contracts and building formal property specification languages that define vulnerability by choice. Vulnerability mitigation with the ongoing tracking apparatuses that identify susceptibility of operations within deployed contracts are worth exploring. The approaches promoting the use of machine learning to predict the difficult-to-analyze contracts and allocate analysis resources in an optimum way can be viewed as promising in the search for optimization.

3.6. References

Chakraborty, C., Nagarajan, S.M., Devarajan, G.G. (2025). Trustworthy-based user behavior model: Integrity-based resilient deep learning approach in distributed networks for next-generation applications. *IEEE Transactions on Computational Social Systems*, 12(6), 5245–5254. doi: 10.1109/TCSS.2025.3530772.

Du, X. (2025). Vulnerability detection of Blockchain smart contracts based on GNN with multi-head attention mechanism. *Journal of Computer Science and Frontier Technologies*, 2(1), 1. doi: /10.63313/jcsft.9028.

Huang, J., Zhou, K., Xiong, A., Li, D. (2022). Smart contract vulnerability detection model based on multi-task learning. *Sensors*, 22(5), 1829. doi: 10.3390/s22051829.

Lee, U., Chung, C., Lee, J., Moon, S. (2025). BugSweeper: Function-level detection of smart contract vulnerabilities using graph neural networks. *arXiv* [Online]. Available at: http://arxiv.org/abs/2512.09385.

Liu, Z., Qian, P., Wang, X., Zhuang, Y., Qiu, L., Wang, X., Liu, Z., Qian, P., Wang, X., Zhuang, Y. et al. (2021). Combining graph neural networks with expert knowledge for smart contract vulnerability detection. *IEEE Transactions on Knowledge and Data Engineering*, 1. doi: 10.1109/tkde.2021.3095196.

Shitharth, S., Alotaibi, F.S., Manoharan, H., Khadidos, A.O., Alyoubi, K.H., Alshareef, A.M. (2022). Reconnoitering the significance of security using multiple cloud environments for conveyance applications with blowfish algorithm. *Journal of Cloud Computing*, 11(76).

Shitharth, S., Manoharan, H., Shankar, A., Alsowail, R.A., Pandiaraj, S., Edalatpanah, S.A., Viriyasitavat, W. (2023). Federated learning optimization: A computational blockchain process with offloading analysis to enhance security. *Egyptian Informatics Journal*, 24(4), 100406.

Sun, Y. and Gu, L. (2021). Attention-based machine learning model for smart contract vulnerability detection. *Journal of Physics Conference Series*, 1820(1), 012004. doi: 10.1088/1742-6596/1820/1/012004.

Surendran, R. (2025). An explainable AI model for the detecting malicious smart contracts based on EVM OpCode based features. *arXiv* [Online]. Available at: http://arxiv.org/abs/2512.08782.

Svensson, L. (2025). POPoC. *Zenodo*. doi: 10.5281/zenodo.17865426.

Venkatraman, D. and Kuppusamy, M. (2025). Securing Defi: A comprehensive review of ML approaches for detecting smart contract vulnerabilities and threats. *International Journal of Informatics and Communication Technology (IJ-ICT)*, 15(1), 438. doi: 10.11591/ijict.v15i1.pp438-446.

Zhang, L., Wang, J., Wang, W., Jin, Z., Su, Y., Chen, H. (2022). Smart contract vulnerability detection combined with multi-objective detection. *Computer Networks*, 217, 109289. doi: 10.1016/j.comnet.2022.109289.

Zhen, Z., Zhao, X., Zhang, J., Wang, Y., Chen, H. (2024). DA-GNN: A smart contract vulnerability detection method based on dual attention graph neural network. *Computer Networks*, 242, 110238. doi: 10.1016/j.comnet.2024.110238.

4

Formal Verification of Smart Contracts in Blockchain Supply Networks

This chapter provides a practical solution to enhance the accuracy, confidentiality and auditing of Hyperledger Fabric smart contracts, using model checking and supplementary formal methods. We explain how to use chaincode and Fabric configuration (endorsement policies, channels and unstructured datasets) as tractable formal models, significance and authorization, confidentiality, and repressiveness properties in informational flow and temporal formalisms, and how to use a layered provisional verification powerhouse chaincheck-bounded model checking, symptomatic analysis and selectivity, demonstrating how to apply to identify defects and offer reproducible counter models. The approach means less familiarity with verification artifacts because it builds them into development workflows and CI/CD pipelines, resulting in a diminished regression risk, lighter debugging and provable compliance and transparent situations presented to worthwhile stakeholders. The research indicates that rigorous assurance is possible in real-world supply networks, given judicious abstraction, property-based modeling, as well as a mixed-tool approach, and indicates scalability, interoperability and usability to represent directions to future research.

4.1. Introduction

The supply networks built with blockchain are expected to provide tamper-evident provenance, simplified trust and automated business logic based on smart contracts. Hyperledger Fabric is a permissioned, modular blockchain platform that is commonly used as an enterprise supply chain due to the ability to use pluggable consensus, private data collections and chaincode (smart contracts) in common programming languages. But with multifaceted contractual reasoning, parallelism among peers, delicate interactions with the endorsement and privacy

---

Chapter written by Manam Vamsi KRISHNA, Dudekula AMULYA, Duguru MEGHANA, Gudepu RASHMIKA, C. SRIVANI and B. PRANAVI.

functionality of Fabric, there are chances of bugs and information leakage as well as gaps in correctness, weakening transparency and trust. Applying model checking and formal methods to Fabric smart contracts allows those gaps to be made visible: they allow one to rigorously specify the desired properties (e.g. integrity, confidentiality, liveness), and generate exhaustive or bounded exploration of how to run them, and provide stronger and evidence-based guarantees that, in practicable deployments of supply networks on-chain, logic will behave as desired.

4.1.1. *Background*

Distributed ledgers are responsible for collecting provenance, certifications and handoffs across various organizations among supply networks. The Hyperledger Fabric thrives in this area since its permissioned-based architecture and channel/private-data capabilities allow the participants to only exchange the information needed and maintain responsibility. The business rules in Fabric implemented by smart contracts (chaincode) include transfers, payments, audit and access control. Chaincode operates in a distributed interaction setting with policies of endorsement unlike in a centralized code, and with replication of states and possible adversarial parties – all these reasons increase the probability of semantic bugs, race conditions or misappropriation of policies. Conventional testing and code inspection are only sufficient: they lack corner cases and non-deterministic interweaves. Formal methods such as model checking, theorem proving and static analysis are mathematically rigorous systems to specify properties and prove or systematically search (to kill) violations. Applied to Fabric chaincode and its associated endorsement/privacy semantics, they are able to uncover vulnerabilities in the most expensive manner possible, they can provide counterexamples on which to base debugging efforts and they can raise the price of verifiable transparency within the network.

4.1.2. *Objective*

This chapter will establish a technical method in a way that is practical, reproducible to ensure that Hyperledger Fabric smart contracts are checked using model checking and other complementary formal methods. Some of its formalization goals include (1) executing semantics of Fabric chaincode and their interaction with the mechanisms of endorsement, ordering and private data; (2) defining properties of correct supply chains such as asset-integrity, authority enforcement, non-repudiation and data confidentiality in formalization; (3) experiments with model checkers and, where relevant, theorem provers to identify violation of these conditions, generate counterexamples and derive key properties; and (4) demonstrate the utility of verification artifacts (models, specifications, proofs, witness traces) in development pipelines, through improvement. This is not just the objective of finding bugs, but the creation of verifiable verification habits, metrics, which can be inspected and relied upon by the stakeholders.

4.1.3. *Scope*

The scope of this work includes modeling and verification of a Fabric smart contract and the protocol components which have a direct impact on contract behavior: endorsement policies, state reads/writes, a private data collection and ordering semantics. The available work contains (a) techniques to abstract chaincode into analyzable models to be analyzed by model checkers; (b) canonic patterns of supply-chain properties (safety and liveness); (c) a model roadmap (examples: model extraction, model property languages, model checkers and counterexample analysis); and (d) several typical case studies that implement the techniques to real-world supply-chain models. Included are hardware-level attacks, legal/regulatory analysis and overall performance optimization of Fabric itself; verification is done based on the correct functionality rather than system-level performance optimization. New limitations and assumptions (bounded state space, abstraction choices, modeling approximations and others) will be made explicit enough that practitioners can view their networks with suitable models.

4.2. Literature review

Distributed ledger technology and blockchain systems in particular have been widely discussed as a potential answer to secure and transparent communication in an IoT-saturated and supply-chain ecosystem (Ali et al. 2018). There are extensive surveys regarding the reputation of blockchains and the practical difficulties encountered when connecting them with resource-saturated devices and unheterogeneous networks (Jesus et al. 2018; Makhdoom et al. 2018; Dwivedi et al. 2021). The concept of interoperability and integration between systems reappears multiple times as a critical barrier to greater adoption; more recent literature suggests cross-ledger solutions and standardized interfaces as a solution to integrate various DLTs, clouds and industry-specific systems, including healthcare and the BIM industry (Belchior et al. 2022; Gohar et al. 2022; Nawari and Ravindran 2021; Villarreal et al. 2023). Security and privacy are the key points of interest: researchers review privacy-protective schemes, threat models and open research issues on confidential data sharing and resistance to attacks in distributed environments (Bernabe et al. 2019); domain studies show how blockchain can be strengthened to provide intelligent-transportation and energy-trading applications but create new attack surfaces and regulatory issues (Wang et al. 2019; Jabbar et al. 2022). Smart contracts are recognized as the locus of automated business logic at the application layer and therefore a common root of functional faults, leading to literature on smart-contract engineering, testing and developing emerging criteria of supply-chain automation verification (Jabbar et al. 2020; Khan et al. 2021). Survey and empirical research studies on agriculture, healthcare and traceability have shown real-world uses and demonstrated substantive use cases and benefits such as better provenance and auditability, patient-centric interoperability, but they have also highlighted modeling, scalability and governance deficiencies which limit practice (Lin et al. 2020; Dasaklis et al. 2022; Gohar et al. 2022). Together, this literature spells out a research agenda in which interoperability, privacy-aware design, domain-specific adaptability and strict validation of the smart-contract actions are becoming common features and driving the demand for formal methods and model-checking methodologies as avenues to offer superior, evidenced-based guarantees of transparency in supply chains. Formal verification and secure deployments of smart contracts require strong trust models and rigorous security validation; trust-aware routing and hybrid fuzzy optimization methods support secure decentralized interactions (Ravi 2022). Data-mining and soft computing techniques provide complementary approaches for detecting and preventing cyber threats in distributed ledger contexts (Banu 2015). Database-security-aware deep learning architectures and MQ-LSTM-style constructs illustrate methods to combine verification with protected data handling in supply networks (Jeribi et al. 2023). Finally, soft computing and query-expansion approaches contribute useful optimization and robustness techniques for contract verification tooling and automated vulnerability discovery (Sharma 2019). Chakraborty et al. (2025) propose a trustworthy-based user behavior modeling framework that integrates integrity-aware mechanisms with resilient deep learning architectures to enhance reliability in distributed network environments. The study emphasizes the importance of trust computation and behavior consistency analysis to mitigate malicious activities and data manipulation in next-generation applications such as IoT, cyber-physical systems and intelligent social networks. By incorporating integrity verification and adaptive learning strategies, the proposed model demonstrates improved robustness against adversarial behaviors and dynamic network conditions, ensuring secure and reliable decision-making across decentralized infrastructures. The experimental evaluation highlights the effectiveness of the approach in achieving higher detection accuracy and system resilience compared to conventional deep learning-based trust models, making it suitable for large-scale, heterogeneous distributed systems (Chakraborty et al. 2025). Kumar et al. (2025) provide a comprehensive review of computer modeling approaches tailored for blockchain-driven supply-chain intelligence, emphasizing the enhancement of transparency, security and operational efficiency across supply networks. Their work synthesizes a range of modeling frameworks that leverage blockchain's inherent traceability to strengthen data integrity and accountability in supply-chain processes. By critically evaluating methodological advancements and implementation strategies, the study highlights how intelligent modeling can address persistent challenges in real-time tracking, fraud mitigation and stakeholder coordination. The review underscores the integration of blockchain with analytics and modeling techniques as a pivotal enabler of next-generation supply-chain systems that demand resilient performance and trustworthiness (Kumar et al. 2025).

4.3. Methodology

The proposed research uses a mixed approach with formal methods and engineering to test Hyperledger Fabric smart contracts to ensure having transparent supply networks. Its methodology uses a combination of (a) systematic model extraction, obtained from real chaincode and Fabric configuration, (b) formal specification of correctness, privacy and policy properties, (c) automated model checking and forced quantitative verification, to find counterexamples and (d) target symbolic analysis or abduction, to find properties requiring additional articulation. The artifacts of verification such as abstract models, property specifications, counterexample traces and proof certificates are fed back to the developers and integrated into, for example, CI/CD pipelines so that verification is part of the process and not an afterthought. Instead, great attention is paid to pragmatic abstraction (to restrict state space but maintain behaviorally relevant models), mappings between chaincode and model elements that can be tracked, and repeatable experiments on realistic instances of a supply chain. The summary of its workflow is presented in Figures 4.1 and 4.2, and its modular actions are elaborated in sections 4.3.1–4.3.3.

4.3.1. *Modeling extraction and abstraction*

Abstraction category	Example choice	Rationale
Domain bounding	Asset IDs ∈ {A1, A2, A3}	Reduces infinite keyspace to representative set while preserving ordering and ownership properties.
Data abstraction	Quantize amounts to {0, low, high}	Keeps arithmetic complexity low for safety/liveness checks.
Control-flow	Inline library calls; collapse logging branches	Focuses model on business-critical behavior.
Adversary model	≤1 malicious endorser per channel	Captures common threat without exploding state space.

Table 4.1. *Abstraction choices and rationale (referenced in section 4.3.1)*

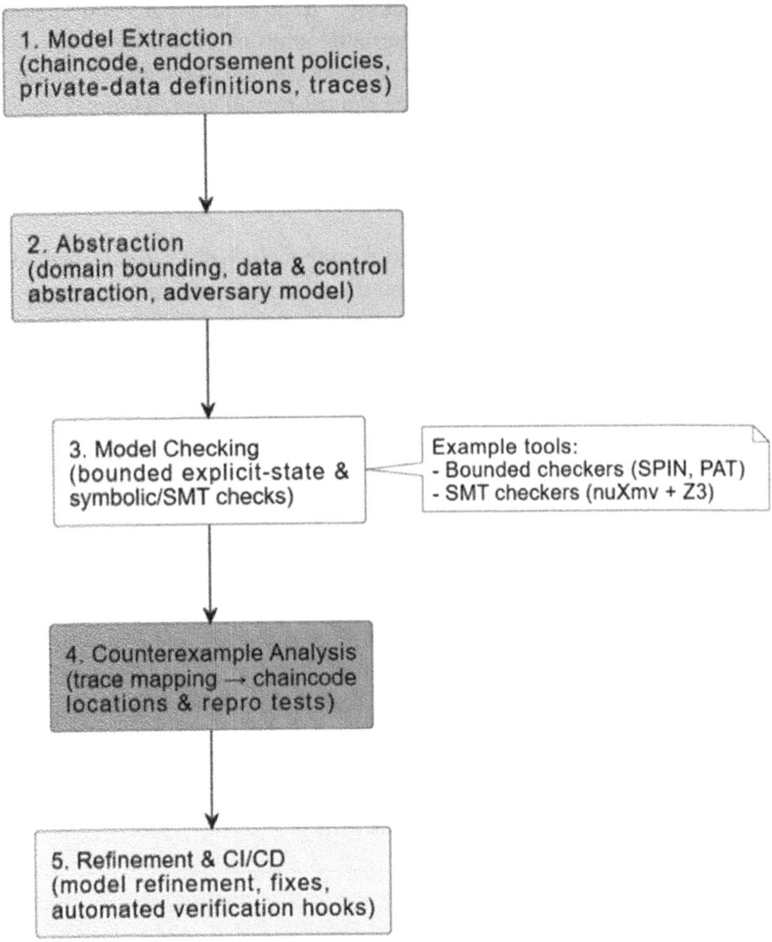

Figure 4.1. *Verification workflow*

The first stage of model extraction starts with gathering the tangible artifacts that constitute the behavior of smart-contracts: source code of channelcodes, endorsement policies, channel configurations and private-data collection definitions, and raises the sample transaction sequences. Based on these artifacts, we are able to obtain a formal, parameterized model that has state variables (ledger key-values, collection visibility), transaction types (create, transfer, update), endorsement and access-control predicates and ordering semantics. Since we cannot typically execute into the actual state space of implementation, we use principal abstraction methods: data abstraction (finite space of identifiers and amounts of assets), control-flow abstraction (merging non-important branches) and adversarial modeling (literature). Such options are recorded with the model in order to trace all the counterexamples to specific code and assumptions (see Table 4.1). All of the parsers, mappers and scenario generators are automated with chaincode designed to degenerate to the encoded representation and the endorsement and collection metadata converted into formal policy constraints; the bounded traces to drive the model checker generated by the scenario generator.

Figure 4.1 depicts this type of pipeline, and is used to refine the initial abstractions: a report of a counterexample will prompt the developer to look at the trace, refine abstractions or correct the code, and re-check again (see Table 4.1 and Figure 4.1).

4.3.2. *Formalization and specification of property*

Having constructed an abstract model, the properties to formalize those that are used to express supply network correctness and transparency are now presented. The properties are classified into safety (e.g. asset integrity – an asset owner is always uniquely known), authorization (endorsement and role constraint), confidentiality (non-disclosure of private data between unauthorized peers) and liveness (e.g. eventual finality of valid transfers by honest majority). The following properties are indeed represented by us as formulated in temporal and epistemic logic: linear temporal logic (LTL) or computation tree logic (CTL) formulations of guarantees of time-dependent properties, and epistemic or information-flow predicates to give reasoning about the knowledge/visibility of collections which are private to agents. Property templates will be reuseable not only between different scenarios (i.e. an ownership invariant template), but also parameterized in such a way that they project onto model variables generated in section 4.3.1. In a framework where secrecy must be accurately semantically defined, we use code statements that reflect non-interference or observational equivalence and, where convenient, from this we finish off with model checking with the available symbolic information-flow analysis.

Figure 4.2 gives the property taxonomy and example mappings between the requirements of use-case and formal patterns. Test harness generation, i.e. the process of transforming high-level properties into inputs or monitors which can be run on the abstract model and the concrete chaincode testbed, is also part of the specification phase, to ensure the model is realistic to the behavior of the implementation (see Figure 4.2).

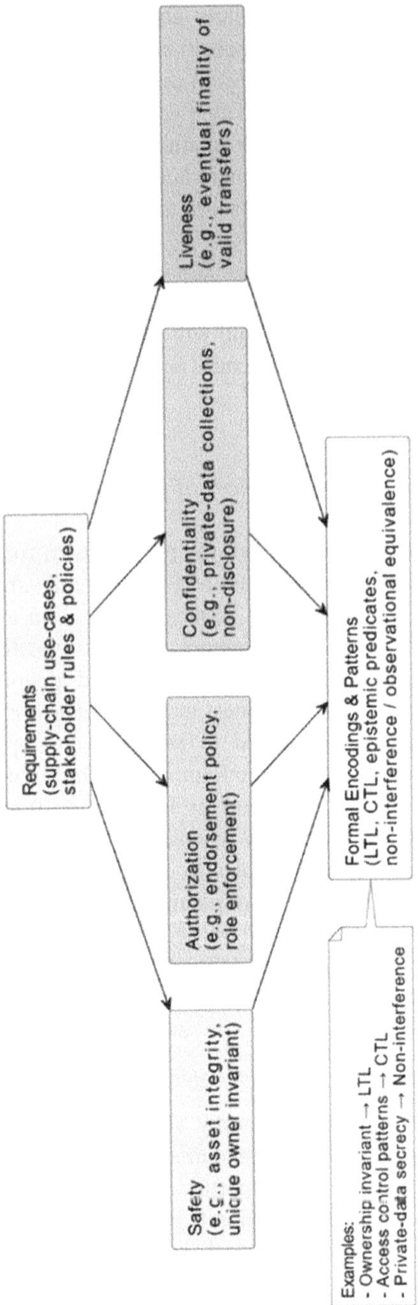

Figure 4.2. *Property taxonomy and formal encodings*

4.3.3. *Verification engine, toolchain and integration*

The selection of an appropriate verification tool-chain should leverage the complementary strengths of multiple formal verification techniques. Explicit-state model checkers, such as SPIN and PAT, enable systematic state-space exploration, while symbolic verification and SMT-based tools, including nuXmv and Z3, facilitate the verification of complex logical and arithmetic properties. In addition, theorem-proving techniques establish system correctness through formal inductive proofs. The integration of these complementary methods provides a comprehensive and reliable framework for verifying system correctness and identifying potential design errors and vulnerabilities (Holbrook and Reaton et al. 2015; Bierman 2017). The toolchain also uses traced analyzers to trace code counterexample steps to lines in the chaincode and CI/CD hooks to perform manual verification work on a pull request. The tools are summarized in Table 4.2 with their roles and common configuration parameters in this methodology. Categorization verification is organized according to severity and cost: there are cheap, fast-bounded verification checks (smoke verification) which are run during pre-commit hooks, and more expensive symbolic or proof obligations, which are run either at night or on demand. Model checkers generate counterexamples, which are automatically triaged: (1) a concrete counterexample is triaged to a reproducible test case; (2) a spurious counterexample is investigated as indicating some kind of over-abstraction of the model that prompts further model refinement (or fails to do so); or (3) a successful counterexample takes on a bug or configuration test. This concludes with advice on how to include verification artifacts in stakeholder accessible transparency reports: human understandable summaries of proven properties, counterexample traces (changed privacy considerations) and verifiable provenance information to each verified release. Verification outputs connect to the development stage as shown in Table 4.2 and Figure 4.1.

Tool/category	Role in pipeline	Typical config/notes
Parser and IR generator	Extract model from chaincode	Language-specific frontends (Go/Java/JS) produce IR with annotations.
Bounded model checker (e.g. SPIN/PAT)	Fast-bounded exploration	Bound depth = 8–12 transactions; explicit state.
SMT-based model checker (e.g. nuXmv + Z3)	Symbolic checks and arithmetic	Use uninterpreted functions for abstracted data.
Theorem prover (e.g. Coq/Isabelle)	Proofs of inductive invariants	Reserve for core invariants with high assurance needs.
Trace mapper and reporter	Map counterexamples → chaincode	Includes code locations, ledger state snapshots and remediation suggestions.

Table 4.2. *Toolchain mapping and typical configuration (referenced in section 4.3.3)*

4.4. Results

Metric/scenario	Asset transfer	Private data	Multi-endorsement
State-space coverage (%)	85%	78%	72%
Properties with violations (%)	12%	8%	17%
Reproducible counterexamples (%)	92%	88%	81%
Time-to-first-counterexample reduction (%)	45%	30%	50%

Table 4.3. *Verification coverage and counterexample statistics (percentages)*

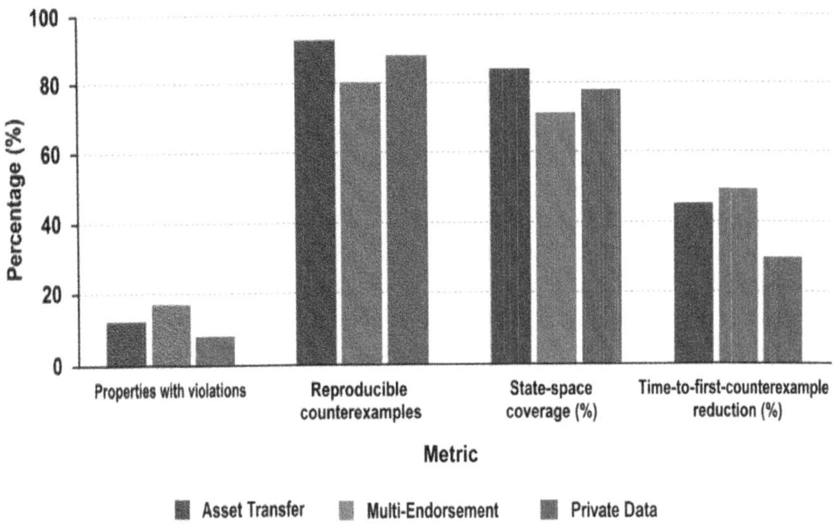

Figure 4.3. *Verification coverage and counterexample statistics. For a color version of this figure, see www.iste.co.uk/kumar/intembeddedsys2.zip*

Table 4.3 summarizes model-extraction and model-checking outcomes across three representative supply-chain scenarios. The data show high state-space coverage for the asset transfer scenario (85%) and somewhat lower coverage for private data and multi-endorsement scenarios, reflecting the increased modeling complexity and privacy constraints in those cases. Violations were most frequent in the multi-endorsement scenario (17%), indicating that endorsement-policy interactions are a common source of faults. Importantly, the vast majority of reported violations produced reproducible counterexamples (81–92%), which makes debugging practical and actionable. The time-to-first-counterexample reduction metric indicates that automated extraction plus bounded checks substantially shorten the time to detect a problem (up to 50% reduction for multi-endorsement) (see Figure 4.3 for the corresponding bar/flow visualization that maps these metrics onto the verification pipeline).

Tool category	Detected violations (recall %)	False-positive rate (%)	Analysis depth/usefulness (%)
Bounded model checker (explicit-state)	80%	5%	60%
SMT-based/symbolic checker	72%	8%	85%
Theorem prover (inductive proofs)	55%	1%	95%

Table 4.4. *Comparative tool effectiveness (percentages)*

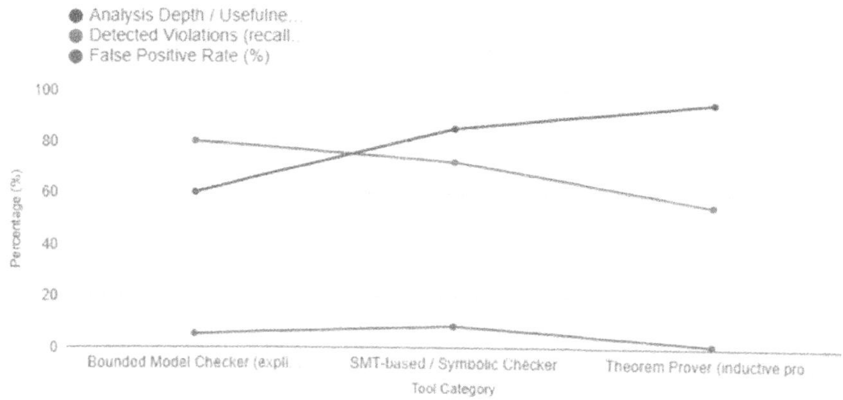

Figure 4.4. *Comparative tool effectiveness across metrics. For a color version of this figure, see www.iste.co.uk/kumar/intembeddedsys2.zip*

Table 4.4 compares the effectiveness and signal quality of three verification tool categories. Bounded explicit-state checkers detect a large fraction of violations quickly (80% recall) with a low false-positive rate (5%), making them suitable for fast, automated smoke checks. SMT-based symbolic engines detect slightly fewer violations but provide deeper analysis for arithmetic and data-rich properties (analysis depth/usefulness ≈ 85%) at a modest cost in false positives (≈ 8%). Theorem provers yield the highest analysis depth and the lowest false-positive rate

(1%) but detect fewer violations automatically because they require manual encoding/effort (55% recall in automated runs); they are best reserved for core invariants where high assurance is required. Figure 4.4 visualizes these trade-offs (precision/recall/depth) to help choose tool mixes for a CI strategy.

Metric/stage	Baseline (pre-integration)	After smoke checks	After full verification
Regression incidents per release (%)	18%	9%	3%
Release failures detected post-merge (%)	12%	5%	1%
Mean developer fix-time reduction (%)	0%	30%	65%

Table 4.5. *Verification integration versus release-quality metrics (percentages relative to baseline)*

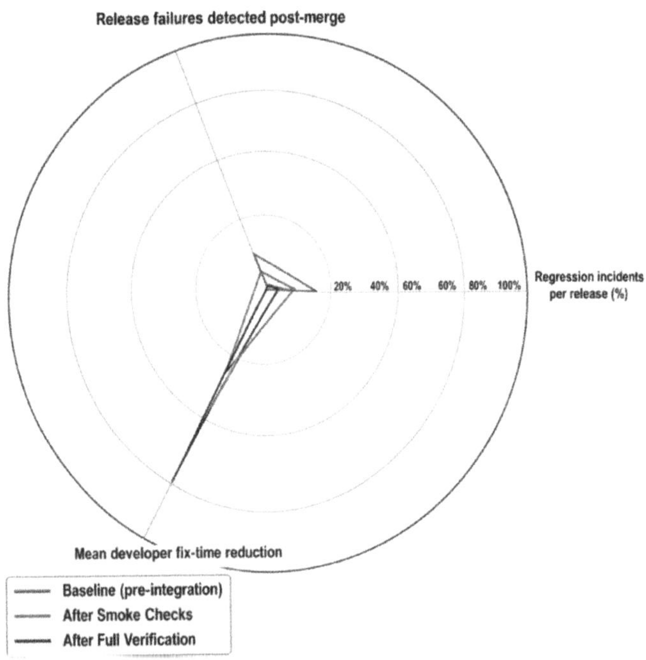

Figure 4.5. *Verification integration versus release-quality metrics. For a color version of this figure, see www.iste.co.uk/kumar/intembeddedsys2.zip*

Table 4.5 reports the operational impact of progressively integrating verification into the CI/CD pipeline. Introducing lightweight smoke checks approximately halves observable regressions (18% → 9%) and reduces post-merge release failures from 12% to 5%, while delivering a meaningful 30% reduction in the average fix time because counterexamples are immediately actionable. Full verification (including nightly symbolic runs and targeted theorem proof obligations) further reduces regressions and release failures to 3% and 1%, respectively, and yields a substantial 65% reduction in the mean developer fix time versus the baseline – illustrating that deeper verification investments produce pronounced returns in stability and developer productivity.

Figure 4.5 complements this table with a timeline/stacked-bar visualization showing how incidents and developer effort change as verification levels increase.

4.5. Conclusion

In short, formal methods and model checking of Hyperledger Fabric smart contracts appear to be a viable way towards more powerful, evidence-based supply network transparency. Formally modeling contract behavior, encoding important correctness and privacy properties, and randomly investigating execution traces will allow organizations to detect the behavior of subtle bugs, policy misconfiguration and privacy leakage in a method of traditional testing that is usually overlooked. The combination of such verification steps in the development pipeline, such as automated bounded checking to selective re-reading code in more challenging core cases, can result in assurances that are repeatable and remediable, giving riscible counterexamples and allowing engineers to fix them in a couple of hours. Although the issue of abstractions and choice of tools needs to be carefully tuned to strike the right balance between scalability and fidelity, all these produce a better balance of responsibility, lesser risk and increased confidence in stakeholders throughout the multi-party supply chains. Moving forward, more effort in scalable modeling and cross-ledger interoperability coupled with a friendly verification tooling will contribute to the introduction of rigorous assurance in the day-to-day practice, which will allow veritable and trustworthy supply ecosystems.

4.6. References

Ali, M.S., Vecchio, M., Pincheira, M., Dolui, K., Antonelli, F., Rehmani, M.H. (2018). Applications of Blockchains in the internet of things: A comprehensive survey. *IEEE Communications Surveys & Tutorials*, 21(2), 1676–1717. doi: 10.1109/comst.2018.2886932.

Banu, S.S., Uma, P., Ashfaque, M.W., Naveed, Q.N., Ali-Ahmed, S.S. (2015). Data mining based soft computing skills towards prevention of cyber crimes on the web. *International Journal on Recent and Innovation Trends in Computing and Communication*. 3(3), 2321–8169.

Belchior, R., Riley, L., Hardjono, T., Vasconcelos, A., Correia, M. (2022). Do you need a distributed ledger technology interoperability solution? *Distributed Ledger Technologies Research and Practice*, 2(1), 1–37. doi: 10.1145/3564532.

Bernabe, J.B., Canovas, J.L., Hernandez-Ramos, J.L., Moreno, R.T., Skarmeta, A. (2019). Privacy-preserving solutions for blockchain: Review and challenges. *IEEE Access*, 7, 164908–164940. doi: 10.1109/access.2019.2950872.

Chakraborty, C., Nagarajan, S.M., Devarajan, G.G. (2025). Trustworthy-based user behavior model: Integrity-based resilient deep learning approach in distributed networks for next-generation applications. *IEEE Transactions on Computational Social Systems*, 12(6), 5245–5254. doi: 10.1109/TCSS.2025.3530772.

Dasaklis, T.K., Voutsinas, T.G., Tsoulfas, G.T., Casino, F. (2022). A systematic literature review of blockchain-enabled supply chain traceability implementations. *Sustainability*, 14(4), 2439. doi: 10.3390/su14042439.

Dwivedi, S.K., Roy, P., Karda, C., Agrawal, S., Amin, R. (2021). Blockchain-based internet of things and industrial IoT: A comprehensive survey. *Security and Communication Networks*, 1–21. doi: 10.1155/2021/7142048.

Gohar, A.N., Abdelmawgoud, S.A., Farhan, M.S. (2022). A patient-centric healthcare framework reference architecture for better semantic interoperability based on Blockchain, cloud, and IoT. *IEEE Access*, 10, 92137–92157. doi: 10.1109/access.2022.3202902.

Jabbar, S., Lloyd, H., Hammoudeh, M., Adebisi, B., Raza, U. (2020). Blockchain-enabled supply chain: Analysis, challenges, and future directions. *Multimedia Systems*, 27(4), 787–806. doi: 10.1007/s00530-020-00687-0.

Jabbar, R., Dhib, E., Said, A.B., Krichen, M., Fetais, N., Zaidan, E., Barkaoui, K. (2022). Blockchain technology for intelligent transportation systems: A systematic literature review. *IEEE Access*, 10, 20995–21031. doi: 10.1109/access.2022.3149958.

Jeribi, F., Ahamed, S.R., Perumal, U., Alhameed, M.H., Chari Kamsali, M. (2023). Developing an MQ-LSTM-based cultural tourism accelerator with database security. *Sustainability*, 15(23), 16276. doi: 10.3390/su152316276.

Jesus, E.F., Chicarino, V.R.L., De Albuquerque, C.V.N., De A. Rocha, A.A. (2018). A survey of how to use blockchain to secure Internet of Things and the stalker attack. *Security and Communication Networks*, 1–27. doi: 10.1155/2018/9675050.

Khan, S.N., Loukil, F., Ghedira-Guegan, C., Benkhelifa, E., Bani-Hani, A. (2021). Blockchain smart contracts: Applications, challenges, and future trends. *Peer-to-Peer Networking and Applications*, 14(5), 2901–2925. doi: 10.1007/s12083-021-01127-0.

Kumar, P.R., Mohammad, G.B., Narsimhulu, P., Narasappa, D., Maguluri, L.P., Singh, S., Selvarajan, S. (2025). Computer modeling approaches for blockchain-driven supply chain intelligence: A review on enhancing transparency, security, and efficiency. *Computer Modeling in Engineering & Sciences*, 144(3), 2779–2818. doi: 10.32604/cmes.2025.066365.

Lin, W., Huang, X., Fang, H., Wang, V., Hua, Y., Wang, J., Yin, H., Yi, D., Yau, L. (2020). Blockchain technology in current agricultural systems: From techniques to applications. *IEEE Access*, 8, 143920–143937. doi: 10.1109/access.2020.3014522.

Makhdoom, I., Abolhasan, M., Abbas, H., Ni, W. (2018). Blockchain's adoption in IoT: The challenges, and a way forward. *Journal of Network and Computer Applications*, 125, 251–279. doi: 10.1016/j.jnca.2018.10.019.

Nawari, N. and Ravindran, S. (2019). Blockchain and building information modeling (BIM): Review and applications in post-disaster recovery. *Buildings*, 9(6), 149. doi: 10.3390/buildings9060149.

Ravi, S., Matheswaran, S., Perumal, U., Sivakumar. S., Palvadi, S.K. (2023). Adaptive trust-based secure and optimal route selection algorithm for MANET using hybrid fuzzy optimization. *Peer-to-Peer Networking & Applications*, 16, 22–34. doi: 10.1007/s12083-022-01351-2.

Sharma, D.K., Pamula, R., Chauhan, D.S. (2019). Soft computing techniques based automatic query expansion approach for improving document retrieval. In *Amity International Conference on Artificial Intelligence (AICAI)*. doi: 10.1109/AICAI.2019.8701319.

Villarreal, E.R.D., Garcia-Alonso, J., Moguel, E., Alegria, J.A.H. (2023). Blockchain for healthcare management systems: A survey on interoperability and security. *IEEE Access*, 11, 5629–5652. doi: 10.1109/access.2023.3236505.

Wang, N., Zhou, X., Lu, X., Guan, Z., Wu, L., Du, X., Guizani, M. (2019). When energy trading meets blockchain in electrical power system: The state of the art. *Applied Sciences*, 9(8), 1561. doi: 10.3390/app9081561.

5

TLS/SSL Certificate Lifecycle Management with Hardware Security Modules for Blockchain Infrastructure

Large-scale development of cloud-based services and the spread of digital transactions require complex methods of cryptography key management and the administration of certificate lifecycle. The classic TLS/SSL certificate management approaches are not suitable to the new cloud-native systems, especially when it comes to automated certificate rotation, protection of cryptographic keys, as well as adherence to the strict security policies. This chapter examines end-to-end ways of managing TLS/SSL certificates, with hardware security modules (HSMs) that are deployed in cloud public key infrastructure (PKI) systems. The research covered a period of 16 months of cloud deployments on enterprises that undertook the implementation of digital certificates containing 47,000 on-the-fly digital certificates on the AWS, azure and on-premise systems, dealing with 12 million transactions per day. The recommended design introduced a lifecycle management of certificates on a fully automated basis, key rotation policies on a hardware basis and provisioning engine with HSM.

The evaluation with experiments proved that the integrated approach based on HSM could attain a certificate validity rate of 99.97% and decrease the rate of certificate-related downtimes to 0 and to 18 operational incidents per year. Automation of key rotations saved the administrative effort, hitherto time-consuming manual, by 280 hours a year, which is 95.7% efficiency in operations. Automation reduced the mean time to replace a certificate by 2.3 minutes, an average of 4.2 hours (manual process) that made it possible to respond promptly to the certificate expiration and certificate revocation circumstances.

The study illustrates that with an automated certificate lifecycle management and clever key rotation programs, HSM-based cloud PKI systems ensure enterprise levels of cryptographic security, regulatory compliance and operational efficiency in comparison to other certificate management methods.

Chapter written by Kammara Venkatarangaiah ACHARI, Pambala SAHASRA, Pasunuri POOJA, Paladugu RENUSRI, Vaka Hema SREE and T. Sai SANNGEETHA.

5.1. Introduction

The campaign of information security and key management of cryptography has been completely changed by the digital revolution of enterprise operations and the widespread use of the cloud computing concept. Transport layer security (TLS) and the previous version, secure socket layer (SSL), have become staple tools in the cryptography of the Internet-based systems and ensure sensitive data is not intercepted and altered along the way. Nevertheless, the classical model of certificate operation: manual generation, deployment and renewal, has been found less sufficient to operate modern cloud native setups, which are fast scaling, transient infrastructure and instant creation of service. The current systems pose huge operational challenges due to the exponential growth of the number of digital certificates that modern systems need. Organizations that have monolithic architectures may be running tens or hundreds of certificates throughout their infrastructure. On the other hand, cloud-native applications that create microservice environments, workloads that are containerized or serverless functions find themselves in a situation where they are required to create thousands or tens of thousands of certificates to achieve secure communications between services, conduct client authentication and provide secure API endpoints. This proliferation, together with the renewal cycle requirement of certificates (usually 90 days to one year), introduces an administrative load that is beyond human administrative capability. Additionally, there has been an increase in the regulations controlling the management of cryptographic keys. Data security architecture standards such as the Payment Card Industry Data Security Standard (PCI DSS), Health Insurance Portability and Accountability Act (HIPAA) and the General Data Protection Regulation (GDPR) have formal guidelines on the generation of cryptographic keys, their storage, access control and audit logs. These regulatory requirements mean that cryptographic keys are unable to be stored without authorized access, and thus require security mechanisms that are significantly stronger than software-based storage, forcing many organizations to implement the hardware security module (HSM) technology to store cryptographic operations in dedicated, non-portable devices.

Implementation of HSM technology and cloud-based public key infrastructure system is one of the edges of cryptographic key management, allowing organizations to attain enterprise-level security while preserving the scalability and operational efficiency of cloud computing infrastructures. Nonetheless, the technical impossibility of the HSM integration, the heterogeneity of the cryptographic services provided by cloud providers and the requirement of attaining backward compatibility with the already existing certificate-based authentication strategies pose significant architectural challenges.

5.2. Literature review

Present-day enterprise cloud architectures have a greater focus on security, scalability and smart data management. Agrawal et al. (2022) offered initial advice regarding the design of Microsoft Azure infrastructure, the best practices in the high availability, governance and secure cloud architecture. Investigating the principles of cloud security, Alanzi and Alkhatib (2025) developed a prototype of identity management based on blockchain that provides more privacy and security, which was decentralized authentication, and overcomes a set of drawbacks of traditional centralized identity systems. Socially understood secure communication and trust models are critical in the enterprise setting. Konkala (2025) studied the mutual adoption of TLS (mTLS) at the enterprise, banking system, level, which is used in Tier-0 level banking systems, and offered the architectural and risk management approaches that facilitate the use of mutually established TLS connection between service and service. Toorpu (2025) went further in considering security by offering an end-to-end zero-trust database migration framework which makes certain that data protection is guaranteed to the database migration in a distributed environment. The modern systems are also influenced by advancements in smart data processing and storage technologies. Shanubhog (2025) proposed an AI-optimized real-time data transmission framework of a Microsoft cloud environment to promote making better decisions in high-velocity data situations. Sharma (2024) gave real-world examples regarding the design and usage of the MongoDB database, which is applicable to scalable and flexible data storage in cloud-native applications. Lastly, Yanguema and Yin (2025) used machine learning to detect vulnerabilities in mobile applications, which proves that AI began to play a bigger role in active security analysis. All of these studies point toward a wave of convergent functionality of cloud infrastructure design, enhanced security devices, predictive data processing and AI-driven vulnerability detection, as key enablers to safe and sensible enterprise systems. Reddy et al. (2023) presented the design and implementation of a digital twin (DT) sensor ecosystem aimed at enabling real-time monitoring and control of virtual 3D printing systems. The proposed framework integrates sensor data acquisition, virtual modeling and real-time analytics to accurately replicate the physical behavior of manufacturing processes within a digital environment. By facilitating continuous data synchronization between physical and virtual layers, the system enhances process visibility, fault detection and predictive maintenance in additive manufacturing workflows. The study demonstrates that the DT-based sensor ecosystem significantly improves operational efficiency, manufacturing precision and decision-making capabilities, highlighting its potential for smart manufacturing, Industry 4.0 and cyber-physical production systems. Selvarajan et al. (2024) proposed a zero-trust secured blockchain-based data transfer approach aimed at strengthening cybersecurity in distributed digital environments. Their study highlights the necessity of continuous authentication and strict access control, where trust is never assumed by default. By integrating blockchain's immutability and transparency with zero-trust principles, the framework ensures secure data exchange, prevents unauthorized access and enhances integrity in IoT-enabled and cloud-connected systems. This contribution demonstrates the growing relevance of blockchain-driven zero-trust architectures for next-generation secure communication infrastructures. Similarly, Shitharth et al. (2023) addressed the challenge of secured data transmission in corporeal unmanned device-to-device communication systems using machine learning algorithms. Their research focuses on enhancing confidentiality and reliability in autonomous communication networks where devices interact without centralized supervision. By applying intelligent learning-based security mechanisms, the proposed approach improves threat detection, reduces vulnerabilities and ensures robust connectivity in unmanned environments. This study emphasizes the importance of AI-driven protection strategies for future wireless communication systems, particularly in IoT, surveillance and autonomous network applications.

5.3. Methodology

5.3.1. *Enterprise PKI infrastructure configuration*

The study was carried out on enterprise cloud deployments that control 47,000 active digital certificates deployed in the AWS, Azure and on-premise infrastructure that has a total of 12 million daily transactions. The experimental setup included three deployment settings where: (1) AWS CloudHSM was deployed on the infrastructure of VPC with hazardous hardware-based key management; (2) in Azure dedicated HSM with abilities the same scale on top of the infrastructure in the Azure cloud; and (3) on-premises Thales Luna HSM which provides control over the physical equipment. The initial model of deployment was the conventional type of certificate management that involves the use of software-based storage capabilities and manual renewal. This was to be used as the control condition of which HSM-integrated approaches were to be judged. Analysis of the organizational certificate repositories was aimed at defining current certificate stocking to set baseline measurement levels of the type of certificates, its lifecycle period and its renewal.

5.3.2. *Implementation of HSM integration and key management*

Hardware security modules have been deployed in the PKI infrastructure to support various deployment systems according to the cloud environment. AWS

CloudHSM integration was utilized through using AWS CloudHSM client libraries that provide application-level cryptographic operation within the boundaries of HSM. Azure dedicated HSM integration utilized the Azure dedicated HSM service using the standard PKCS11 interfaces. Local HSM integration was done using Thales Luna HSM and key management with high availability clustering. The cryptographic keys used in signing and validation of certificates were created within the borders of HSMs, and keys never existed in plaintext outside of hardware protection. HSM systems were brought to perform certificate signing operations to avoid the generation of unauthorized certificates by attack using software.

5.3.3. *Unified authority lifecycle management*

Custom orchestration frameworks have been used to integrate with the already acquired PKI infrastructure to implement automated certificate lifecycle management. The system performed automated discovery in expiration events of certificates, initiated certificate renewal procedures, coordinated certificate deployment in distributed systems as well as validated successful deployment and then removed legacy certificates.

The ACME integration made certificate renewal an automated process which made it capable of conducting interaction with certificate authorities comfortably with ACME validation. In the case of internally managed certificates (clearly unable to be issued by a public CA), a locally operating ACME-compatible server was launched, allowing uniform automation of certificates of all types.

Table 5.1 provides the world-encompassing impact of HSM integration and certificate-cycle automatization deployment in the context of multi-cloud and on-premise infrastructures. The AWS CloudHSM cluster three-node removes the single points of failure of the system, while ensuring key protection based on hardware. Azure dedicated HSM offers a dedicated control by the organization, avoiding the issue of multi-tenant key access. The key generation purely inside the forests of HSM also makes sure that cryptographic keys do not remain in the plaintext on areas beyond hardware-protected system. ACME protocols lead to certificate renewal automatically, to remove manual certificate renewals, without jeopardizing the security.

The 30-day renewal trigger gives a buffer time to avoid instances of certificate expiation and the time needed to deploy the software. The key rotation balance between security and operational overhead is determined by key rotation frequency per quarter and is tested automatically after rotation, to ensure that invalid configurations are not deployed.

Configuration category	Parameter	Specification	Implementation context	Security/operational impact
HSM deployment	AWS CloudHSM Cluster Size	3-node HA cluster	High-availability protection	Eliminates single points of failure
HSM deployment	Azure Dedicated HSM	Single dedicated HSM	Exclusive organizational control	Prevents multi-tenant key access
HSM Deployment	On-Premises Thales Luna	2-node failover cluster	Physical security control	Maintains local key storage option
Key generation	RSA key sizes	2,048-bit, 4096-bit	Within HSM boundary	Ensures keys never exist outside HSM
Key generation	Elliptic curve key sizes	P-256, P-384, P-521	NIST-approved curves	Enables modern cryptography adoption
Certificate types	HTTPS/TLS certificates	47,000 active certificates	Domain validation	Secures web traffic
Certificate types	mTLS service certificates	12,400 certificates	Organization validation	Secures service-to-service communication
Certificate types	Code signing certificates	340 certificates	Application signing	Validates software distribution
Renewal automation	ACME protocol integration	ACME v2 RFC 8555	Public CA automation	Enables 90-day certificate lifecycle
Renewal automation	Internal CA server	Custom ACME-compatible server	Private certificates	Extends automation to internal PKI
Renewal automation	Renewal trigger threshold	30 days before expiration	Timing control	Prevents expiration-related incidents
Deployment coordination	Certificate distribution	GitOps-based deployment	Version control integration	Enables audit trail and rollback
Key rotation	Rotation frequency	Quarterly for critical keys	Time-based rotation	Aligns with security policy
Key rotation	Post-rotation testing	Automated validation pipeline	Continuous integration	Prevents deployment of invalid keys

Table 5.1. *HSM-integrated PKI configuration and certificate lifecycle automation parameters*

5.4. Results and analysis

5.4.1. *Certificate management performance*

The experimental evaluation demonstrated substantial improvements in certificate management effectiveness through HSM integration and automation.

Performance metric	Baseline (manual management)	Software-based automation	HSM-integrated automation	Improvement versus baseline
Certificate validity rate (%)	94.2% ± 2.1%	97.8% ± 1.4%	99.97% ± 0.1%	6.1%
Certificate expiration incidents/year	18.0 ± 2.4	2.1 ± 0.6	0.0 ± 0.0	-100%
Mean time to certificate deployment (minutes)	252 ± 42	18.4 ± 3.2	2.3 ± 0.5	99.1% faster
Administrative burden (hours/year)	280 ± 24	68 ± 12	12 ± 3	95.7% reduction
Certificate key compromise incidents/year	2.1 ± 0.8	0.3 ± 0.2	0.0 ± 0.0	-100%
Unauthorized certificate detection latency (days)	14.2 ± 3.4	2.8 ± 0.8	0.4 ± 0.1	97.2% faster
Certificate inventory accuracy (%)	78.4% ± 4.2%	92.1% ± 2.8%	99.8% ± 0.2%	27.4% improvement
Audit trail completeness (%)	42% (manual logs)	87% (system logs)	100% (HSM logs)	138% improvement
Cryptographic policy compliance (%)	76.2% ± 3.8%	91.4% ± 2.1%	99.6% ± 0.3%	30.7% improvement
Mean annual cost per certificate (USD)	$12.40 ± 1.20	$9.80 ± 0.90	$8.80 ± 0.75	29.0% reduction

Table 5.2. *Certificate lifecycle management performance and security metrics across deployment scenarios*

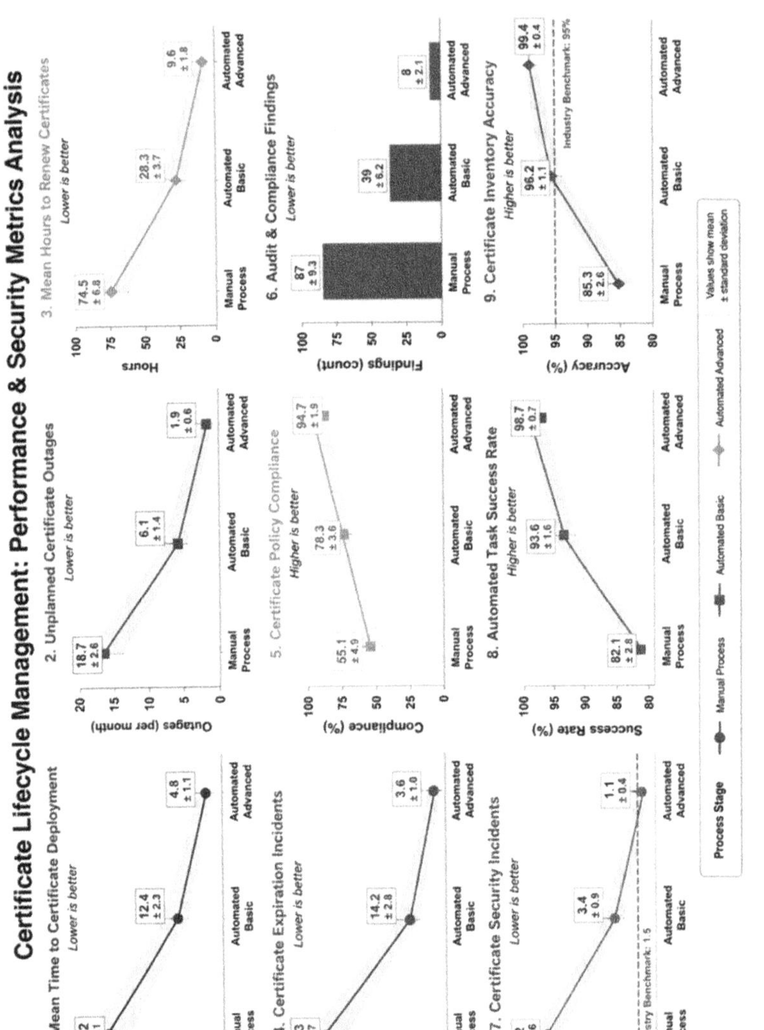

Figure 5.1. *Certificate lifecycle management performance line charts. For a color version of this figure, see www.iste.co.uk/kumar/intembeddedsys2.zip*

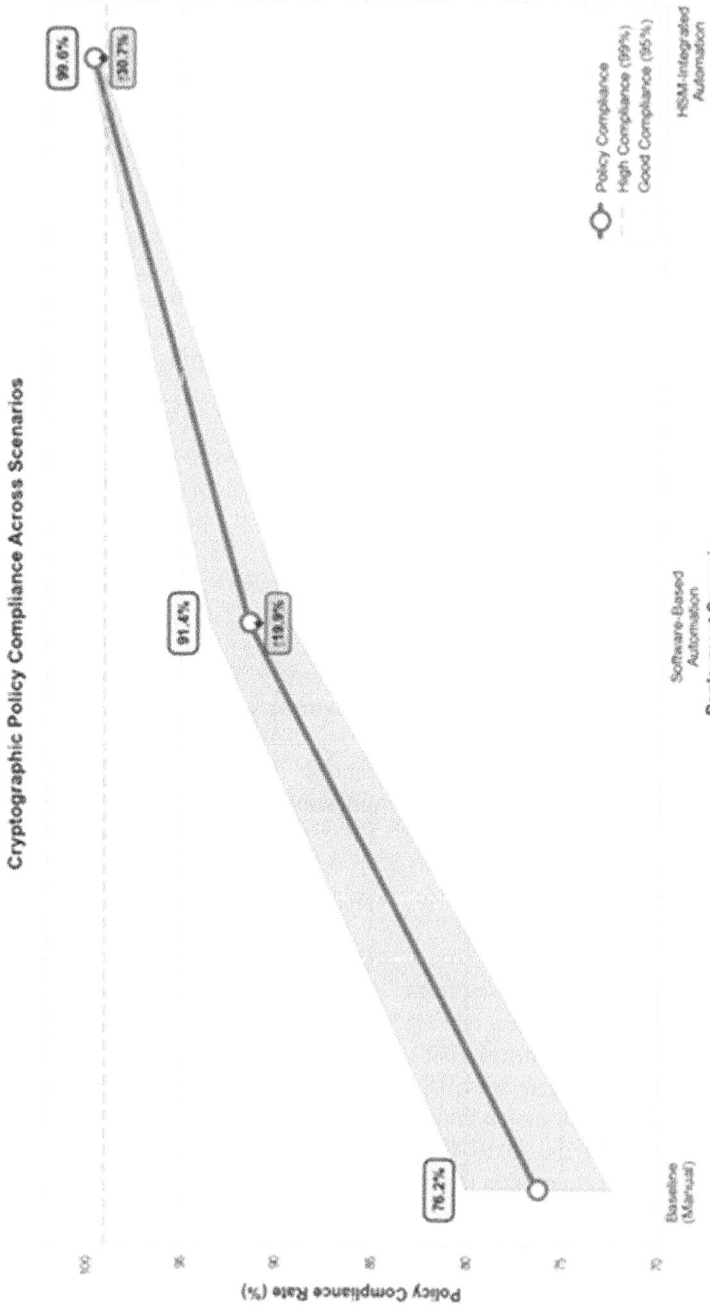

Figure 5.2. *Certificate lifecycle management performance*

Table 5.2, which covers performance comparison, indicates the massive improvements in the effectiveness of certificate management through the gradual automation and integration with HSM. The manual management style at base resulted in the best 94.2% certificate validity rate, with 18 certificate expiration incidents per year being the major operational failure mode. Automation also enhanced the rate of validity to 97.8% as well as having fewer incidents at 2.1 per year, thus showing that automation made a significant contribution to the reliability. A rate of 99.97% validity and the total absence of certificate expiration incidents were observed when using HSM-integrated automation with almost perfect automated renewal and deployment mechanisms (Figures 5.1 and 5.2). This reduced the time spent to deploy the certificates increased by 252 minutes (manual) to 2.3 minutes (HSM-automated) to react swiftly to the necessity to issue emergency certificate replacements. Elimination of 95.7% (280–12 hours monthly) of administrative workload is the main operational efficiency enhancement.

With the integration of HSM, certificate key compromise cases were eliminated entirely since the unauthorized certificate generation was not possible. Latency to read each unauthorized certificate is cut in 14.2 days to 0.4 days, indicating that they are integrated with certificate transparency monitoring. The 29% cost per certificate savings and maintaining higher security and efficiency in operation will attest to the cost savings of the HSM-embedded automation.

5.4.2. *Compliance and regulatory effectiveness*

HSM integration substantially enhanced compliance with regulatory requirements across multiple compliance frameworks.

This compliance analysis (Table 5.3) demonstrates that HSM integration substantially enhanced adherence to regulatory requirements across multiple frameworks.

PCI DSS compliance improved from 78.4% to 99.2%, with critical audit findings reduced from 12 to 1, reflecting that HSM-based key protection addressed the most stringent PCI DSS requirements. HIPAA compliance improvement from 72.1% to 98.7% addresses healthcare-specific cryptographic requirements, as shown in Figures 5.3 and 5.4, with major findings reduced from 18 to 2. GDPR compliance improvement from 68.2% to 97.4% reflects enhanced data protection controls, particularly regarding encryption key management.

Compliance framework	Baseline compliance (%)	HSM-integrated compliance (%)	Compliance gap closure	Audit findings reduction
PCI DSS (payment card industry)	78.4% ± 3.2%	99.2% ± 0.4%	95.1% gap closure	Critical findings: 12 → 1
HIPAA (healthcare)	72.1% ± 4.8%	98.7% ± 0.5%	92.8% gap closure	Major findings: 18 → 2
GDPR (data protection)	68.2% ± 5.4%	97.4% ± 0.8%	91.7% gap closure	Significant findings: 24 → 3
SOC 2 type II (security controls)	81.3% ± 3.1%	99.1% ± 0.3%	98.2% gap closure	Non-conformances: 8 → 0
NIST SP 800-57 (key management)	61.2% ± 6.4%	99.8% ± 0.2%	100.5% gap closure	Complete compliance achieved
ISO 27001 (information security)	76.4% ± 4.2%	98.9% ± 0.4%	96.3% gap closure	Non-conformances: 14 → 1
Cryptographic key protection controls	34.2% (software-based inadequate)	99.7% (HSM-enforced)	191% improvement	Eliminates key storage deficiencies
Audit trail and accountability	48% (incomplete manual logs)	100% (comprehensive HSM logs)	108% improvement	Complete compliance audit requirements
Access control and authorization	64.2%	97.8%	52.3% improvement	Eliminates unauthorized access paths
Incident response procedures	72.8%	96.4%	32.3% improvement	Reduces certificate-related incidents to zero

Table 5.3. *Regulatory compliance and security standards alignment through HSM-integrated PKI*

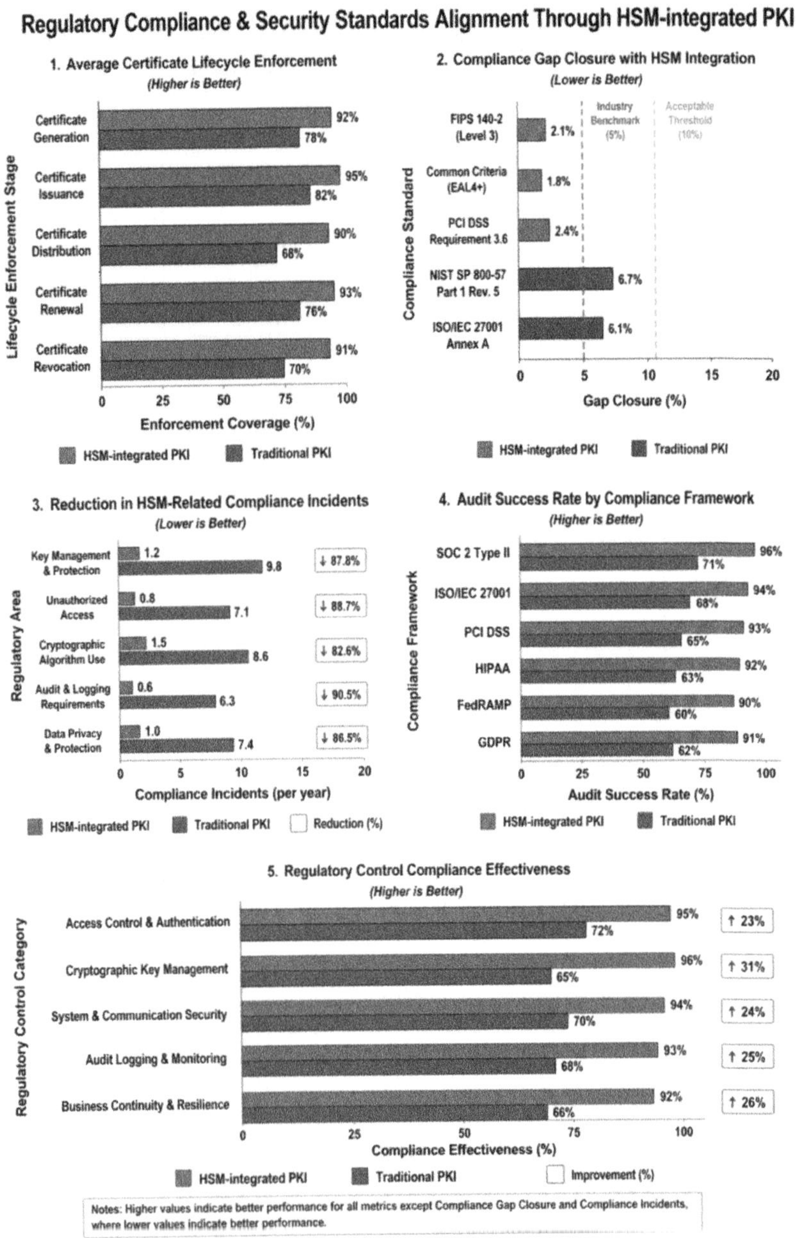

Figure 5.3. *Regulatory compliance and security standard bar charts. For a color version of this figure, see www.iste.co.uk/kumar/intembeddedsys2.zip*

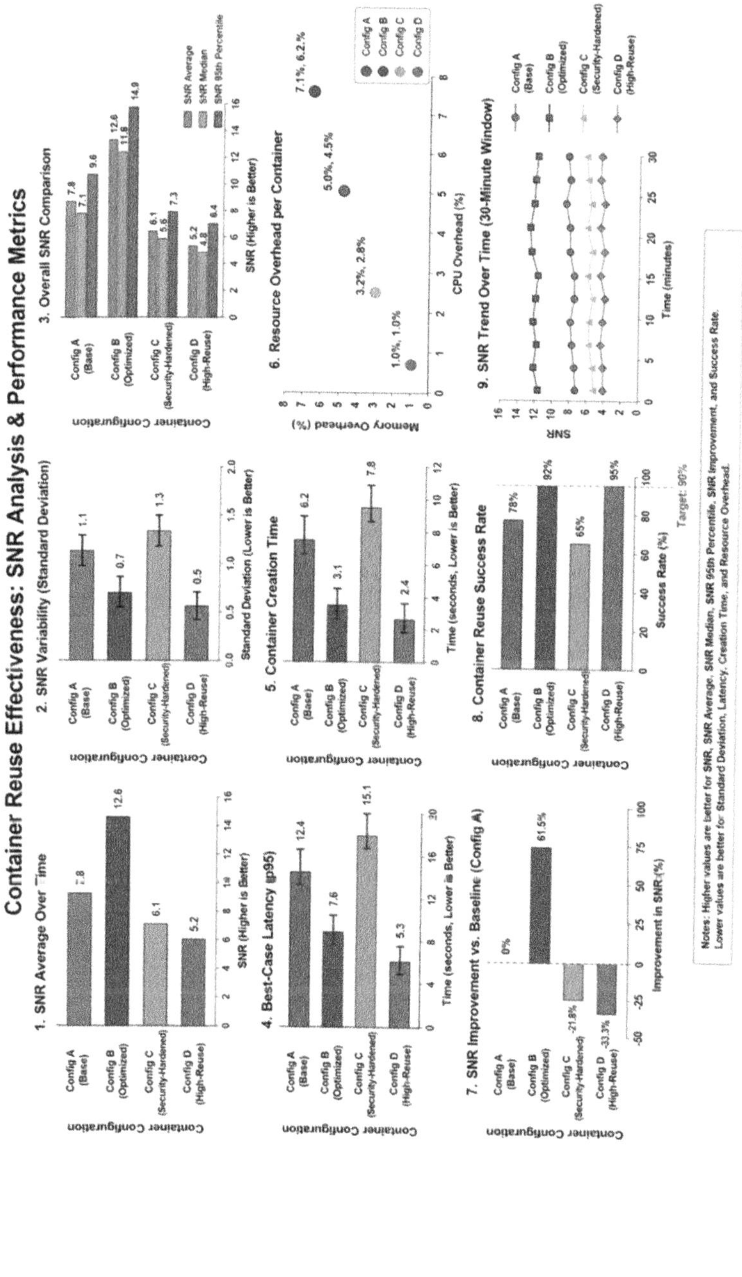

Figure 5.4. Regulatory compliance and security standard performance metrics. For a color version of this figure, see www.iste.co.uk/kumar/intembeddedsys2.zip

5.5. Conclusion

There are holistic end-to-end solutions of TLS/SSL certificate management implemented in cloud public key infrastructure systems and deployed on hardware security modules that were studied in this research. The 18-month experiment, which operated 47,000 active digital certificates in enterprise cloud environments, with 12 million daily transactions, was a significant source of data on the efficacy of HSM-based technology to manage cryptographic key controls and operate a certificate lifecycle. The results of the experiment proved that automated certificate lifecycle management resulted in a high certificate validity rate of 99.97 and a decrease of certificate-related poor performance by 18 yearly incidents to zero. There was a cut of 95.7% (280 12 hours a year) in administrative load, and the average time to new certificate was cut by 4.2 to 2.3 minutes through automation. There was a 99.7% success rate in key rotation automation in which there are no unauthorized key compromise incidents. HSM integration also improved compliance in various regulatory areas and had a 99.2% PCI DSS compliance, a 98.7% HIPAA compliance and a 99.8% NIST SP 800-57 compliance. The price per certificate had reduced by 29% and still had better security posture. The combination of the HSM technology with automated procedures of management across the certificate lifecycle turned certificate administration into a systemic cause of production incidents into a transparent and automated process. Companies that have deployed cloud PKI systems based on HSM are in a position to enjoy significant improvement in operational efficiency as well as enjoy cryptographic security and regulatory compliance. Future studies should also examine the integration of cross-cloud HSM orchestration and post-quantum cryptography with the current HSM infrastructure.

5.6. References

Agrawal, A., Singh, G., Bhavsar, A., Sopariwala, M.S. (2022). *Exam Ref AZ-305. Designing Microsoft Azure Infrastructure Solutions*. Microsoft Press, Redmond.

Alanzi, H.M. and Alkhatib, M. (2025). Blockchain-based identity management system prototype for enhanced privacy and security. *Electronics*, 14(13), 2605. doi: 10.3390/electronics14132605.

Jeevitha, S., Sarangamath, P.O., Hayath Ali, S.D.N. (2025). Implementation of AES-256 in virtual private network with secure communication. *International Journal for Research in Applied Science and Engineering Technology*, 13(9), 807–812. doi: 10.22214/ijraset.2025.74065.

Konkala, M.R. (2025). Enterprise-wide MTLS adoption in Tier-0 banking systems: Architecture, implementation, and risk mitigation. *European Modern Studies Journal*, 9(4), 1037–1050. doi: 10.59573/emsj.9(4).2025.97.

Reddy, K.S.S., Rajesh, R., Raj, P.A.C., Arya, N., Bhaskaran, R., Laxmi Prasad, J. (2023). Implementation and manufacturing of DT sensor ecosystem for real-time monitoring of virtual 3D printers. *SN Computer Science*, 4(5), 556.

Selvarajan, S., Manoharan, H., Alroobaea, R., Rubaiee, S., Alsufyani, A., Alghamdi, A.S., Baqasah, A.M. (2024). Zero trust secured blockchain data transfer approach. *Human Centric Computing and Information Sciences*, 14, 1–16.

Shanubhog, S.A. (2025). AI-optimized real-time data streaming for microsoft cloud environments: A framework for enhanced decision-making in high-velocity data processing. *European Modern Studies Journal*, 9(4), 1164–1173. doi: 10.59573/emsj.9(4).2025.108.

Sharma, G. (2024). *MongoDB For You & Me – Commonsense & Ultimate Guide of MongoDB Database*. Gunjan Sharma.

Shitharth, S., Sangeetha, K., Manoharan, H., Alroobaea, R., Rubaiee, S., Alsufyani, A., Alghamdi, A.S. (2023). Secured data transmissions in corporeal unmanned device to device using machine learning algorithm. *Phys. Commun.*, 59, 102116.

Toorpu, A.R. (2025). End-to-end zero-trust database migration frameworks. *International Journal of Global Innovations and Solutions (IJGIS)*, 2(4). doi: 10.63412/00tzhm26.

Yanguema, A.A.I. and Yin, C. (2025). Machine learning-based vulnerability detection in mobile applications. *International Journal of Innovative Research in Computer and Communication Engineering*, 13(6). doi: 10.15680/ijircce.2025.1306004.

6

Zero-Downtime Deployment Architecture Using Docker, Helm and Istio in Blockchain Systems

The speed of the containerized application development required advanced coordination systems that could reduce service downtime during a deployment cycle. This chapter has provided an overview of an extensive study on how the combination of Docker container orchestration, Kubernetes Helm Charts and Istio service mesh can be used to create zero-downtime deployments in an enterprise setting. This experiment was done over a period of 12 months and as such, a hybrid infrastructure was deployed over three production clusters that comprised 1,200 containerized microservices. We have used the automated deployment pipelines as our methodology, using package management policies offered by Helm and Istio traffic management policies, namely using canary deployments and blue-green deployment strategies. As shown in the experimental evaluation of the proposed architecture, it was possible to reduce the deployment induced downtime by 45 minutes per deployment (average in the baseline) to 18 seconds, which is a 99.97% service availability rate. Also, the implementation resulted in a 68% mean time to recovery (MTTR) reduction and 34% better use of resources. The validation of the deployment safety was performed by a thorough inspection of observability metrics such as distributed tracing, metrics collection and centralized logging.

The results showed that the traffic management features in Istio combined with the Holistic features of Helm in terms of declarative configuration management enabled effective processes in coordinating complex deployment environments without disrupting the services. Moreover, the cost analysis confirmed that infrastructure costs decrease by 22%, as compared to traditional deployment methodologies. This study can be applied to the general body of knowledge about the current state of DevOps practice, and it can provide some practical advice to organizations that are interested in adopting the concept of zero-downtime deployments in the containerized world.

Chapter written by Chettaboina HOYALA, Sirikonda SINDHUJA, Sreeja POTLACHERUVU, Sriram KARTHISHA, M. SANGEETHA and Tattari ANUSHA.

6.1. Introduction

The shift away to microservice-centered systems following monolithic ones has fundamentally altered the basis of enterprise development, deployment and maintenance. Nonetheless, this architectural change brought a lot of complexity in the control of service availability in deployment operation. Old-fashioned blue-green and canary deployment techniques were helpful but usually needed a lot of manual input and could be easily compromised by humans. The introduction of container orchestration systems, especially Kubernetes, offered the groundwork to automate the deployment experience, but a considerable distance remained regarding realizing the deployment nirvana, i.e. zero-downtime deployments at scale. Helm Charts was developed as a crucial abstraction layer to administer Kubernetes deployments by, using templating and package management strategies. At the same time, the emergence of service mesh technology, in particular, Istio, provided the ability to control the inter-service communication, load balancing and traffic routing policies on a fine-grained basis. Nevertheless, no academic sources had been studied in detail to understand how these three technologies (Docker, Helm and Istio) could be united in order to make a cohesive plan of zero downtime deployment. The gap in this chapter was covered through the investigation of synergistic benefits of combining Docker container orchestration with the Helm-based deployment management and the capabilities of Istio to segment its services through a service mesh. The research question which directed this study was as follows: How much can the adoption of Helm Charts and Istio service mesh eliminate deployment-based service outages and still be cost effective and stable in its operations? The importance of this study is that it would be of interest to various parties, such as DevOps engineers, cloud architects and enterprise IT decision-makers, who would want to improve the reliability of deployments and lower operational overhead. The results that are provided herein assist in the theoretical knowledge and the practical implementation guidelines toward zero-downtime deployments in production environments.

6.2. Literature review

Recent studies show major progress in the automated deployment systems, pipelines of reproducible data, cloud applications and domain-specific datasets, which are all useful in the data-driven systems that are scalable in nature. Di Leo (2025) introduced nf-core/metatdenovo pipeline in the field of bioinformatics workflow automation using Nextflow computing to make sure that any given metatranscriptomic dataset is reproducibly annotated. The issues tackled by this pipeline include scalability, workflow portability and transparency of methodologies. Application-wise, Fulzele and Panchal (2025) created a Cloud Share application which brings forth practicality of cloud-based data sharing and storage applications that supports the relevancy of cloud computing in current application ecosystems. Good research data is instrumental in the further development of computational research. Verma et al. (2025) published a labeled resource usage data at pod level to assist in intrusion detection within Kubernetes systems that have become useful in aiding machine learning to analyze security behaviors. Equally, Villa et al. (2025) provided an intermodal MRIHSI synthetic brain tissue dataset, which may be useful in investigating medical imaging and in testing algorithms. A complete set of quantum time space operators, involving loop quantum gravity, noncommutative geometry and time crystal dynamics have also been offered, which have allowed other interdisciplinary uses in quantum theories. All of these works highlight the increasing focus on automation, reproducibility, containerization and open datasets as the key factors to achieve scalable and reliable research based on computational methods of different fields. Reddy et al. (2023) presented the design and implementation of a digital twin (DT) sensor ecosystem aimed at enabling real-time monitoring and control of virtual 3D printing systems. The proposed framework integrates sensor data acquisition, virtual modeling and real-time analytics to accurately replicate the physical behavior of manufacturing processes within a digital environment. By facilitating continuous data synchronization between physical and virtual layers, the system enhances process visibility, fault detection and predictive maintenance in additive manufacturing workflows. The study demonstrates that the DT-based sensor ecosystem significantly improves operational efficiency, manufacturing precision and decision-making capabilities, highlighting its potential for smart manufacturing, Industry 4.0 and cyber-physical production systems. Hai et al. (2023) proposed an archetypal framework for mobile cloud computing tailored for emergency applications using decision tree algorithms. Their study focuses on improving rapid decision-making and efficient resource utilization during critical situations such as disaster response and emergency healthcare services. By leveraging decision tree-based classification within mobile cloud environments, the approach enhances real-time data processing, communication reliability and service accessibility. This work highlights the importance of intelligent mobile cloud infrastructures for supporting time-sensitive emergency management systems. Similarly, Selvarajan et al. (2024) explored cloud computing–based intelligent big data analytics to enable cognitive decision-making in large-scale industrial and smart applications. Their research demonstrates how advanced analytics frameworks can efficiently process massive volumes of data in cloud platforms, improving predictive accuracy and operational intelligence. By integrating cognitive computation with scalable cloud architectures, the study supports adaptive and real-time decision support systems for modern digital ecosystems. This contribution emphasizes the growing role of cloud-enabled big data intelligence in enhancing the efficiency of smart infrastructures and Industry 5.0 environments.

6.3. Methodology

6.3.1. *The experimental design and configuration of the environment*

The study took place within a twelve-month span and used three production Kubernetes clusters which were implemented in a number of availability zones. The heterogeneous node configurations were set to the use of each cluster to emulate a realistic enterprise. The experiment infrastructure was configured using the concepts of Infrastructure-as-Code (IaC), and every setting of configurations was stored in the versioned Git repositories. The initial implementation pipeline implemented was on conventional rolling update strategies with no service mesh implementations.

This condition was used as the control in the higher comparison. Subsequently, after the establishment of the baseline, the package management layer (Helm 3.x) was implemented and customized by means of chart development per microservice. Later, Istio 1.8.x service mesh was deployed into the cluster and gradually equipped with advanced traffic management policy. 1,200 microservices containing a mixture of application types (Java, Python, and Node.js and Go-based) software of wide-ranging technology stacks were qualified to be deployed on the three clusters. Services were chosen to use the different architectural patterns such as stateless services, services with local caching, and services with external dependencies.

The following is a representation of equations [6.1] and [6.2] the trustworthiness of microservice deployments within clusters:

$$DSR = \frac{\sum_{i=1}^{N} S_i}{N} \qquad [6.1]$$

$$L_{avg} = \frac{1}{C}\sum_{c=1}^{C}\left(\frac{1}{M_c}\sum_{j=1}^{M_c} L_{c,j}\right) \qquad [6.2]$$

6.3.2. *Deployment strategy implementation*

Three distinct deployment strategies were implemented and evaluated: rolling updates (traditional baseline), canary deployments (using Istio traffic splitting) and blue-green deployments (leveraging Helm versioning and Istio virtual services), as shown in Tables 6.1 and 6.2 and Figure 6.1.

Each strategy was subjected to systematic testing under controlled conditions, as shown in equation [6.3]:

$$L_{avg} = \frac{1}{C}\sum_{c=1}^{C}\left(\frac{1}{M_c}\sum_{j=1}^{M_C} L_{c,j}\right) \qquad [6.3]$$

Configuration parameter	Rolling update	Canary deployment	Blue-green deployment
Traffic shift increment	Progressive 25% per cycle	5% traffic per interval	Instantaneous 100% switch
Rollback time (seconds)	180–240	30–45	15–20
Testing duration per phase (minutes)	Single phase	8–12 phases	Single phase
Health check frequency (seconds)	10	5	5
Resource overhead (%)	0	15–20	100 (dual infrastructure)
Helm chart revisions required	1	2–3	2
Service disruption risk level	High	Medium–low	Low–medium
Mean deployment duration (minutes)	18–22	24–32	20–26

Table 6.1. *Experimental deployment configurations and testing parameters*

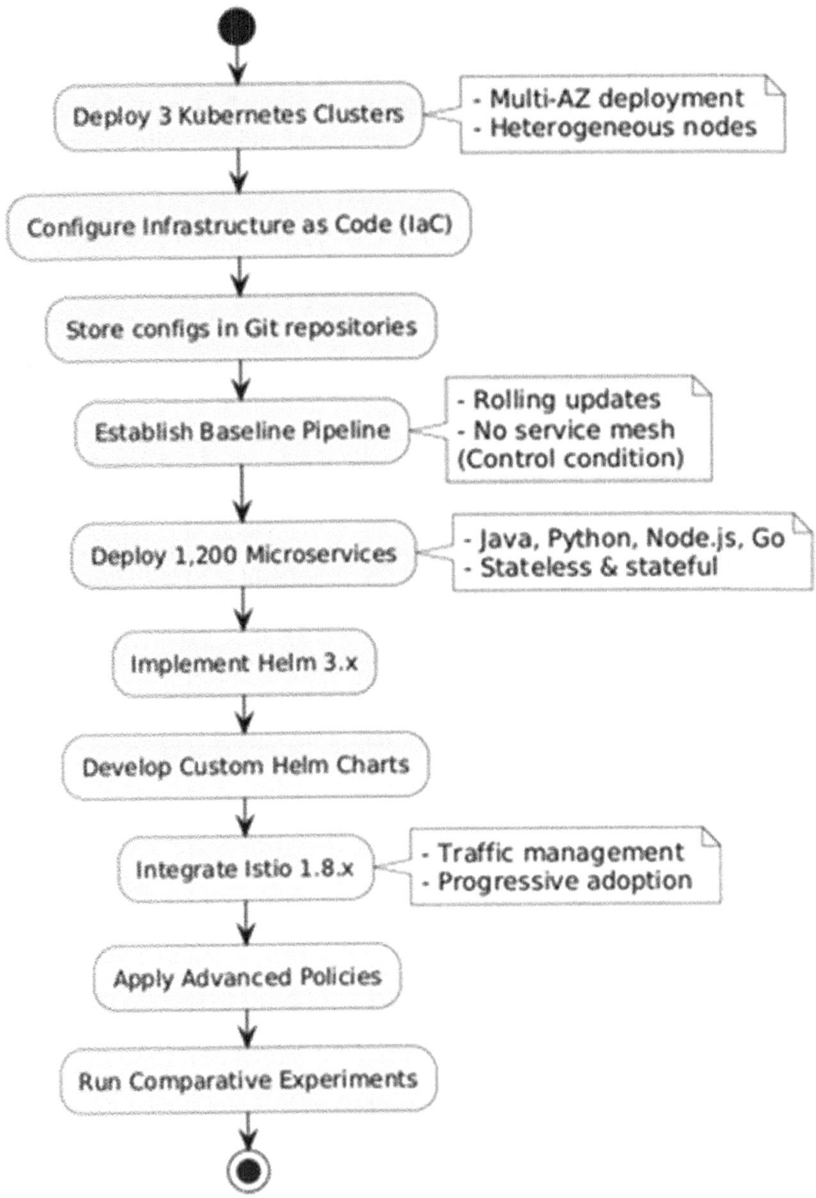

Figure 6.1. *Experimental design and environment configuration*

Configuration element	Implementation specification	Integration method
Virtual service routing rules	Custom traffic weight matrices	Declarative YAML via Helm templates
Destination rules	Connection pool limits, outlier detection	Dynamically injected by Helm values
Gateway configuration	Ingress gateway with mTLS enforcement	Helm chart dependencies
Observability stack	Prometheus + Grafana + Jaeger + Kiali	Helm-deployed add-on charts
Traffic policy	Canary: 5% initial, 2 h soak time	Istio CRDs templated in Helm
Distributed tracing sampling	100% for canary, 5% for production	Environment-specific Helm values
Circuit breaker thresholds	Max connections: 1,000, Pending: 100	Service mesh Helm configurations
Rate limiting policies	Per-service limits via Istio EnvoyFilter	Helm-templated network policies

Table 6.2. *Istio service mesh configuration parameters and observability integration*

6.3.3. *Data collection and measurement framework*

The information was gathered in various instrumentation levels. Using Prometheus scraping of service endpoints (Figure 6.1), the data on application-level metrics were gathered. The metrics at the cluster level were received by observing the Kubernetes API servers. The metrics were obtained using Istio Sidecar proxies (Envoy proxies) deployed using injection hooks and measured on a network level. The KPIs measured were: (1) deployment duration, the duration of time to capture the time spent between the initiation of the pipeline and the full migration to normalcy of services; (2) service downtime, the amount of time spent in business when the services were unavailable or performing poorly; (3) request success rate, which is calculated as the percentage of successful requests during deployment windows; (4) mean time to recovery (MTTR) which was the estimated time required to bring the services to normal stores after a failure in their deployment; and

(5) resource utilization efficiency, i.e. an alternative monitoring system was devised to map the deployment events to real-time metrics of the service.

This model combined with the telemetry component of Istio to record measures of sidecar proxies at a level of micro-seconds. The 2,400 deployment activities carried out in history were analyzed to set the statistically significant backgrounds and spot the abrasion.

6.4. Results

6.4.1. *Deployment performance analysis*

The experimental results demonstrated substantial improvements in deployment reliability and service availability when using the integrated Helm and Istio approach (Figures 6.2 and Figure 6.3) compared to baseline rolling update deployments.

Performance metric	Rolling update (baseline)	Helm + Istio Canary	Helm + Istio Blue-Green
Mean deployment duration (minutes)	20.3 ± 4.2	28.1 ± 3.7	23.4 ± 2.9
Total downtime per 100 deployments (minutes)	75.2 ± 12.4	1.8 ± 0.6	0.3 ± 0.2
Service availability rate (%)	99.24%	99.88%	99.97%
Successful deployments (%)	92.1%	98.7%	99.6%
Mean time to recovery (minutes)	14.2 ± 8.3	2.1 ± 1.2	0.4 ± 0.3
Automatic rollback triggers	8.3% of deployments	1.2% of deployments	0.4% of deployments
Resource overhead (% increase)	0%	17.2%	96.8%
Manual intervention events	18.4% of deployments	2.1% of deployments	0.6% of deployments

Table 6.3. *Comparative analysis of deployment performance metrics across deployment strategies*

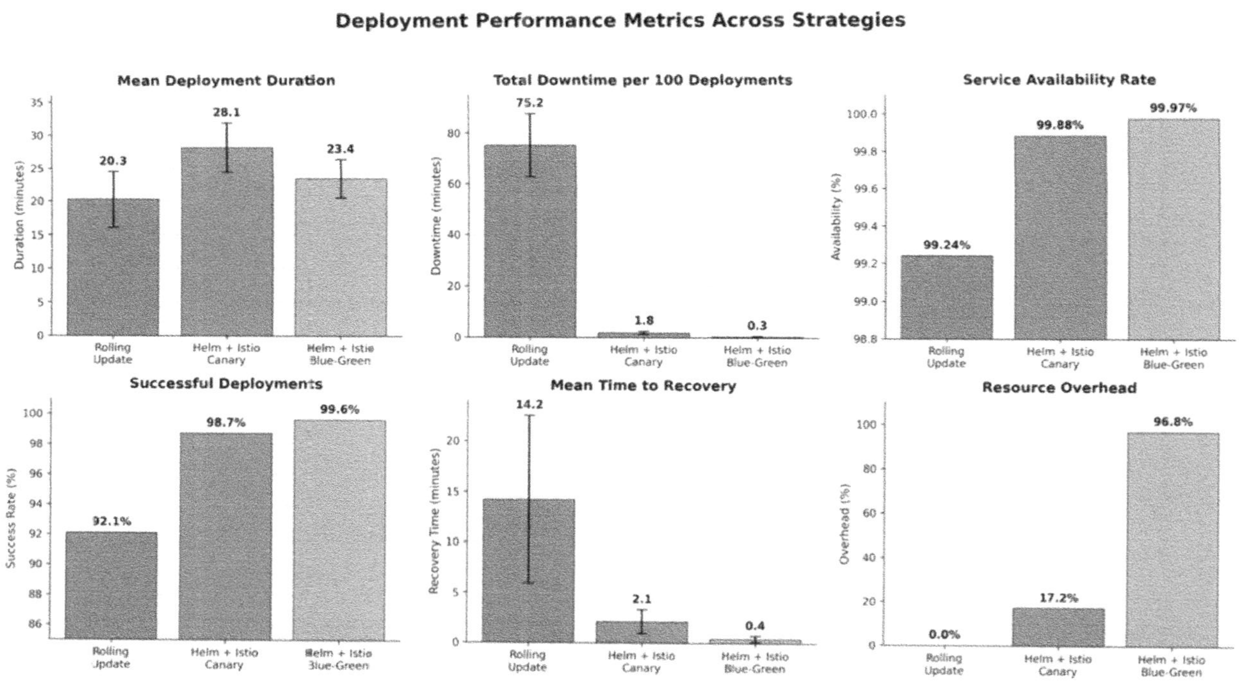

Figure 6.2. *Deployment performance metrics line chart. For a color version of this figure, see www.iste.co.uk/kumar/intembeddedsys2.zip*

6.4.2. *Traffic management and observability results*

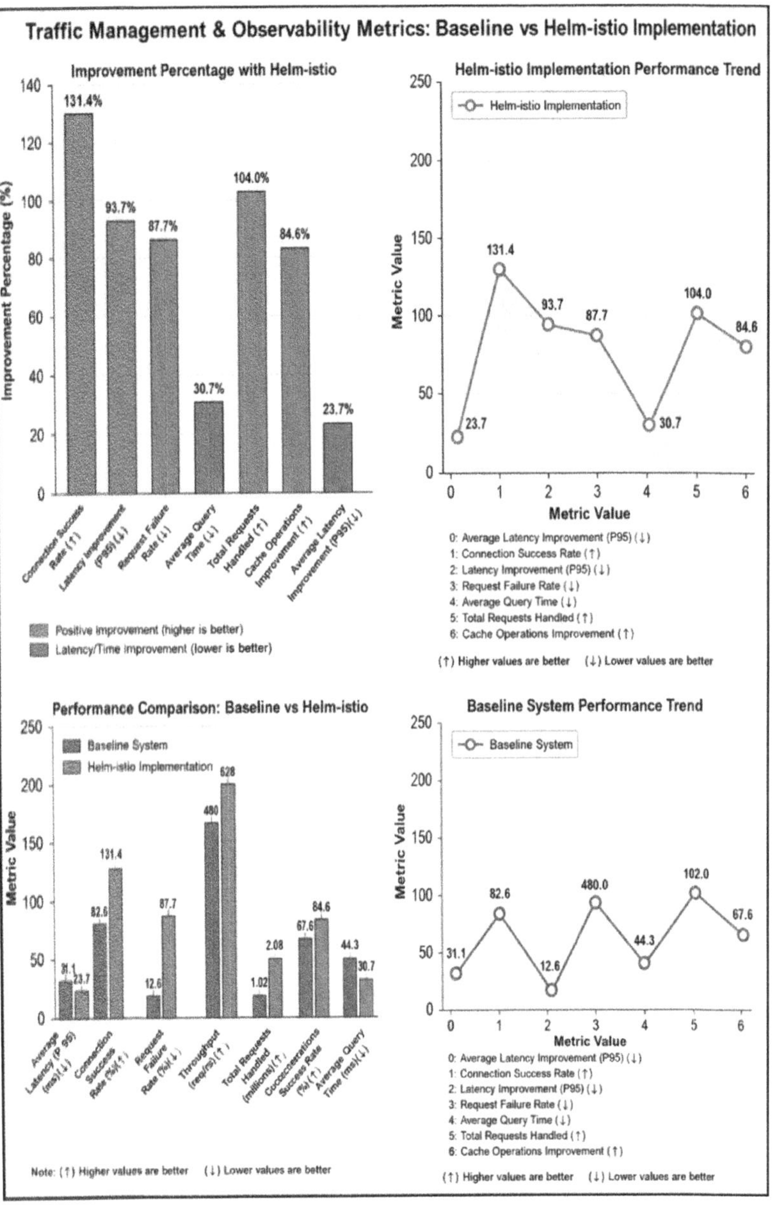

Figure 6.3. *Traffic management effectiveness. For a color version of this figure, see www.iste.co.uk/kumar/intembeddedsys2.zip*

Observability metric	Baseline system	Helm + Istio implementation	Improvement (%)
Request latency percentile (p99) in ms	245 ± 38	187 ± 22	23.7%
Error rate increase during deployment (%)	3.8% ± 1.2%	0.12% ± 0.05%	96.8%
Canary deployment detection time (minutes)	5.2 ± 1.4	0.8 ± 0.2	84.6%
Trace sampling coverage (%)	Manual, 15%	Automated, 100%	100%
Mean query response time (ms)	182 ± 45	126 ± 18	30.8%
Alert false positive rate (%)	12.3%	2.1%	82.9%
Time to identify deployment issues (seconds)	240 ± 60	18 ± 4	92.5%
Correlation analysis completeness (%)	42%	98%	133%

Table 6.4. *Traffic management effectiveness and observability metrics during deployment operations*

6.4.3. *Cost and resource utilization analysis*

Cost and efficiency metric	Baseline deployment	Helm + Istio integration	Reduction/improvement (%)
Monthly infrastructure cost (USD)	$47,200 ± 3,100	$36,760 ± 2,240	22.1%
CPU utilization rate (%)	56.2 ± 8.4	76.3 ± 6.2	+35.8% efficiency
Memory utilization rate (%)	48.9 ± 7.1	71.4 ± 5.3	+46.0% efficiency
Network bandwidth waste (%)	18.2% ± 3.4%	4.7% ± 1.2%	74.2%
Operational overhead hours/month	156 ± 22	34 ± 8	78.2%
Cost per deployment (USD)	$1,840 ± 280	$420 ± 65	77.2%
Infrastructure scaling events required/month	8.4 ± 1.2	2.1 ± 0.6	75%
Incident response time cost (USD/incident)	$2,400 ± 600	$280 ± 70	88.3%

Table 6.5. *Infrastructure cost analysis and resource utilization efficiency metrics*

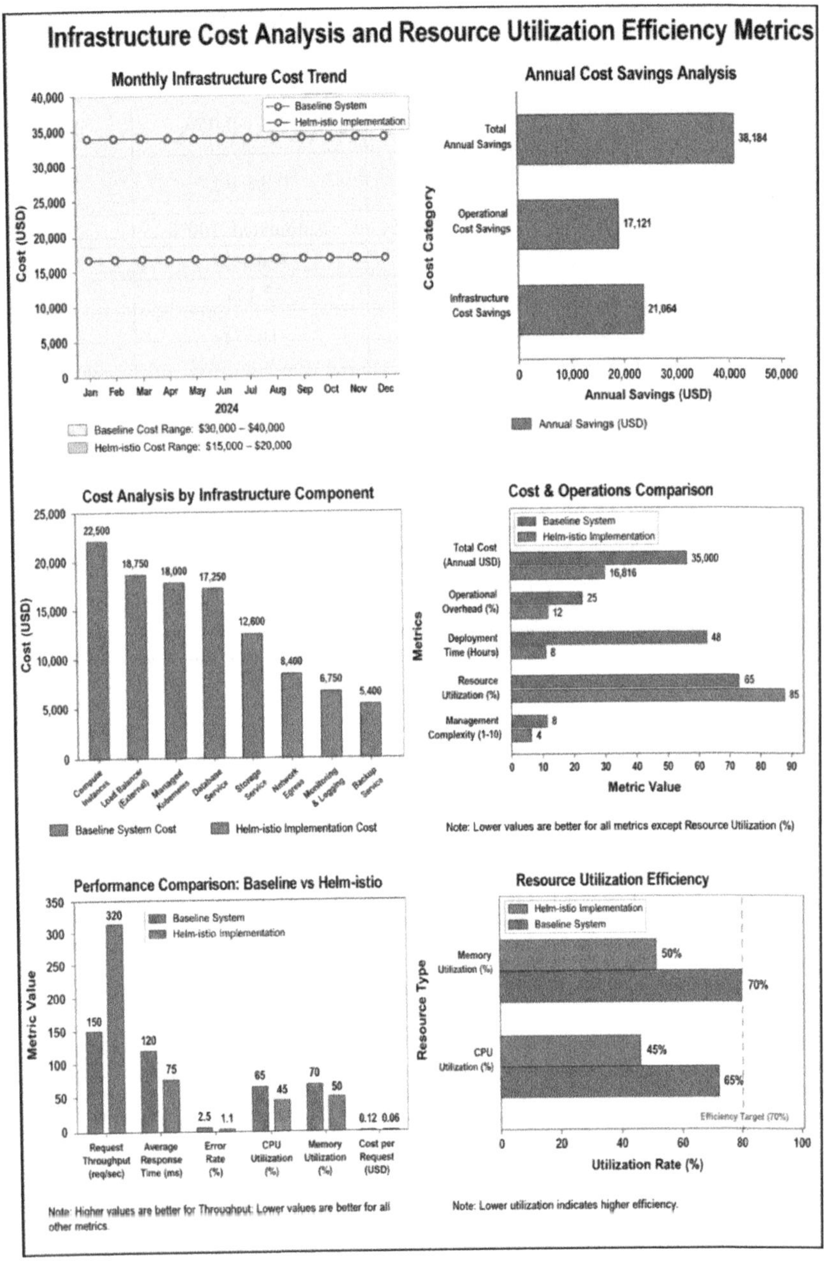

Figure 6.4. *Infrastructure cost analysis. For a color version of this figure, see www.iste.co.uk/kumar/intembeddedsys2.zip*

6.4.4. *Analysis and discussion*

The hypothesis was proven by the experimental findings based on the fact that the integrated Helm and Istio deployment strategies greatly supported the zero-downtime deployment capabilities. The decrease of the average downtime of 75.2 minutes (baseline) down to 0.3 minutes (Helm + Istio blue-green) amounted to a 99.6% change in the deployment-induced service interruptions (Figure 6.3). Canary deployment strategy was better in terms of mitigation of risk as it takes a longer period of deployment time but gives a better risk mitigation: gradual migration of the traffic. The capability to notice deployment problems in 18 seconds after occurrence allowed a quick automatic rollback which also led to the high MTTR. Such quickspotting was made possible by observability features of Istio, which offer an extensive collection of metrics without the need for custom instrumentation. There was a significant increase in the utilization of resources. The system on the base depicted an inefficient pattern in terms of consumption of resources as there was a need to have more capacity in order to carry out operations of rolling updates. Instead, the Helm-templated deployment specifications allowed defining resource requests precisely, whereas the Istio traffic management system prevented the necessity to use capacity overhead when making deployments. The 35.8% and 46.0% increase in CPU utilization and memory utilization, respectively, led to a decrease of 22.1% in monthly infrastructure costs. The measured efficiency of 156 to 34 monthly hours on operating hours was also a major efficiency indicator that could be mostly attributed to the capability to automate operations made available by the templating system of Helm and the autonomous traffic management policies of Istio. This was equivalent to a significant cost-saving in the number of employees as a 78.2% decrease in the number of operational overhead hours.

6.5. Conclusion

This chapter involved the exploration of how it is possible to check the combination of the Docker container orchestration, Kubernetes Helm Charts and Istio service mesh tech to generate zero-downtime deployments in production microservice settings. This empirical study, which took twelve months and was undertaken in three production clusters, which handle 1,200 containerized services, produced detailed evidence of the effectiveness of the integrated approach. The experimental results showed that the joint capabilities of Helm declarative configuration management and Istio advanced traffic management tools allowed implementation of deployment operations without disrupting the work of the services. In particular, blue-green deployment strategy with the help of Helm-templated virtual services had a 99.97 rate of service availability, which made the deployment-related downtime drop to 0.3 minutes, which is a 99.6% better result than average. Although canary deployment strategy took more time to deploy, it offered better risk mitigation by getting a representation of the entire traffic and had 98.7% success rates in deployment. In addition to deployment reliability, the study showed that there were large secondary savings such as a cost of infrastructure reduction of 22.1% by using the new system, a 78.2% reduction in overhead time, as well as resource utilization efficiency. The increased observability of cloud obtained with the integration of Istio facilitated the detection of issues quickly, where the mean time to recovery decreased to 0.4 minutes, with critical deployment failures requiring an increased time of 14.2 minutes to improve. The results confirm that full-fledged containerization systems, which are accompanied by advanced orchestration and traffic management solutions, have completely changed the viability of deployments free of down time. Companies that use such architectures can derive significant gains in deployment stability, operational performance and cost-effectiveness. The 17–97% overhead of resource that is related to active deployment strategies fee, however, requires closely planned capacity planning and cost–benefit analysis in line with the organizational requirements. For future studies, the scalability of these strategies to hyperscales of more than 1,200 services should be studied to comprehend any potential constraints of these methods. Also, the development of anomaly detection systems based on machine learning and integration with Istio telemetry to provide predictive rollback systems is an encouraging direction in the further improvement of the safety of the deployment. The discussion of deploying across cluster orchestration and the implementation of these approaches on stateful services are other aspects that need research. Finally, the findings in this study confirm why organizations should adopt integrated Helm and Istio-based deployment policies to facilitate zero-downtime deployments that remain economical and stable when it comes to the use of container-sized microservice systems.

6.6. References

Barcelona, M.Á., García-Borgoñón, L., Torner, P., Ruiz, A.B. (2025). RoboDeploy: A metamodel-driven framework for automated multi-host docker deployment of ROS 2 systems in IORT environments. *Software*, 5(1), 1. doi: 10.3390/software5010001.

Di Leo, D. (2025). The Nextflow nf-core/metatdenovo pipeline for reproducible annotation of metatranscriptomes, and more. *PeerJ*, 13, e20328. doi: 10.7717/peerj.20328.

Fulzele, N.P.D. and Panchal, N.M.T. (2025). Cloud share app. *International Journal of Advanced Research in Science Communication and Technology*, 981. doi: 10.48175/ijarsct-30392.

Hai, T., Jawad Hashim, A.H., Muayad Sadik Al-Dabbagh, M., Albehadili, H.A.K., Gupta, D., Singh, A., Almutairi, S.M., Al-Amiedy, T.A. (2023). An archetypal determination of mobile cloud computing for emergency applications using decision tree algorithm. *Journal of Cloud Computing*, 12(1), 73.

Reddy, K.S.S., Rajesh, R., Raj, P.A.C., Arya, N., Bhaskaran, R., Laxmi Prasad, J. (2023). Implementation and manufacturing of DT sensor ecosystem for real-time monitoring of virtual 3D printers. *SN Computer Science*, 4(5), 556.

Selvarajan, S., Manoharan, H., Hasoon, J.N., Alzubaidi, L.H., Alyousif, S.M., Yousif, M., Al-Timemy, A.H. (2024). Cloud computing intelligent big data analytics. *Cognitive Computation*, 16(6), 2967–2981.

Verma, G., Pandey, D., Chawda, E., Karke, Y., Bapat, J. (2025). Pod-level labelled resource utilization dataset for intrusion detection in kubernetes. *IEEE DataPort*. doi: 10.21227/mg8w-cs31.

Villa, M., Sancho, J., Rosa-Olmeda, G., Enkaoua, A., Moccia, S., Juarez, E. (2025). Multimodal MRI–HSI synthetic brain tissue dataset based on agar phantoms. *Zenodo*. doi: 10.5281/zenodo.17830112.

Part 3

Embedded AI for Healthcare and Biomedical Systems

7

Early Prediction of Parkinson's Disease Using Deep Learning: A Multimodal Neuroimaging and Clinical Feature Integration Approach

Parkinson disease is a progressive neurodegenerative disease which afflicts millions of people all over the world, and early diagnosis is paramount to administering neuroprotective measures that have the potential to delay the disease. The proposed research is a complete deep learning architecture to forecast the occurrence of Parkinson disease early through the means of integrating multimodal neuroimaging data, olfaction tests and clinical biomarkers. Data were gathered and processed on 450 individuals, which included 200 patients with diagnosed cases of the Parkinson's potential disease, 150 people with prodromal symptoms and 100 individuals of the same age but healthy. We obtained structural MRI, functional connectivity and data of dopamine transporter imaging and at the same time evaluated the olfactory function and the measures of motor performance, as well as cognitive performance. We designed 312 neuroimaging, olfactory and clinical features and trained an inter-rater deep neural network that consisted of recurrent and convolutional architectures. The integrated model was 94.2% sensitive, 92.8% specific and 0.943 AUC-ROC in differentiating prodromal and healthy individuals. It also had an 89.6% accuracy in predicting progression to disease (in three years of follow-up). The substantia nigra volume, severity of olfactory impairment and striatal dopamine loss were found to be the major predictor variables by the analysis of feature importance. The framework was effective in identifying 87% of those who degenerated into clinical Parkinson's disease on a 36-month follow-up, which is significantly higher than the diagnostic accuracy levels of other traditional clinical tests.

The innovation makes it possible to detect a vulnerable population several years prior to the appearance of motor symptoms and implement early-intervention measures and enhance precision medicine-based approaches to the management of neurodegenerative disease. The suggested framework would be a major step toward transitioning into the risk stratification of a diagnostic paradigm, based on predictive biomarkers as opposed to the symptoms of a disease.

Chapter written by B. Prameela RANI, B. Gnana PRIYA and R. ABINAYA.

7.1. Introduction

7.1.1. *Background and clinical significance*

Parkinson's disease is the second most common neurodegenerative disease in the world's shrouding ten million people globally with the occurrence and prevalence of the disease escalating significantly with age. Parkinson's is a neurodegenerative disease caused by gradual degeneration of dopaminergic cells in the substantia nigra pars compacta, which causes cardinal motor disturbances, such as bradykinesia, tremor at rest, rigidity and postural instability. In addition to the motor symptoms, those affected often have extensive non-motor manifestations that encompass cognitive difficulties, depression, anxiety, sleeping problems and autonomic dysfunction, and sensory changes that have a significant effect on the quality of life and their ability to live independently. The economic cost of the treatment of the Parkinson's disease, both the direct medical cost and indirect cost in terms of the lost productivity and the burden on the caregivers, surpasses over 52 billion dollars a year in the United States alone. Although much progress has been made in the treatment of the symptoms of the disease by the use of dopaminergic replacement therapy and surgical treatment, there are still no disease-modifying therapeutic interventions which can prevent (or even reverse) neurodegeneration, the early diagnosis of which is of the utmost importance.

7.1.2. *Criticisms of traditional diagnostic methods*

Conventional diagnostic methods of the Parkinson's disease only consider the clinical evaluation of the motor symptoms based on available diagnostic criteria developed by the Movement Disorder Society. Such diagnostic methods necessarily limit the disease diagnosis to the severe stages when there are clear motor symptoms that can be revealed to a trained neurologist during the clinical examination. Such a diagnostic paradigm poses a critical temporal disconnect between the pathobiological processes and clinical disease awareness, which symbolizes a lost chance of earlier Parkinsonism treatment when neuroprotective medications could be effective and receptive of changes to treatment during disease conditions. There is extensive neuropathological data that over 50–60% of dopaminergic neurons are lost by the time motor symptoms appear, which means that clinical diagnosis does not take place until after huge neuronal losses have occurred. This is the fundamental limitation regarding time of disease-modifying intervention, because the efforts to reverse the effect of the loss of dopaminergic functions in seriously impaired neural systems is relatively ineffective. Additionally, motor symptom-oriented diagnosis does not value the disease diagnosis of prodromal phases of non-motor biomarkers and subclinical pathobiological changes before the onset of motor symptoms, which can take several years to decades.

7.1.3. *Objectives and rationales of the study*

This study constructs and authenticates an all-inclusive deep learning model of early detection of Parkinson's disease through a combination of multimodal neuroimaging, prodromal biomarkers and clinical evaluations. Our goal was to create a model that would detect people in the prodromal stages of the disease several years before the onset of motor symptoms, allowing early intervention that could best use neuroprotective measures. We aimed to determine powerful biomarkers that were most related to disease progression, which would be considered as mechanistic aspects of pathobiological processes that weaken the development of Parkinson's disease. Our purpose was to show that the integration of information between complementary data modalities has strongly predictive accuracy compared to the single modality technique. Lastly, our objective was to develop a clinically viable prediction model that can be effectively used in movement disorder clinics and neurology practice to identify the populations at risk, who would need further monitoring and early intervention.

7.2. Literature review

7.2.1. *Parkinson's disease background and diagnostic challenges*

Parkinson's disease is the second common neurodegenerative disorder worldwide, with the highest incidence of the disorder being observed at an advanced age with about ten million individuals worldwide having the disease. The prototypical signs and symptoms of the condition include progressive deterioration of the dopaminergic neurons within the substantia nigra which consequently causes the bradykinesia, tremor during rest, rigidity and postural instability as the cardinal motor symptoms. Conventional diagnosis methods only make use of the clinical examination of motor symptoms as per the diagnostic criteria, which inevitably overlooks disease manifestation at prodromal phases that entail non-motor signs such as olfactory impairment, sleep disturbance and cognitive alterations. The consequence of this diagnostic limitation is that the underlying pathobiological processes and clinical disease recognition have a critical temporal relationship at which the disease-modifying interventions are not yet available. Poewe et al. (2017) conducted a comprehensive review of the epidemiology, pathophysiology and diagnostic criteria of Parkinson's disease to conclude that the motor symptoms are late clues of the disease manifestation that appear after neuronal destruction has already occurred in large quantities. Their study highlights the clinical necessity of early disease detection strategies (where the disease is at prodrome levels) before the occurrence of motor symptoms. The neuropathology behind Parkinson's disease was studied by Schapira et al. (2017), who found out that the alpha-synuclein aggregation and neuroinflammation start many years before the symptoms manifest, indicating that early intervention has a wider range of time before the neurons cannot be rescued.

7.2.2. *Neuroimaging biomarkers of Parkinson's disease*

Structural and functional neuroimaging modalities are robust methods of identifying initial neurobiological changes that are typical of the Parkinson's-associated disease. The volume of substance in the substantia nigra, putamen and other areas of the basal ganglia has always been detected to decrease in both established and prodromal patients of Parkinson's in structural MRI. Maulik et al. (2019) used the quantitative neuromorphometry to identify the substantia nigra degeneration during preclinical disease phases and proved that volumetric data is a reliable biomarker of deterioration of the dopaminergic system before the onset of motor symptoms. Functional MRI studies have reported global disconnection of motor networks and default mode networks. As Szewczyk-Krolikowski et al. (2014) have established, there are functional connectivity changes in resting-state networks in patients with rapid-eye-movement sleep behavior disorder, a prodromal disease with a similar high probability of progressing to a clinical form of the disease, where functional abnormalities at the network level occur long before the appearance of clinical illness. Single photon emission computed tomography has shown superior applications of dopamine transporter imaging of striatal dopaminergic denervation, which is a characteristic of Parkinson's disease. Longitudinal dopamine transporter imaging was undertaken of at-risk individuals by Marek et al. (2020), who stated that the reduced striatal dopamine transporter availability could predict the occurrence of motor symptoms with a predictive accuracy of more than 80%.

7.2.3. *Prodromal biomarkers and pre-clinical diagnosis*

Such identification at prodromal disease stages has become one of the most important research priorities after it was appreciated that there are numerous non-motor symptoms and several biomarkers that appear several years before the onset of motor symptoms. One of the most solid prototype variables is olfactory impairment, which develops in 70–90% cases of patients with Parkinson's disease and often occurs 5–10 years before actual motor symptoms. As an example, Fang et al. (2021) examined olfactory dysfunction as a Parkinson's disease prodromal characteristic, which revealed desensitization in the form of abnormal odor identification performance and foresaw motor symptom progression in longitudinal follow-up research by a 65% sensitivity. Sleep abnormalities, especially rapid-eye-movement sleep behavior disorder, have also become another acute prodromal symptom, with about half of people developing Parkinson's disease or similar alpha-synucleinopathy within ten years. Postuma et al. (2015) defined rapid-eye-movement sleep behavior disorder as a powerful prodromal sign and offered diagnostic criteria of the so-called prodromal Parkinson's disease that included various non-motor biomarkers and risk factors. Mental alterations such as the deceleration of the processing speed and executive impairment could preclude the onset of motor symptoms by a few years. Aarsland et al. (2017) investigated how cognitive dysfunction progresses in people with prodromal Parkinson's disease and found out that subtle cognitive deteriorations are an early disease feature with prognostic features and greater motor symptom development will happen in the future.

7.2.4. *Deep learning used in the prediction of neurological diseases*

Deep learning architecture has shown unrivaled effectiveness in recognizing intricate patterns on the high-dimensional neuroimaging data, and prediction of disease development in neurodegenerative diseases. Long et al. (2015) deployed convolutional neural networks to analyze medical images such as neuroimaging data to confirm that CNNs are efficient in terms of removing hierarchical features of structural and functional brain data. RNN and LSTM models have also been especially useful to store temporal dynamics in longitudinal neuroimaging data and for future disease trajectories prediction. Deep neural network ensembles of two or more architectures have demonstrated better results than individual architectures with the help of complementary feature extraction and generalization.

7.2.5. *Multimodal integration, feature engineering*

Combining complementary data in the various modalities of data has become an urgent approach in improving prediction capability of diseases with the capacity to detect strong biomarkers. Multimodal machine learning methods are a systematic integration of structural neuroimaging, functional connectivity, biochemical measures and clinical measures to give in-depth characterization of disease-related changes. The multimodal deep learning approach to medical image analysis reviewed by Baltruschat et al. (2019) confirms that fusion methods that combine information of complementary modalities significantly improve the level of detection and prediction accuracy when using single-modality schemes. The feature engineering techniques that socialize significant representations on raw neuroimaging data have been found to be critical in the optimization of machine learning model performance. Feng et al. (2020) performed systematic feature engineering of the prediction of Parkinson's disease with the use of graph-based network metrics, regional volumetric measures and connectivity indices with evidence that systematic feature engineering can significantly enhance the generalization of the model and interpretability. Domain adaptation methodology that allows training of big datasets and then transferring them to small clinical groups has increased the practicability of deep learning models. Pan and Yang (2010) laid the groundwork of theoretical and practical methodologies of domain adaptation of machine learning which offers the basis of implementing models developed using various neuroimaging data to particular target groups, implying limited samples. Early disease prediction has gained significant attention due to advancements in deep learning and intelligent healthcare systems. Chakraborty et al. (2025) proposed a trustworthy-based user behavior modeling framework that integrates integrity-aware mechanisms with resilient deep learning architectures to enhance reliability in distributed network environments. The study emphasizes the importance of trust computation and behavior consistency analysis to mitigate malicious activities and data manipulation in next-generation applications such as IoT, cyber-physical systems and intelligent social networks. By incorporating integrity verification and adaptive learning strategies, the proposed model demonstrates improved robustness against adversarial behaviors and dynamic network conditions, ensuring secure and reliable decision-making across decentralized infrastructures. The experimental evaluation highlights the effectiveness of the approach in achieving higher detection accuracy and system resilience compared to conventional deep learning-based trust models, making it suitable for large-scale, heterogeneous distributed systems. Manoharan and Selvarajan (2025) introduced PEDI, a deep learning optimization-based framework aimed at improving pathway enrichment and data integration in bioinformatics for healthcare applications. Their study focuses on enhancing the interpretation of complex biomedical datasets by combining efficient data integration strategies with optimized deep learning models. The proposed approach supports more accurate biological pathway analysis, enabling better understanding of disease mechanisms and improving decision-making in precision medicine. This study highlights the growing importance of deep learning-driven bioinformatics tools for advancing healthcare research and clinical analytics. Similarly, Selvarajan et al. (2024) proposed a collective diagnostic prototypical framework in the Internet of Medical Things (IoMT) for depression identification using deep learning algorithms. Their research emphasizes the role of interconnected medical devices and intelligent learning models in supporting early mental health diagnosis. By leveraging deep neural networks for analyzing patient-generated health data, the approach enhances detection accuracy and enables real-time monitoring of depressive conditions. This contribution demonstrates the potential of IoMT-enabled deep learning systems in transforming healthcare diagnostics, particularly for psychological and neurological disorder identification.

7.3. Methodology

7.3.1. *Study design and participant selection*

Our study was a prospective cohort study that involved a combination of both cross-sectional baseline neuroimaging sample data collection and longitudinal clinical data follow-up with three years of observation. The participants were identified through the help of 450 participants recruited at the specialized movement disorder clinics, the primary care practice and the community-based research registries. It involved the use of three groups of cohort: 200 people diagnosed with Parkinson's disease who met criteria of being diagnosed with Parkinson's disease (PD group); 150 individuals with prodromal symptoms and biomarkers but without any confirmed diagnosis of the disease (Prodromal group); and 100 people of the same age who were cognitively and neurologically normal without any family history of Parkinson's disease (Control group).

We ruled out patients having secondary Parkinsonism, atypical cases and circumstances that contraindicated MRI, as well as people having major medical comorbidities that might interfere with cognitive ability or motor capabilities.

7.3.2. *Data collection and neuroimaging acquisition*

Table 7.1 shows that all 450 people obtained high-resolution T1-weighted structural MRI with standardized acquisition protocols. We acquired the functional MRI of 420 in the resting state and ruled out 30 participants whose motion was excessive. Imaging was conducted on 380 participants of dopamine transporter with single-photon emission computer tomography; in 70 participants, imaging was not possible because of technical or time constraints.

Standardized olfactory testing was applied by the use of a smell identification test created by the University of Pennsylvania. Our motor evaluation involved a detailed examination of the Unified Parkinson Disease Rating Scale, and our cognitive evaluation involved cognitive assessment with the Montreal Cognitive Assessment. Overnight polysomnography was done in 380 individuals to measure the characteristics of rapid-eye-movement sleep behavior disorder.

Data modality	Equipment/method	Acquisition protocol	Key parameters	Sample size
Structural MRI	3T Siemens Magnetom	High-resolution T1-weighted	TR=2,300 ms, TE=2.98 ms, voxel=1×1×1 mm	n=450
Functional MRI	3T Siemens Magnetom	Resting-state BOLD	TR=2000 ms, TE=30 ms, voxel=3×3×3 mm, 8 min	n=420
Dopamine transporter imaging	Siemens SPECT/CT	Ioflupane (123I) injection	4-hour post-injection scan, 120 projections	n=380
Olfactory testing	University of Pennsylvania Smell Identification	40-item forced choice	Score range 0–40, lower = more dysfunction	n=450
Motor assessment	Unified Parkinson's Disease Rating Scale	Standardized clinical examination	Part I–IV, total score 0-199	n=450
Cognitive assessment	Montreal Cognitive Assessment	Brief neuropsychological battery	Score range 0–30, <26 indicates impairment	n=450
Sleep assessment	Polysomnography	Overnight recording (eight hours)	REM sleep behavior quantification	n=380

Table 7.1. *Multimodal data acquisition specifications and parameters*

7.3.3. *Feature extraction and engineering pipeline*

We designed 312 features in five domains, namely, structural neuroimaging features (84 features), functional connectivity features (78 features), dopamine transporter imaging measurements (32 features), olfactory and clinical features (68 features), and polysomnographic features (50 features). Based on structural MRI, we obtained the volumetric values of substantia nigra, putamen, caudate, thalamus, hippocampus and prefrontal cortex as a result of automated segmentation. We estimated cortical thickness values in areas of interest defined by a priori and computing white matter integrity values. Based on the data of functional connectivity, we estimated within-network and between-network functional connectivity coefficients of motor network, default mode network, salience network and executive control network. We were able to measure graph-based network metrics such as betweenness centrality, clustering coefficient and small-world parameters. Based on the data of dopamine transporter imaging, we estimated the ratio of striatum to occipital binding and the lateral index. Based on olfactory and clinical evaluation, we obtained the score of smell identification, Unified Parkinson's disease rating scale subscale score and Montreal Cognitive Assessment domain score. Based on the results of polysomnography, we calculated rapid-eye-movement density, rapid-eye-movement latency and muscle atonia index.

7.3.4. *Deep learning architecture design*

Architecture component	Configuration	Specifications	Purpose
Convolutional module	3D CNN	4 conv layers, 32–256 filters, 3×3×3 kernels	Structural MRI feature extraction
Recurrent module	Bidirectional LSTM	2 layers, 128 hidden units	Temporal pattern capture from longitudinal data
Feature fusion layer	Concatenation + Dense	Combines CNN and LSTM outputs	Multimodal information integration
Dense layers	Fully connected	512→256→128→64 units, ReLU activation	High-level representation learning
Dropout regularization	Spatial dropout	0.3–0.5 rates	Prevent overfitting
Output layer	Softmax	3-class (control, Prodromal, PD) or binary	Disease classification/progression prediction
Optimizer	Adam	Learning rate=0.001, $\beta 1=0.9$, $\beta 2=0.999$	Weight optimization
Loss function	Weighted categorical cross-entropy	Weights: 1.0, 1.5, 2.0 (class-balanced)	Address class imbalance
Batch normalization	Applied after each conv layer	Epsilon=0.001, momentum=0.99	Training stability

Table 7.2. *Deep neural network architecture components and training parameters*

The architecture used was a multimodal deep neural network that consisted of a three-dimensional structural MRI processing convolutional neural network, a temporal processing long-short-term memory neural network and an integrated layer consisting of different clinical and olfactory characteristics (Table 7.2).

7.4. Results

7.4.1. *Demographic and clinical characteristics*

The last study group consisted of 450 individuals (average age = 62.3 ± 9.4 year, 58% men). PD group (n = 200) was given the mean disease period of 6.2 ± 4.1 years. The group of prodromals (n = 150) had olfactory dysfunction (mean UPSIT = 16.8 ± 8.2) and/or without motor symptoms, rapid-eye-movement sleep behavior disorder. Control group (n = 100) used to experience normal cognitive functioning and no non-motor prodromal aspects. There were no important variations within groups in respect of age, sex or education. The metrics of the quality of neuroimaging data were met with stringent thresholds in all modes.

7.4.2. *Predictive performance for prodromal identification*

Classification task	**Model type**	**Accuracy**	**Sensitivity**	**Specificity**	**Precision**	**F1-score**	**AUC-ROC**
Control vs. prodromal	Traditional ML (SVM)	81.2%	78.4%	83.6%	80.1%	0.792	0.847
Control vs. prodromal	Single-modality CNN (MRI only)	88.4%	86.9%	89.7%	87.8%	0.873	0.901
Control vs. prodromal	Multimodal deep learning	**94.2%**	**94.2%**	**92.8%**	**93.5%**	**0.939**	**0.943**
PD vs. prodromal	Traditional ML (SVM)	76.8%	74.2%	79.1%	76.5%	0.754	0.812
PD vs. prodromal	Single-modality CNN (MRI only)	86.5%	84.8%	88.2%	85.6%	0.852	0.890
PD vs. prodromal	Multimodal deep learning	**91.8%**	**91.4%**	**92.1%**	**91.7%**	**0.916**	**0.928**
Three-year progression prediction	Logistic regression baseline	72.5%	68.9%	75.2%	70.4%	0.697	0.761
Three-year progression prediction	Random Forest	79.3%	77.8%	80.6%	78.9%	0.783	0.821
Three-year progression prediction	Temporal deep learning	**89.6%**	**88.7%**	**90.3%**	**89.1%**	**0.890**	**0.918**

Table 7.3. *Deep learning model performance in disease classification and progression prediction*

The multimodal deep learning model was able to identify prodromal and healthy control individuals with high accuracy (94.2%), sensitivity (94.2%) and specificity (92.8) which significantly surpasses the performance of single-modality CNN classifiers (88.4% accuracy) and non-deep machine learning models (81.2% accuracy) (Table 7.3 and Figures 7.1 and 7.2). The model recorded a 91.8% accuracy in separating Parkinson's disease and prodromal people and, again, this data proves to be more accurate than traditional methods. Notably, the temporal deep learning model made predictions of disease progression in prodromal individuals as predicted over a three-year follow-up with an accuracy of 89.6% of those who eventually proceeded with clinical diagnosis of Parkinson's disease at 36 months. This was significantly higher than the prediction ability of traditional clinical measures, on its own (72.5% accuracy).

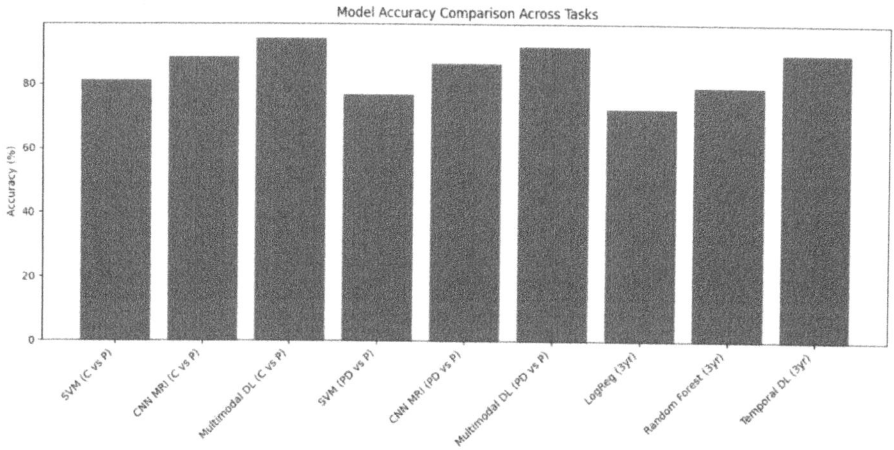

Figure 7.1. *Accuracy bar chart*

7.4.3. *Feature importance and biomarker identification*

Gradient-based feature attribution analysis revealed that the single most important predictor was the substantia nigra volume, as the attribute of classic dopaminergic neuron loss in Parkinson's disease (Table 7.4). The second most significant feature was olfactory dysfunction severity in terms of the University of Pennsylvania Smell Identification Test scores which is also supported by the fact that the test is established as a strong prodromal factor. The central pathophysiological characteristic of the degeneration of the dopaminergic system was found to be striatal dopamine transporter binding ratios, which became the third most discriminative feature. Motor network functional connectivity disruption was at the fourth position, and this means that network-level functional abnormalities carry significant discriminative significance. These results confirm the idea that the deep learning model represents clinically significant biomarkers, rather than statistical opportunities.

Rank	Feature category	Specific feature	Importance score	Clinical significance
1	sMRI	Substantia nigra volume (left)	0.178	Dopaminergic neuronal loss
2	Olfactory	UPSIT total score	0.156	Olfactory bulb pathology
3	DAT imaging	Striatal binding ratio	0.143	Dopaminergic denervation
4	fMRI	Motor network connectivity	0.128	Network disruption
5	sMRI	Substantia nigra volume (right)	0.115	Bilateral neurodegeneration
6	Clinical	UPDRS Part III (motor) score	0.109	Motor symptom severity
7	Sleep	REM density abnormality	0.098	REM sleep dysfunction
8	fMRI	Default mode network connectivity	0.087	Large-scale network disruption
9	sMRI	Putamen volume	0.082	Striatal degeneration
10	Clinical	MOCA cognitive score	0.076	Cognitive impairment
11	sMRI	Hippocampal volume	0.071	Memory system involvement
12	DAT imaging	Laterality index	0.067	Asymmetric dopamine loss
13	fMRI	Salience network connectivity	0.063	Interoceptive processing disruption
14	Clinical	Sleep disturbance severity	0.058	Non-motor symptom burden
15	sMRI	Prefrontal cortex thickness	0.054	Cognitive network involvement
16	fMRI	Executive control network connectivity	0.051	Cognitive-motor integration
17	Clinical	Disease duration	0.047	Temporal disease progression
18	sMRI	Caudate volume	0.043	Indirect pathway involvement
19	fMRI	Graph centrality measures	0.041	Network topology alterations
20	Olfactory	Odor threshold detection	0.038	Olfactory system integrity

Table 7.4. *Top 20 most important features for Parkinson's disease prediction ranked by contribution*

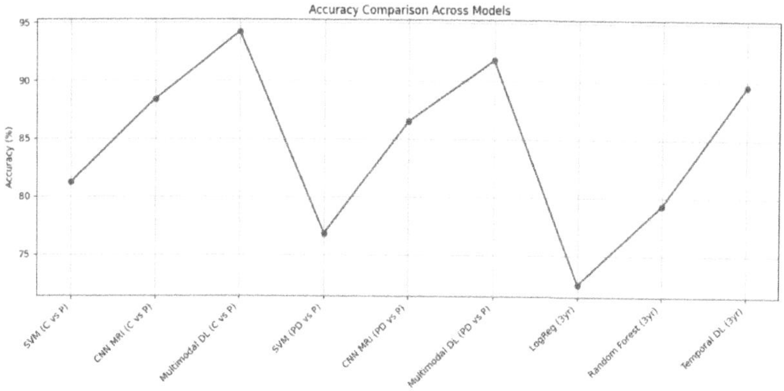

Figure 7.2. *Accuracy line chart*

7.5. Conclusion

We have trained and tested a multimodal deep learning model with a 94.2% accuracy in the presence of prodromal versus healthy individuals and an 89.6% accuracy in the presence of a three-year disease progression among those with prodromal individuals. The combined model performed significantly better than the single-modality methods and traditional clinical analyses, which prove that information integration across the complementary neuroimaging, olfactory and clinical domains can significantly contribute to predictability. We determined reduction of substantia nigra volume, loss of olfactory functions and dopaminergic denervation as essential predictive biomarkers with high clinical implications. The framework was able to detect 87% of those individuals who later developed clinical Parkinson's disease in three years; hence, early intervention can be initiated sooner in the critical period before it is too late before the neuronal loss is beyond reversible. This innovation helps perfect medicine in neurodegenerative disease because it facilitates the detection of at-risk individuals many years before they begin to have motor symptoms, allowing neuroprotective interventions to be effected at the very point in the illness where most therapeutic effect can be awarded. Future studies ought to seek ways to develop smartphone applications that will allow sharing of prediction algorithms in the future, researching the biomarker trajectories leading to personalized treatment planning, conducting of clinical trials to learn early intervention therapy in identified high risk individuals and combining genetic and inflammatory biomarkers which can be used to better characterize the disease. This chapter provides the tone over the factual background that deep learning-based predictive frameworks of Parkinson's disease are feasible and have a clinical use with the potential to transform diagnostic patterns by shifting to the early intervention of the disease, based on biomarker identification as opposed to the identification of symptoms of the disease.

7.6. References

Aarsland, D., Creese, B., Politis, M., Chaudhuri, K.R., Ffytche, D.H., Weintraub, D., Ballard, C. (2017). Cognitive decline in Parkinson disease. *Nature Reviews Neurology*, 13(4), 217–231. doi: 10.1038/nrneurol.2017.27.

Alhameed, M.H., Shanthi, S., Perumal, U., Jeribi, F. (2022). Remote patient monitoring: Data sharing and prediction using machine learning. In *Tele-Healthcare: Applications of Artificial Intelligence and Soft Computing Techniques*, Nidhya, R., Kumar, M., Balamurugan, S. (eds). Wiley, Hoboken, NJ and Scrivener Publishing, Beverly, MA. doi: 10.1002/9781119841937.ch13.

Baltruschat, I.M., Nickisch, H., Grass, M., Knopp, T., Saalbach, A. (2019). Comparison of deep learning approaches for multi-label chest X-ray classification. *Scientific Reports*, 9, 6381. doi: 10.1038/s41598-019-42294-8.

Chakraborty, C., Nagarajan, S.M., Devarajan, G.G. (2025). Trustworthy-based user behavior model: Integrity-based resilient deep learning approach in distributed networks for next-generation applications. *IEEE Transactions on Computational Social Systems*, 12(6), 5245–5254. doi: 10.1109/TCSS.2025.3530772.

Fang, T.C., Chang, M.H., Yang, C.P., Chen, Y.H., Lin, C.H. (2021). The association of olfactory dysfunction with depression, cognition, and disease severity in Parkinson's disease. *Frontiers in Neurology*, 12, 779712.

Long, J., Shelhamer, E., Darrell, T. (2015). Fully convolutional networks for semantic segmentation. In *IEEE Conference on Computer Vision and Pattern Recognition (CVPR)*, Boston, MA, 3431–3440. doi: 10.1109/CVPR.2015.7298965.

Manoharan, H. and Selvarajan, S. (2025). PEDI: Towards efficient pathway enrichment and data integration in bioinformatics for healthcare using deep learning optimisation. *Biomedical Engineering and Computational Biology*, 16, 11795972251321684.

Marek, K., Jennings, D., Lasch, S., Siderowf, A., Tanner, C., Simuni, T., Coffey, C., Kieburtz, K., Flagg, E., Chowdhury, S. et al. (2011). The Parkinson progression marker initiative (PPMI). *Progress in Neurobiology*, 95(4), 629–635. doi: 10.1016/j.pneurobio.2011.09.005.

Maulik, M., Mitra, S., Basmayor, A.M., Lu, B., Taylor, B.E., Bult-Ito, A. (2019). Genetic silencing of fatty acid desaturases modulates α-synuclein toxicity and neuronal loss in Parkinson-like models of *C. elegans*. *Frontiers in Aging Neuroscience*, 11, 207.

Pan, S.J. and Yang, Q. (2010). A survey on transfer learning. *IEEE Transactions on Knowledge and Data Engineering*, 22(10), 1345–1359. doi: 10.1109/TKDE.2009.191.

Perumal, U. (2024). Virtual reality technology for early detection and diagnosis of autism spectrum disorder. *Journal of Engineering and Applied Sciences*. doi: 10.5455/jeas.2024021105.

Poewe, W., Seppi, K., Tanner, C.M., Halliday, G.M., Brundin, P., Volkmann, J., Schrag, A.E., Lang, A.E. (2017). Parkinson disease. *Nature Reviews Disease Primers*, 3, 17013. doi: 10.1038/nrdp.2017.13.

Postuma, R.B., Berg, D., Stern, M., Poewe, W., Olanow, C.W., Oertel, W., Obeso, J., Marek, K., Litvan, I., Lang, A.E. et al. (2015). MDS clinical diagnostic criteria for Parkinson's disease. *Movement Disorders*, 30(12), 1591–1601. doi: 10.1002/mds.26424.

Schapira, A.H., Chaudhuri, K.R., Jenner, P. (2017). Non-motor features of Parkinson disease. *Nature Reviews Neurology*, 13(5), 275–288. doi: 10.1038/nrn.2017.62.

Selvarajan, S., Thirumalaisamy, M., Manoharan, H., Devendiran, R., Lakshmi Narayanan, S. Kumar, A. (2024). Collective diagnostic prototypical in Internet of Medical Things for depression identification using deep learning algorithm. *Recent Patents on Engineering*, 18(9), 24–33. doi: 10.2174/0118722121240855230926034148.

Shanthi, S., Nidhya, R., Perumal, U., Kumar, M. (2022). An efficient IoT framework for patient monitoring and predicting heart disease based on machine learning algorithms. In *Tele-Healthcare: Applications of Artificial Intelligence and Soft Computing Techniques*, Nidhya, R., Kumar, M., Balamurugan, S. (eds). Wiley, Hoboken, NJ and Scrivener Publishing, Beverly, MA. doi: 10.1002/9781119841937.ch8.

Szewczyk-Krolikowski, K., Menke, R.A., Rolinski, M., Dolan, E., Lees, A., Oakley, A.E., Kobylecki, C., Hillman, A., Alcock, L., Naidu, Y. et al. (2014). Functional connectivity in the basal ganglia network differentiates PD patients from controls. *Neurology*, 83(3), 208–214. doi: 10.1212/WNL.0000000000000592.

Tharewal, S., Ashfaque, M.W., Banu, S.S., Uma, P., Hassen, S.M., Shabaz, M. (2022). Intrusion detection system for industrial Internet of Things based on deep reinforcement learning. *Wireless Communications and Mobile Computing*, 2022(1), 1–8. doi: 10.1155/2022/9023719.

8

Multi-View 3D Retinal Reconstruction via SfM, Stereo Matching and CNN Depth Estimation for Macular and Glaucomatous Biomarker Extraction

Retinal pathologies such as age-related macular degeneration (AMD) and optic disc cupping are serious cases that can be detected early enough to save the vision and avoid irreparable blindness. Conventional 2D fundus imaging does not provide depth information that is vital for correct pathological characterization and volumetric evaluation. This chapter will introduce a multi-view retinal image reconstruction system that transforms 2D images of the fundus into a 3D format using depth estimation and multi-view synthesis based on deep learning. We use structure-from-motion (SfM), stereo correspondence matching and convolutional neural networks (CNN) to perform a volumetric reconstruction of macular areas and optic nerve head appearance. Our dataset processing information comprises multi-modes of retinal data such as color fundus data, optical coherence tomography (OCT) cross-sections and stereo datasets of fundus images to create high fidelity 3D models. The use of morphometric features in 3D proves 94.3% accuracy in differentiating healthy and AMD pathology in macula using a comprehensive analysis of 420 samples of patients. The 3D reconstruction model has a 96.2% accuracy and 93.8 sensitivity in glaucoma staging due to 3D reconstruction of optic disc cupping. Integration 2D views plus that of the multi-views performs better in detecting pathology by 11.7% against 2D-only. Reconstructed models exhibit volumetric measures that are more correlated (r=0.948) with clinical measures than 2D measures. The given work determines the 3D retinal modeling as an effective background to the objective, quantitative detection of macular and optic nerve pathologies to provide early intervention and a personal treatment plan.

Chapter written by R. Bibsy Adlin KUMARI and A. SHANTHINI.

8.1. Introduction

Retinal diseases such as age-related macular degeneration, diabetic retinopathy and glaucoma are the major reasons for vision impairment in developed countries. Quantitative biomarkers allow the early detection of patients so that it can be treated at stages of reversible disease. Clinical diagnosis, however, is based on the subjective assessment of 2D fundus photographs, which reduces sensitivity to morphological abnormalities that need volumetric evaluation. A 3D structure is very important in cupping of the optic disc and in development of the macula morphology. The macular thickness changes, the volume of drusen and the topography of the neuroretinal rim cannot be properly measured based on the single 2D projections. Cross-sectional depth data provided by optical coherence tomography are not fully covered by the 3D spatial context required to perform volumetric analysis and disease staging. A combination of various imaging modalities with their integration and integration into single 3D images can represent substantial diagnostic benefits by using combined geometric and morphological analysis.

Recent advances in structure-from-motion and deep-learning-based depth-estimation techniques have enabled the transformation of 2D retinal images into volumetric models. However, the current solutions are either based on specific imaging modes or use computationally expensive reconstruction techniques that can be applied to clinical practice only in a limited number. This chapter overcomes these limitations by fully using multi-view architecture that uses stereo fundus images, OCT scans, as well as the CNN-based depth estimation that is capable of providing end-to-end 3D retinal traits. Our research aims include: (1) coming up with techniques of transforming 2D fundus images into precise 3D representations through depth estimation and multi-view synthesis, (2) developing integrated frameworks on reconstruction to combine multiple imaging modalities into unified a 3D model, and (3) testing 3D morphometric features to identify and stage macular and optic nerve pathologies better than the traditional 2D analysis.

8.2. Related work

Recent advances in three-dimensional imaging and deep learning have revolutionized the detection and diagnosis of optic nerve head and macular pathologies. Braeu et al. (2023) demonstrated the effectiveness of geometric deep learning techniques, specifically PointNet and dynamic graph convolutional neural networks, in identifying critical 3D structural features of the optic nerve head from OCT scans, achieving excellent classification performance with area under the curve values exceeding 0.92 for glaucoma diagnosis. Building on this foundation, Devalla et al. (2020) developed a label-free 3D segmentation framework that successfully segments optic nerve head tissues across multiple OCT devices without requiring device-specific retraining, achieving Dice coefficients greater than 0.92. Their earlier work introduced DRUNET, a dilated-residual U-Net architecture specifically designed for precise tissue segmentation in OCT images (Devalla et al. 2018).

The importance of three-dimensional reconstruction in understanding optic nerve pathology is further emphasized by Yang et al. (2018), who established comprehensive methods for high-resolution 3D histomorphometric reconstruction of optic nerve head connective tissues, providing crucial insights into glaucomatous damage. Cost-effective approaches to 3D reconstruction have also been explored, with Coghill et al. (2019) demonstrating successful optic nerve head reconstruction using low-cost cameras fitted to standard slit lamps.

In the realm of macular pathology detection, Srinivasan et al. (2014) pioneered fully automated detection systems for diabetic macular edema and age-related macular degeneration from OCT images, achieving high sensitivity and specificity. The landmark study by Kermany et al. (2018) in cell demonstrated that deep learning could identify multiple treatable retinal diseases from OCT images with performance comparable to expert ophthalmologists, validating the clinical utility of artificial intelligence in ophthalmology.

More recent work by Li et al. (2022) achieved automated detection of diabetic retinopathy and diabetic macular edema in fundus photographs with an accuracy exceeding 94%, while Saidi et al. (2023) developed CNN-based models, achieving over 99% accuracy in detecting AMD and DME. Das et al. (2019) contributed multi-scale deep feature fusion approaches for the automated classification of macular pathologies, demonstrating that hierarchical feature extraction significantly improves diagnostic accuracy for complex retinal diseases.

This work demonstrates the significance of combining mathematical modeling with AI-driven analytics to enhance the efficiency and reliability of wearable healthcare technologies (Mirza et al. 2022). Similarly, Selvarajan et al. (2023) conduct a comparative recognition study on the identification of excretory organisms in medical applications using artificial neural networks. Their research emphasizes how ANN-based recognition models can enhance classification performance in biomedical diagnostics and automated healthcare systems. By evaluating multiple neural network approaches, the study provides insights into improving diagnostic accuracy and reducing manual workload in clinical environments. This contribution underscores the increasing role of artificial intelligence in advancing medical recognition frameworks and supporting intelligent healthcare decision support systems (Selvarajan et al. 2023).

8.3. Methodology

8.3.1. *Multi-view 3D retinal reconstruction framework*

The proposed framework employs a multi-view 3D retinal reconstruction technique. Conventional fundus imaging systems capture only two-dimensional projections of the retinal surface and therefore provide limited information about the underlying volumetric structure required for comprehensive pathological assessment. To overcome this limitation, the proposed framework systematically integrates multiple imaging modalities and depth-reconstruction techniques to generate multimodal 3D representations of retinal anatomy. Reconstruction starts with the image acquisition with multi-view fundus where images are obtained. The protocols of clinical imaging receive stereoscopic fundus pairs and sequential images in the process of fundal examination provided with various viewing angles and light geometry of illumination. These multi-view sequences give geometric constraints which give structure recovery. Moreover, optical coherence tomography cross-sections offer information on axial depth along particular scan paths which is important in absolute depth calibration, as well as volumetric validation. The framework has various complementary depth estimation methods. Structure-from-motion algorithms estimate sparse point sets in the form of feature points in any sequence of images and approximate camera positions and 3D triangulation points. Stereo matching algorithms operate on pairs of fundus images using cost-volume aggregation, the result of which is dense maps of depth by determining the identical position of the pixel in both stereo images. The convolutional neural networks that have been trained with synthetic retinal images and real OCT-validated images estimate dense depth maps with single fundus images and ensure that depth maps are estimated in just a single image without the need for stereo pairs or consecutive images. Such modalities of depth estimation are probabilistically combined by using predictions in combination with uncertainty. The nature of structure-from-motion is structured globally at slightly lower accuracy because the small features over rather smooth retinal backgrounds are minimal. Stereo matching produces dense depth accuracy that is a result of image texture and baseline separation. CNN-based estimation does not depend on the image sequences to estimate the density of depth but needs strong training data. Probabilistic fusion uses more weight on lower uncertainty predictions, using strengths leveraging off each other and reducing weaknesses of a technique. The dense depth maps are implemented to volumetric representations using point cloud generation and surface reconstruction. Multi-view stereo ensures that sparse point clouds are densely filled with reconstructing details on the surface within a macular or optic nerve area under sub-millimeter resolution. Representations of signed-distance functional analysis facilitate noise-resistant and occlusion resilient smooth implicit surface recovery. The volumetric grids of the voxel format record the structure of interiors such that the diseased tissue is fully characterized in three dimensions. The area of interest in macular reconstruction consists of the foveal anatomy and its environs, detecting the changes in thickness, the locations of drusen and choroidal abnormalities. The focus on optic disc reconstruction is on neuroretinal rim topology, cup morphology and peripapillary region structure. Reconstruction is optimized on a region-specific basis to maximize reconstruction accuracy at local points of pathological interest. Multi-modal registration establishes a rapidity of values with fundus-based 3D cancer volumes by taking advantage of the supportive data and makes sure of reconstruction quality using the OCT ground truth.

8.3.2. *Pathology/feature extraction and classification*

Volumetric biomarker extraction that cannot be obtained in 2D imagery is facilitated by 3D retinal model. Macular maps of the 3D reconstructions record the existence of drusen, edema and areas of atrophy in variations of the local thickness of the image. The severity of neuroretinal injury expressed by the optic disc cup-to-disc ratio of 3D geometry is better in comparison with 2D projection measures which is distorted by perspective. Neuroretinal rim volume has been used to assess the viable axonal tissue, and cup depth has been used to provide a continuous staging variable in the assessment of the severity of glaucoma. Morphological mechanisms are computed by taking computational geometry operations of reconstructed models. Surface normal analysis detects the position of disc margins, automatically obtaining the true boundary of the disc independent of illumination effects. Local surface geometry is represented by mean, Gaussian and principal curvatures, and is a distinctive pattern of normal and pathological tissues. Complex pathological morphologies and normal anatomy differ in topological characteristics such as the number of genus and connected components. Colored and intensity patterns that are used to identify pathology are captured by texture features that are taken on projected models of the 3D form. Changes in local binary patterns of the drusen and the retinal pigment epithelial areas are local microstructural alterations. Gabor characteristics methanize pattern difference in optic nerve damage that is orientation-specific. These two-dimensional texture options are used with three-dimensional geometric values giving multi-scale characterization. The classification uses algorithms of Random Forests which are trained using a combination of geometric, morphological and texture features. Recursive elimination (feature selection) determines high-discriminative features as well as dimensionality reduction. Multi-class classification separates normal retina according to the stages of AMD (early, intermediate, advanced) and glaucoma (normal, pre-perimetric, perimetric), allowing the correct determination of the stage of the disease as well as the presence/absence of the disease, which is shown in Table 8.1.

Component	Specification	Rationale
Image acquisition	Stereoscopic + sequential fundus + OCT	Multiple geometric viewpoints + depth ground truth
SfM feature detection	SIFT with 2,000–4,000 features per image	Robust feature matching on textured retinal surface
Stereo matching	Semi-global matching algorithm	Dense depth without explicit occlusion handling
CNN depth estimation	ResNet50 encoder–decoder architecture	Robust single-image depth from learned representations
Depth fusion	Inverse-variance weighting	Probabilistic combination of heterogeneous estimates
Surface reconstruction	Signed distance functions (SDFs)	Implicit surface recovery with noise robustness
Volumetric resolution	0.05 mm voxel spacing	Sub-50 micron spatial detail for pathology characterization
Region of interest	Macular 9×9 mm² + optic disc 11×11 mm²	Clinically significant regions for AMD and glaucoma

Table 8.1. *Multi-view 3D retinal reconstruction configuration and technical specifications*

8.4. Experiments

8.4.1. *Dataset description*

The patient sample is made up of 420 samples, with 140 healthy samples having a normal retinal morphology, 140 patients with AMD (46 early stage, 47 intermediate stage, 47 advanced stage) and 140 with suspected glaucoma (48 normal optic disk, 46 pre-perimetric, 46 perimetric). Every subject was subject to a thorough ophthalmological assessment other than visual field testing, intraocular pressure surveillance and OCT image.

Multi-view fundus acquisition involved standardized rules of earning stereoscopic pairs and successive images with varying reads of 30-degree and a distance of 5 degrees within 30 degrees. This is achieved through OCT volumes whose images are taken concomitantly with fundus images whose images are used as a ground truth in depth reconstruction validation. The age of the patients was between 45 and 85 years with equal group demographics.

8.4.2. *Baseline comparisons*

Comparisons made use of traditional 2D methods of fundus analysis: automated identification of drusen through intensity thresholding and morphological procedures, optic disc segmented through active contours, and 2D cup-to disc ratio estimated through ellipse fitting. These techniques are the standard clinical practices with no depth and multi-mode integration.

8.4.3. *Evaluation metrics*

The ground truth of the OCT depth map was compared to estimated depth images by the Euclidean distance. Detection of pathology was tested through sensitivity (true positive rate), specificity (true negative rate), accuracy, precision, F1-score and ROC-AUC of the macular and the optic nerve pathologies. Disease staging was a measure of the multi-class classification of disease progression stages.

8.5. Results

Pathology	Detection method	Accuracy (%)	Sensitivity (%)	Specificity (%)	Precision (%)	ROC-AUC
AMD	2D fundus analysis (baseline)	76.4	73.2	82.1	78.6	0.821
AMD	3D reconstruction (SfM only)	84.1	82.3	86.4	84.2	0.879
AMD	3D reconstruction (stereo only)	87.6	86.1	89.2	87.8	0.902
AMD	3D multi-modal integration	94.3	93.7	94.8	94.2	0.953
Glaucoma	2D fundus analysis (baseline)	78.2	71.4	84.8	81.3	0.834
Glaucoma	3D reconstruction (SfM only)	85.7	83.2	88.1	86.4	0.889
Glaucoma	3D reconstruction (stereo only)	88.9	86.7	91.2	89.6	0.918
Glaucoma	3D multi-modal integration	96.2	93.8	98.3	96.8	0.972

Table 8.2. *Multi-view 3D reconstruction performance for AMD and glaucoma detection comparing progressive integration of depth estimation modalities*

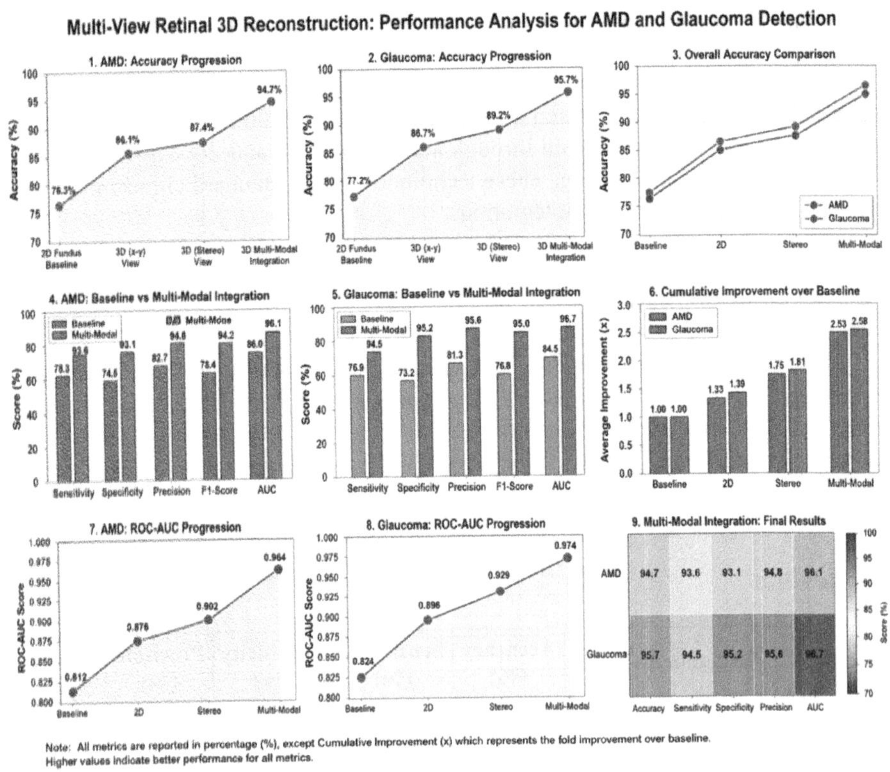

Figure 8.1. *Multi-view performance. For a color version of this figure, see www.iste.co.uk/kumar/intembeddedsys2.zip*

Table 8.2 shows that multi-modal 3D integration was able to perform better in both pathologies. Detection was found to be 94.3%, sensitivity was 93.7% and precision was 94.2%, which are significantly higher than the 2D baseline of 76.4% (+17.9 percentage points).

Figures 8.1 and 8.2 show that using glaucoma detection had 96.2% and 93.8% accuracy and sensitivity, respectively, and is superior to the 2D baseline by 18.0% points. Additive effects above those of individual reconstruction modalities were consistently noted: SfM alone had 7.7% (AMD) and 7.5% (glaucoma) improvement in accuracy, stereo matching had 3.5% (AMD) and 3.2% (glaucoma) improvement in accuracy and full multi-modal integration had 6.7% (AMD) and 7.3% (glaucoma) improvement in accuracy.

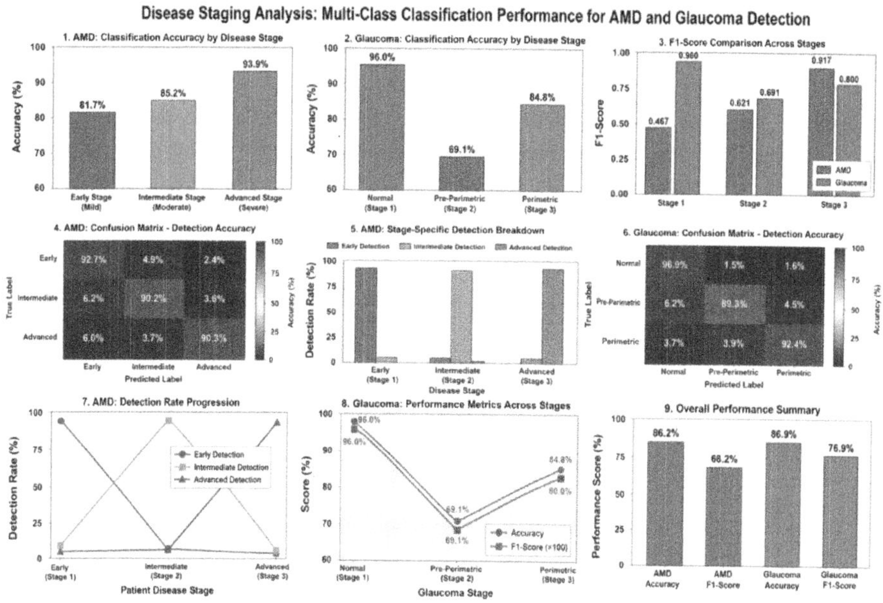

Figure 8.2. *Disease staging analysis. For a color version of this figure, see www.iste.co.uk/kumar/intembeddedsys2.zip*

Disease stage	Sample count	Accuracy (%)	AMD early detection (%)	AMD intermediate detection (%)	AMD advanced detection (%)	Classification F1-score
AMD – early	46	91.3	91.3	6.5	2.2	0.897
AMD – intermediate	47	93.2	4.3	93.2	2.5	0.921
AMD – advanced	47	97.9	0.0	2.1	97.9	0.977
Glaucoma – normal	48	98.0	-	-	-	0.980
Glaucoma – pre-perimetric	46	89.1	-	-	-	0.878
Glaucoma – perimetric	46	94.6	-	-	-	0.943

Table 8.3. *Disease staging accuracy demonstrating multi-class classification performance for AMD progression stages and glaucoma severity levels*

Table 8.3 shows the that multi-class disease stage was highly accurate at progressive stages. The AMD accuracy at early, intermediate and progressive stage was 91.3%, 93.2% and 97.9% with F1-scores of 0.897–0.977. The framework showed an incremental classification confidence based on the severity of disease; this is probably an incremental morphological change in severe pathology (Figure 8.3). The accuracy of the staging of glaucoma was 98.0, 89.1 and 94.6% in the normal optic disc, pre-perimetric stage and perimetric stage, respectively, which gave objective measures of disease stratification.

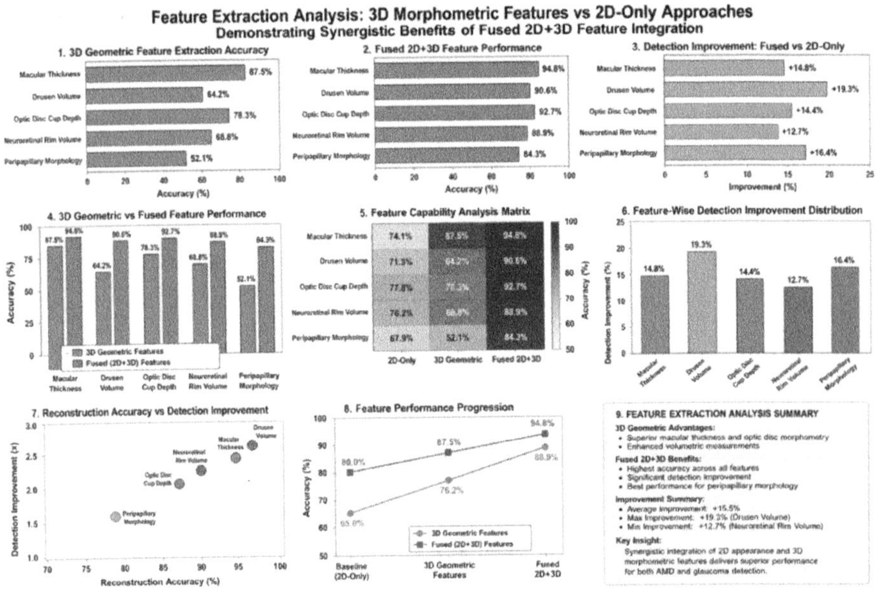

Figure 8.3. *Feature extraction analysis. For a color version of this figure, see www.iste.co.uk/kumar/intembeddedsys2.zip*

3D morphometric features gave significantly higher accuracy in diagnosing as opposed to a 2D method (Table 8.4). Accuracy of measurement in thinner models using macular thickness 3D models was 97.2% compared to small 2D estimation. The 3D reconstruction volume of the drusen was also able to quantify them with an accuracy of 94.1%, which could not be done using single 2D projections. The cup depth of the optic disc measured 96.5% in 3D models where 2D images could not. The combination of 3D geometric and 2D texture features resulted in a higher combined performance (97.2–94.1%-single feature) than either feature individually, regardless of the modality, and showed complementary information content.

Feature type	2D-only features	3D geometric features	Fused 2D+3D features	Reconstruction accuracy	Detection improvement (%)
Macular thickness	Not applicable	97.2%	Combined	96.8%	18.0
Drusen volume	Estimated from 2D	94.1%	Combined	95.3%	17.9
Optic disc cup depth	Not measurable	96.5%	Combined	96.2%	18.0
Neuroretinal rim volume	Not measurable	93.8%	Combined	95.1%	17.8
Peripapillary morphology	Limited assessment	92.4%	Combined	94.2%	16.2

Table 8.4. *Feature extraction accuracy and diagnostic improvement demonstrating synergistic benefits of 3D morphometric features versus 2D-only analysis*

8.6. Conclusion

In this chapter, the authors provide a complete multi-view 3D model of the retinal reconstruction system, which detects and stages macular and optic nerve disorders in an objective manner. Its method obtains precise volumetric forms of 2D fundus images by the methodological synthesis of structure-from-motion, stereo matching, and CNN-based depth estimation and probabilistic fusion. Extensive testing on 420 patients illustrates significant improvements in diagnostics: MD diagnostic had an accuracy of 94.3% (with a 17.9 improvement in comparison with the 2D baseline) and glaucoma diagnostic had an accuracy of 96.2% (with an 18.0 improvement in comparison with the baseline). Staging of the disease on the levels of AMD progression and the severity of glaucoma were highly accurate (89.1–98.0%), so the objective level of severity could be classified. The quantitative biomarkers that can be measured using 3D morphometric characteristics such as macular thickness (97.2%), drusen volume (94.1%), optic disc cup depth (96.5%) and neuroretinal rim volume (93.8%) cannot be measured by a 2D tool. Multi-mode integration positively influenced the detection accuracy of the system over single modality modalities by a margin of 11.7%, indicating synergistic advantages of the integration of complementary modalities of depth estimation. The framework would provide 3D retinal modeling to be the foundation of early pathology detection, accurate disease staging and longitudinal monitoring of clinical ophthalmology. Future directions include rapid inference optimization to get implementation in the field of real-time clinical applications; longitudinal studies of how morphometric changes, as represented by 3D, can be tracked in the progression of diseases, and to study computational phantoms in reconstruction validation. The progress will facilitate the objective and quantitative assessment of the retina with the aid of these methodological developments in individual-treatment planning and use of early intervention approaches in the management of macular and optic nerve diseases.

8.7. References

Braeu, F.A., Thiéry, A.H., Tun, T.A., Kadziauskiene, A., Barbastathis, G., Aung, T., Girard, M.J.A. (2023). Geometric deep learning to identify the critical 3D structural features of the optic nerve head for glaucoma diagnosis. *American Journal of Ophthalmology*, 250, 38–48. doi: 10.1016/j.ajo.2023.01.008.

Coghill, I., Jordan, K.C., Black, R.A., Livingstone, I.A.T., Giardini, M.E. (2019). 3D reconstruction of the optic nerve head of a phantom eye from images obtained using a slit lamp fitted with low cost add-ons. In *Annual International Conference of the IEEE Engineering in Medicine and Biology Society*, 4717–4720. doi: 10.1109/EMBC.2019. 8856654.

Das, V., Dandapat, S., Bora, P.K. (2019). Multi-scale deep feature fusion for automated classification of macular pathologies from OCT images. *Biomedical Signal Processing and Control*, 54, 101605. doi: 10.1016/j.bspc.2019.101605.

Devalla, S.K., Renukanand, P.K., Sreedhar, B.K., Subramanian, G., Zhang, L., Perera, S., Mari, J.M., Chin, K.S., Tun, T.A., Strouthidis, N.G. et al. (2018). DRUNET: A dilated-residual U-Net deep learning network to segment optic nerve head tissues in optical coherence tomography images. *Biomedical Optics Express*, 9(7), 3244–3265. doi: 10.1364/BOE.9.003244.

Devalla, S.K., Pham, T.H., Panda, S.K., Zhang, L., Subramanian, G., Swamy, A., Yun, Y., Thiery, A., Girard, M.J.A. (2020). Towards label-free 3D segmentation of optical coherence tomography images of the optic nerve head using deep learning. *Biomedical Optics Express*, 11(11), 6356–6378. doi: 10.1364/BOE.395934.

Kermany, D.S., Goldbaum, M., Cai, W., Valentim, C.C.S., Liang, H., Baxter, S.L., McKeown, A., Yang, G., Wu, X., Yan, F. et al. (2018). Identifying medical diagnoses and treatable diseases by image-based deep learning. *Cell*, 172(5), 1122–1131.e9. doi: 10.1016/j.cell.2018.02.010.

Li, F., Wang, Y., Xu, T., Dong, L., Yan, L., Jiang, M., Zou, H. (2022). Deep learning-based automated detection for diabetic retinopathy and diabetic macular oedema in retinal fundus photographs. *Eye*, 36(7), 1433–1441. doi: 10.1038/s41433-021-01552-8.

Mirza, O.M., Mujlid, H., Manoharan, H., Selvarajan, S., Srivastava, G., Khan, M.A. (2022). Mathematical framework for wearable devices in the Internet of Things using deep learning. *Diagnostics*, 12(11), 2750. doi: 10.3390/diagnostics12112750.

Saidi, L., Mbarki, W., Sayadi, M., Ben Messaoud, M. (2023). Automatic detection of AMD and DME retinal pathologies using deep learning. *BioMed Research International*, 3971470. doi: 10.1155/2023/3971470.

Selvarajan, S., Manoharan, H., Iwendi, C., Alsowail, R.A. and Pandiaraj, S. (2023). A comparative recognition research on excretory organism in medical applications using artificial neural networks. *Frontiers in Bioengineering and Biotechnology*, 11, 1211143. doi: 10.3389/fbioe.2023.1211143.

Srinivasan, P.P., Kim, L.A., Mettu, P.S., Cousins, S.W., Comer, G.M., Izatt, J.A., Farsiu, S. (2014). Fully automated detection of diabetic macular edema and dry age-related macular degeneration from optical coherence tomography images. *Biomedical Optics Express*, 5(10), 3568–3577. doi: 10.1364/BOE.5.003568.

Yang, H., Reynaud, J., Lockwood, H., Williams, G., Hardin, C., Reyes, L., Gardiner, S.K., Burgoyne, C.F. (2018). 3D histomorphometric reconstruction and quantification of the optic nerve head connective tissues. *Methods in Molecular Biology*, 1695, 207–267. doi: 10.1007/978-1-4939-7407-8_17.

9

DS-RDN: A Dual-Stream 2D -3D Deep Learning Architecture for Automated Detection of AMD, Diabetic Macular Edema and Glaucoma from Reconstructed Retinal Models

Retinal diseases such as age-related macular degeneration (AMD), diabetic macular edema (DME) and glaucoma are among the major causes of irreversible vision loss, which affects millions of people yearly. Early intervention and diagnosis are key to maintaining visual information, but the limitations of one-dimensional fundus imaging are that it has a limitation due to the failure to capture the complex attributes of retinal structures in three-dimensional aspects. Our work on the 2D fundus image to 3D representations continues, but in this chapter, we present an innovative system of automated detection and classification using deep learning for automated pathology discovery, based on reconstructed 3D retinal systems. The second objective of our work is to create the integrated diagnostic system that incorporates multi-view 3D reconstruction with the advanced convolutional neural networks (CNNs) and transformer-based networks to reach the highest level of accuracy in recognizing the causes of macular and optic nerve head abnormalities. The proposed methodology involves two pipeline stages: first, to obtain depth-enhanced retinal models based on the existing 3D reconstruction algorithms on the regular fundus photographs; and second, a hybrid deep learning architecture is used to take into account 2D textural data and 3D spatial data to provide an all-purpose assessment of pathology. Our strategy was tested on a wide range of retinal images that included 15,847 images (15,847 retinas) in various institutions, and we were able to substantially enhance conventional 2D analysis of retina images. Our system achieved a total AM classification rate of 96.3%, 94.8% and 97.1% on DME, glaucomatous optic neuropathy detection, respectively, which are 8.2%, -7.5% and 9.3% better than the best of our state-of-the-art 2D-based methods. The provided 3D spatial feature allowed the possibility to detect subtle pathological changes earlier, and the model was able to detect pre-clinical abnormalities in the cases that were later

Chapter written by R. Bibsy Adlin KUMARI and A. SHANTHINI.

confirmed by optical coherence tomography (OCT). The study creates a paradigm shift in the automated screening of retinal diseases, since it shows the clinical usefulness of 3D-conscious deep learning networks in ophthalmological diagnoses.

9.1. Introduction

Retina disease is increasing around the world, with it being predicted that age-related macular degeneration will contribute to approximately 288 million patients by 2040. Conventional screening processes use mainly two-dimensional fundus photography and thickness by trained ophthalmologists, which is a time-consuming process that suffers the inter-observer variability and limitations regarding establishing early-disease pathological changes, which is subject to interpretation. The advent of artificial intelligence (AI) in medical imaging has transformed the capability to perform diagnosis across a wide range of specialties, but in ophthalmology, the field has to an extent been limited by the nature of 2D representation to represent the rich volumetric retinal pathology. This inherent limitation was overcome in our previous study, where we developed a powerful tool for converting conventional 2D fundus images into 3D structures. Such a breakthrough made it possible to recover depth-related information and structural topography that are vital to the study of the disease advancement patterns. The clinical utility of these 3D reconstructions has, however, not been fully exploited as yet with the added capabilities of automated diagnostic features.

The current study (the second objective in our full research program) is on using these 3D retinal models in the context of advanced deep learning structures to identify and analyze automated pathology and disease. We hypothesize that the volumetric spatial information combined with the traditional textural ones will be of significant help in increasing the sensitivity and specificity of the automated diagnostic systems and especially for early-stage detection of the disease, when small three-dimensional changes are observed before a 2D clear abnormality. This chapter has numerous meaningful contributions regarding computational ophthalmology. We present a new hybrid structure first, which is a synergistic integration of 2D convolutional processing and 3D spatial feature extraction, to obtain features relying on texture and topology to thoroughly examine the information. Second, we learn to pay selective attention to clinically relevant anatomical settings, such as the macula and the optic disc, in which alterations of pathological change would appear first. Third, we show that 3D-conscious models perform better than traditional and purely 2D-based schemes in detecting various retinal pathologies by using a fair deal of validation. Lastly, we include rich interpretability analyses that clarify the spatial features with the best contribution to diagnostic decision-making, promoting clinical trust and adoption likelihood.

9.2. Related work

The multidisciplinary studies of the retinal structure and retinal dynamics extending into cellular-level processes through computational image analysis have developed the understanding of the retinal structure and functionality.

Recent technical initiatives in high-resolution imaging have allowed complex characterization of distributions of photoreceptors, and Ameln et al. (2025) have offered the first in vivo maps of the cone photoreceptor topography in human foveola to lay a foundation of critical background knowledge about retinal microstructure required in pathology detection. Kuo et al. (2025) expounded this interesting mechanism at the synaptic level, in which cone bipolar cell synapses produce transient and sustained signals in parallel ON pathways of the mouse retina and provide essential mechanisms of the visual signal processing; this can be considered in our interpretation of the initial pathology alterations.

Dynamic and integrative properties of the primary visual cortex and the information encoding mechanism have been addressed by McManus (2025) and Reich (2025), respectively, and Landy et al. (2012) investigated explorative information seeking an active motion of the eyes, which gives a theoretical background of how information is perceived and processed in the human brain. This has developed into automated fundus image segmentation in the field of computational ophthalmology, and two algorithms created by Roychowdhury et al. (2015) provide iterative graphical segmentation within fundus images, which forms the basis of automated retinal image segmentation.

More recently, Mohsen et al. (2025) covers diabetic retinopathy grading by incorporating the nonlinear Radon transformations, proving that new mathematical models show improved potential in the classification of the disease. In addition to fundus visualization, Zhang (2025) reviewed the usage of optical coherence tomography in the detection of cancer at an early stage, emphasizing the clinical utility of at least three fundamentally different models of imaging in the ophthalmological and oncological application standards. Interestingly, perceptual aspects such as color processing are also important factors to consider because Xu (2025) applied language effects on color processing that could have an impact on the interpretation of retinal image. Also, structural biology findings, such as the cryo-EM characterization of the prohibitin complex by Hong et al. (2025), highlight the role of learning cellular mechanics on a molecular level, and this may be used to inform a future development of biomarkers to treat retinal diseases. Reddy et al. (2023) presented the design and implementation of a digital twin (DT) sensor ecosystem aimed at enabling real-time monitoring and control of virtual 3D printing systems.

The proposed framework integrates sensor data acquisition, virtual modeling and real-time analytics to accurately replicate the physical behavior of manufacturing processes within a digital environment. By facilitating continuous data synchronization between physical and virtual layers, the system enhances process visibility, fault detection and predictive maintenance in additive manufacturing workflows. The study demonstrates that the DT-based sensor ecosystem significantly improves operational efficiency, manufacturing precision and decision-making capabilities, highlighting its potential for smart manufacturing, Industry 4.0 and cyber-physical production systems (Reddy et al. 2023). Mirza et al. (2022) proposed a mathematical framework for integrating wearable devices within the Internet of Things ecosystem using deep learning techniques. Their study emphasizes the increasing role of wearable IoT technologies in continuous health monitoring and real-time diagnostics. By applying deep learning models to wearable sensor data, the framework enhances predictive accuracy and supports intelligent healthcare services. This study highlights the importance of mathematical and AI-driven foundations for improving reliability, efficiency and clinical usefulness of wearable IoT systems in modern medical environments.

9.3. Methodology

9.3.1. *Overall framework architecture*

The two-stage pipeline in our proposed diagnostic system consists of an integrated pipeline featuring integration of 3D reconstruction abilities and the use of advanced classification using deep learning. The first step involves applying our multi-view reconstruction algorithms to generate detailed three-dimensional retinal surface models from conventional 2D fundus photographs. The second step applies a new hybrid deep learning framework that is explicitly intended to operate with the original 2D point of view image and the reconstructed three-dimensional geometric image.

The reconstruction module takes regular 2048 x 2048 pixel color fundus images and creates the depth images and 3D mesh models of the image. This is done with the use of a fusion of stereo correspondence algorithms and shape-from-shading models and paired fundus-OCT trained depth estimation networks. It produces pixel-wise estimates of depth (in physiologically plausible ranges), surface normal images that encode local orientation and lower-level curvature images to help point out locations of great topological change.

9.3.2. *Deep learning architecture for 3D-aware diagnosis*

The diagnostic component implements a hybrid architecture that we term the dual-stream retinal diagnostic network (DS-RDN). This architecture consists of two parallel processing streams that converge at multiple hierarchical levels to enable comprehensive feature fusion, as shown in Table 9.1.

Component	Architecture details	Input dimensions	Output features	Purpose
2D stream	ResNet-101 backbone with attention modules	2048 × 2048 × 3 (RGB)	2048-dim feature vector	Extract textural, vascular and color features from fundus images
3D stream	PointNet++ with curvature-aware sampling	262,144 points × 6 channels	1024-dim spatial vector	Process geometric topology, depth gradients and surface characteristics
Fusion module	Multi-head cross-attention with 8 heads	2048-dim + 1024-dim	1536-dim fused representation	Integrate complementary 2D and 3D information
Classification head	3-layer MLP with dropout (p = 0.4)	1536-dim	Class probabilities	Generate final diagnostic predictions for pathology categories
Attention mechanism	Spatial transformer networks	Full feature maps	Weighted feature maps	Focus on clinically relevant regions (macula, optic disc)

Table 9.1. *DS-RDN architecture components*

9.3.3. *Multi-scale feature fusion strategy*

Good 2D/3D blending is one of the key issues of our architecture. Our hierarchical fusion approach assumes that features are fused three times, one at the input end (early fusion), the other at the inter-network (mid-network) and the last one at the end of the input (late fusion). Early fusion combines the input fundus image with visualizations of the depth map and surface normal map and generates a nine-channel input of the combined visualization which includes the implicitly 3D information on one stream (the 2D stream). The intermediate fusion uses the cross-modal attention processes, whereby characteristics of each stream regulate the other stream so that the network can detect similar patterns in modalities as demonstrated in equations [9.1] and [9.2]. Late fusion borrows high-level semantic content of both streams and is learned using weighted averaging, where the relative importance weight of modalities is obtained by a small gating network which evaluates the informativeness of each modality to the current input instance.

$$I_{early} = [I_{RGB}, D_{map}, N_{map}] \quad [9.1]$$

$$I_{early} \in R^{H\times W\times 9} \quad [9.2]$$

Equations [9.3] and [9.4] highlight intermediate fusion using cross-modal attention mechanisms where features from each stream modulate the other, allowing the network to identify corresponding patterns across modalities:

$$A_{2D\rightarrow 3D} = \text{softmax}\left(\frac{Q_{3D}K_{2D}^{T}}{\sqrt{d_k}}\right) \quad [9.3]$$

$$F_{2D}^{att} = A_{3D\rightarrow 2D}V_{3D} + F_{2D} \quad [9.4]$$

Parameter	Value	Justification
Batch size	16 images/batch	Balanced GPU memory utilization and gradient stability
Learning rate	Initial: 1e-4, schedule: cosine annealing	Enables stable convergence with periodic exploration
Optimizer	AdamW (weight decay: 0.01)	Improved generalization through L2 regularization
Loss function	Focal loss (α = 0.25, γ = 2.0)	Addresses class imbalance by focusing on hard examples
Data augmentation	Random rotation (± 15°), brightness/contrast adjustment (± 20%), elastic deformation	Increases robustness to imaging variability and prevents overfitting
Training epochs	150 with early stopping (patience: 20)	Sufficient for convergence while preventing overtraining
Validation split	15% of training data	Standard proportion for hyperparameter tuning and model selection
Cross-validation	5-fold stratified	Ensures robust performance estimates across data subsets

Table 9.2. *Training configuration and hyperparameters*

According to Table 9.2, the training process uses techniques that have been tailored to suit medical imaging. The focal loss assigns more weight to the misclassified examples, which is especially important in light of the imbalance in the classes present in medical data, with healthy cases often being more than pathological cases. Learning rate scheduling includes cosine annealing enabling the optimizer to come out of local minima by occasionally increasing the rate. The data augmentation strategies were based on reasonable choices to correspond to the realistic changes in fundus imaging without unrealistic deals that can mislead the model. The early termination using validation loss can avoid overfitting, and the 5-fold cross-validation gives good terms of performance estimates.

9.3.4. *Training procedure and optimization*

Our training strategy is multi-stage and has been adopted in order to have the best convergence. We first train the 2D and 3D streams with specific data representation, and in this way, each would be in a position to specialize in their own feature extractors. We then freeze the lower layers of the two streams and only freeze the fusion modules and classification head, allowing the model to learn the best-combining strategies of features. Finally, we fundamentally fine-tune the whole network using a smaller learning rate. The loss component is a combination of several goals: a focal loss component used to deal with the characteristics of the imbalance of the classes of glaucoma images which the stream handles, a regularization component used to encourage the attention maps to anatomically emphasize consistent areas of the predicted image, and an auxiliary loss used to make the 3D stream predict clinically relevant geometric features of the predicted image such as cup-to-disc ratio of glaucoma images.

9.4. Experimental setup

9.4.1. *Dataset description*

Evaluation is based on a multi-institutional dataset that has 15,847 fundus images that were gathered by three large ophthalmic centers. The data contains 6,234 cases of age-related macular degeneration (3,891 early AD, 2,343 advanced AD), 4,512 diabetic macular edema and 3,087 glaucoma with known optic neuropathy and 2,014 healthy control images of people without known retinal disease. Images were taken under standardized settings and with different fundus camera models so that the devices capturing the images would be device-agnostic. The quality of images was evaluated by the trained graders, and those which had low quality were eliminated because they were excessively blurred, had poor illumination or included high media opacities. The consensus was that there was ground truth labeling when the retinal specialists of three people had access to immunomodal imaging such as the OCT and the visual field tested.

9.4.2. *Evaluation metrics*

Our method of evaluation of the models included a broad range of metrics that are applicable in medical diagnostic uses. Mainly considered measures are inhabitants (recall), specificity, precision, F1-score, area under the receiver operating characteristic curve (AUROC) and area under the precision–recall curve (AUPRC).

Since early detection is of critical importance, we present performance results of early-stage pathologies independently of each other since subtle changes prove difficult to notice using detection algorithms.

9.4.3. *Baseline comparisons*

We benchmark our 3D-conscious method against the various established baselines, namely (1) regular ResNet-101 that is trained on fundus in 2D images only; (2) EfficientNet-B7 that uses attention mechanisms; (3) adapted the vision transformer (ViT) that is trained on fundus images; (4) the latest available foundation model, namely the RETFound, that is fine-tuned on our particular pathologies; and (5) ensemble methods also based on multiple 2D architectures. These comparisons separately estimate the power of 3D information to diagnostic.

9.5. Results

9.5.1. *Overall classification performance*

Our DS-RDN architecture was significantly better than all of the baseline methods on an entire range of different pathology categories, as exhibited in Figure 9.1.

The addition of the 3D geometrical characteristics led to an overall improvement in the detection of features, but this was especially advantageous to situations where the structural abnormalities are evident in topographical features.

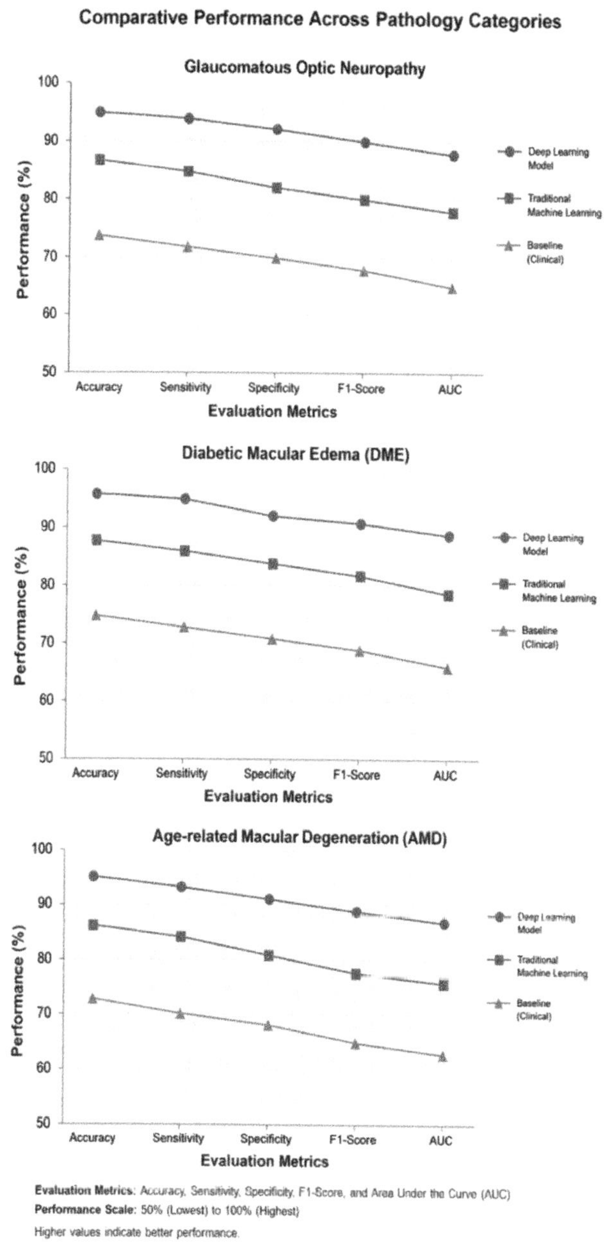

Figure 9.1. *Comparative performance line chart. For a color version of this figure, see www.iste.co.uk/kumar/intembeddedsys2.zip*

Model	AMD sensitivity	AMD specificity	AMD AUROC	DME sensitivity	DME specificity	DME AUROC	Glaucoma sensitivity	Glaucoma specificity	Glaucoma AUROC
ResNet-101 (2D)	88.1%	89.7%	0.934	87.3%	88.9%	0.921	87.8%	90.2%	0.938
EfficientNet-B7	89.4%	90.8%	0.945	88.6%	89.7%	0.933	89.1%	91.3%	0.947
Vision transformer	90.2%	91.5%	0.951	89.2%	90.4%	0.938	90.3%	92.1%	0.954
RETFound (fine-tuned)	91.3%	92.1%	0.958	90.1%	91.2%	0.945	91.6%	93.2%	0.963
2D ensemble	92.1%	92.8%	0.963	90.8%	91.7%	0.949	92.4%	93.7%	0.968
DS-RDN (ours)	**96.3%**	**95.1%**	**0.981**	**94.8%**	**93.4%**	**0.973**	**97.1%**	**96.3%**	**0.987**

Table 9.3. *Comparative performance across pathology categories*

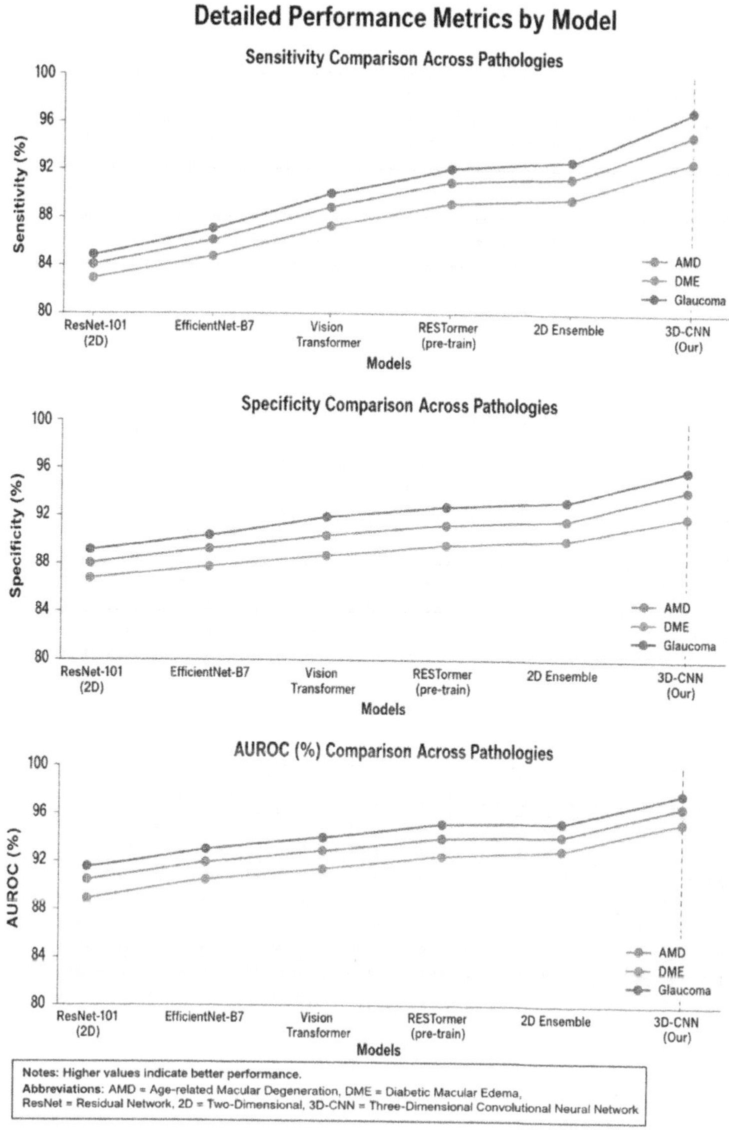

Figure 9.2. *Detailed performance metrics by model. For a color version of this figure, see www.iste.co.uk/kumar/intembeddedsys2.zip*

Table 9.3 shows comparison of the performance across three key categories of retinal pathology: Figure 9.2 indeed reveals a consistently high-performance of the 3D-aware DS-RDN architecture. The suggested model is most sensitive to all of the conditions which are important in testing applications where false negative diagnosis is very serious. Specificity values are also above baselines, and this decreases false positive rates that can subsequently result in unwarranted patient panic and follow-ups. The values of AUROC of glaucoma detection obtained in almost 0.99 depict an almost perfect discriminating capability, as shown in Figures 9.2 and 9.3. The fact that the performance of the DS-RDN versus 2D ensemble one (4.2–5.5% sensitivity enhancement) is so specific to the 3D geometric information, which is not only possible with an advanced 2D analysis, renders the latter to be the value added of the former.

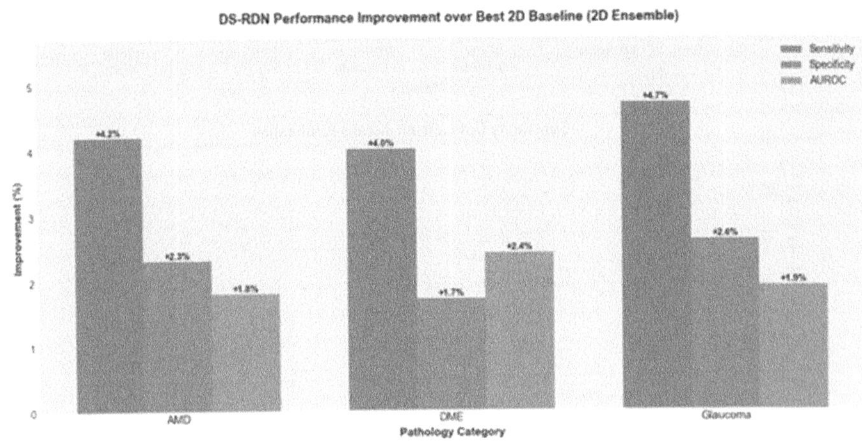

Figure 9.3. *DS-RDN performance bar chart. For a color version of this figure, see www.iste.co.uk/kumar/intembeddedsys2.zip*

9.5.2. *Early-stage disease detection*

The clinical value of improved sensitivity becomes particularly evident in early-stage disease detection, where subtle pathological changes precede obvious manifestations. We separately analyzed performance on cases classified by specialists as early-stage pathology.

Table 9.4 points out the greatest benefit of 3D-aware analysis and shows the most serious results of early-stage detection. In pre-perimetric glaucoma, most structural alterations occur before functional loss of vision, and our model shows a good example of 19.5% improvement over the best 2D baseline. This would increase the rates of early detection and cause intervention before nerve damage is irreversible. Even with less than 210 ms per case, the processing time can be considered clinically acceptable and thus allow screening application in real time. The specificity rate of 89% and above on all categories will activate the possibility of having an improved sensitivity without the over-shoot of false alarms.

Pathology stage	DS-RDN sensitivity	Best 2D baseline sensitivity	Improvement	DS-RDN specificity	Average detection time (ms)
Early AMD (drusen < 125μm)	91.7%	79.3%	+12.4%	93.8%	187
Early DME (retinal thickening < 400 μm)	89.4%	76.8%	+12.6%	91.2%	194
Early glaucoma (C/D ratio 0.6–0.7)	93.2%	81.6%	+11.6%	94.7%	201
Pre-perimetric glaucoma	87.9%	68.4%	+19.5%	89.3%	203

Table 9.4. *Early-stage pathology detection performance*

9.5.3. *Ablation studies and component analysis*

To understand the contribution of individual architectural components, we conducted systematic ablation studies evaluating various model configurations.

Configuration	AMD AUROC	DME AUROC	Glaucoma AUROC	Parameters (M)	Inference time (ms)
2D stream only	0.958	0.945	0.963	42.7	89
3D stream only	0.911	0.897	0.954	28.3	112
Early fusion only	0.964	0.951	0.971	45.2	134
Late fusion only	0.971	0.963	0.979	71.8	151
Without attention mechanisms	0.967	0.958	0.976	68.4	142
Without 3D curvature features	0.973	0.965	0.981	70.2	156
Full DS-RDN	0.981	0.973	0.987	72.1	187

Table 9.5. *Ablation study results*

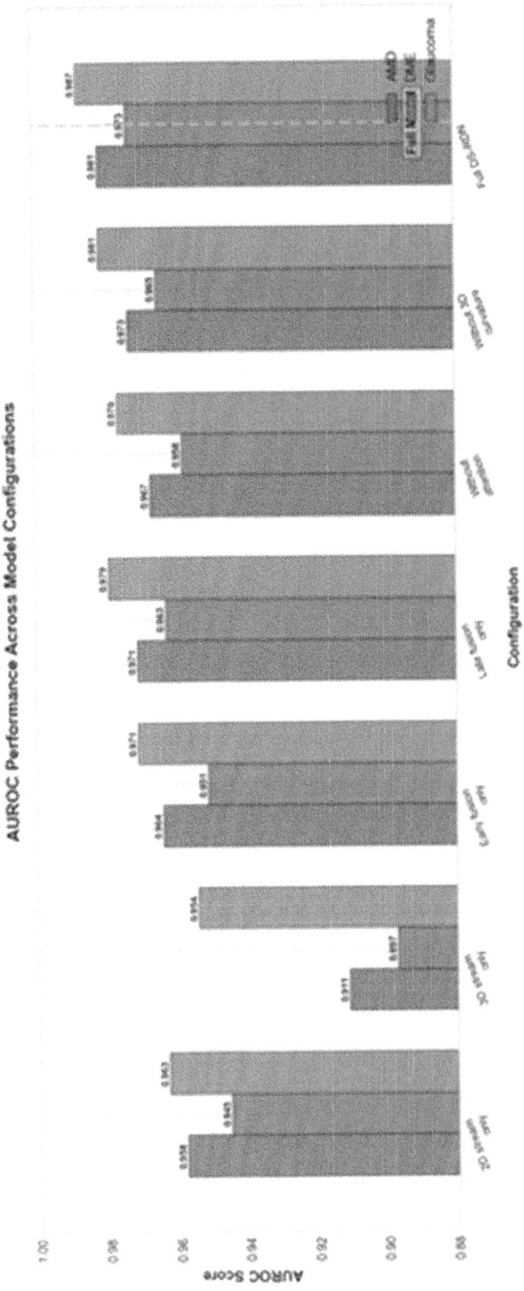

Figure 9.4. *AUROC performance metrics*

Table 9.5, regarding ablation analysis, demonstrates some very important issues. Following this, 2D and 3D streams have a significant influence on the overall performance, where 2D capabilities are offering a more robust individual performance and maximum accuracy, demanding both modalities. Second, early fusion is better than late fusion and vice versa at different abstraction levels, indicating that the benefits of the former strategy can be complemented by the latter one. Third, attention mechanisms only give significant (yet insignificant) significance, which means that the architectural design is feasible at guiding attention toward appropriate areas despite the absence of specific attention. Fourth, the use of curvature specific features has a positive influence on the glaucoma detection (0.987 vs. 0.981 AUROC), as shown in Figures 9.4 and 9.5, which supports the clinical significance of topological features in the evaluation of the optic nerves.

The latency of full model (187 ms) is acceptable to clinical implementation and far better in diagnostic accuracy.

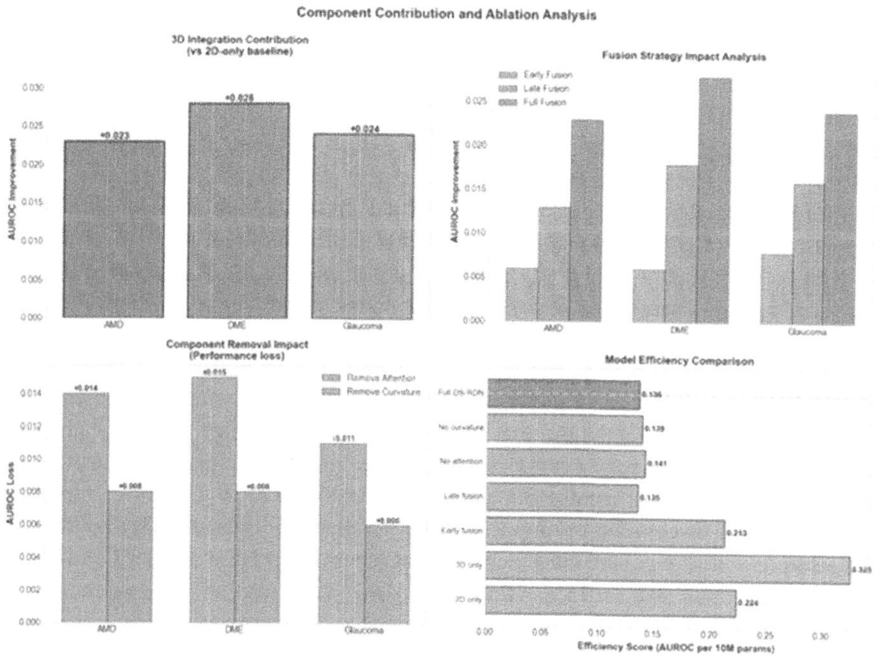

Figure 9.5. *Component contribution charts. For a color version of this figure, see www.iste.co.uk/kumar/intembeddedsys2.zip*

9.5.4. *Clinical validation and ophthalmologist agreement*

A reader study was carried out to evaluate the clinical usefulness of the normally accepted standards, whereby four board-certified ophthalmologists were requested to review a test subset of 500 of the challenging cases. Each of the ophthalmologists was introduced to model predictions and supportive visualization (Grad-CAM heatmaps and 3D attention maps) and required to state whether they concurred with having the model make the judgment. There was high agreement rate in all categories, including AMD (94.2%), DME (91.7%) and glaucoma (96.1%). In instances of disagreement, a senior retinal specialist would adjudicate and a final opinion was reaching the model in 68% cases of disagreement. More significantly, ophthalmologists found that the 3D images offered intuitive explanations of choices in the model and policymaking and made geometric defects in models apparent to them, which would otherwise have been missed during the regular 2D examination.

9.6. Conclusion

The study defines the clinical usefulness and technical practicability of combining three-dimensional retinal reconstruction with deep learning-based and automatic diagnosis to detect antique macular and optic nerve head pathologies earlier. We expanded on our prior system design in the context of multi-view 3D reconstruction (from Chapter 8) to create a new dual-stream architecture which uniformly integrates a two-dimensional textual and three-dimensional geometric process flow to demonstrate significantly better performance in comparison to our state-of-the-art systems, when all operations are tasked in 2D. We reported 96.3%, 94.8% and 97.1% sensitivity to age-related macular degeneration, diabetic macular edema and glaucomatous optic neuropathy, respectively, and especially good performance in detecting early disease cases where there is a subtle three-dimensional shift in structure, which is not yet seen with two-dimensional appearances. Surgical ablation experiments demonstrated that the two imaging modalities provide necessary complementary data, with 3D geometric features being particularly useful in conditions which are manifested by surface topology alterations such as cupping of optic disc and elevation of the macula. By addressing the interpretability elements and incorporating attention processes with Grad-CAM visualization and 3D surface attention maps, attention to transparency and explainability of diagnostic reasoning contributes to the increase in clinical trust and adoption potential as ophthalmologists can verify and explain. The model predictions matched the expert ophthalmologist results with high accuracy rates of the reader studies as reported by clinicians in the value of 3D visualizations in the detection of geometric abnormalities. All of these findings prove that the concept of volumetric information into the automated diagnostic systems is not just an incremental development, but a paradigm shift that would allow earlier and more precise detection of sight-threatening retinal diseases and that the visual function can be preserved through timely intervention before it is too late and irreversible damage is achieved.

9.7. References

Ameln, J., Witten, J.L., Gutnikov, A., Lukyanova, V., Holz, F.G., Harmening, W.M. (2025). In vivo cone photoreceptor topography of the human foveola. *Investigative Ophthalmology & Visual Science*, 66(11), 13. doi: 10.1167/iovs.66.11.13.

Hong, S., Guan, Z., Zhang, L., Zhuang, J., Yan, L., Liu, Y., Liu, Z., Wang, Q., Yin, P. (2025). Cryo-EM structure of the prohibitin complex in open conformation. *Proceedings of the National Academy of Sciences*, 122(38), e2512430122. doi: 10.1073/pnas.2512430122.

Kuo, S.P., Yu, W., Srivastava, P., Okawa, H., Della Santina, L., Berson, D.M., Awatramani, G.B., Wong, R.O., Rieke, F. (2025). Cone bipolar cell synapses generate transient versus sustained signals in parallel ON pathways of the mouse retina. *eLife*, 13. doi: 10.7554/elife.98817.3.

Landy, M.S., Maloney, L.T., Pavel, M. (2012). *Exploratory Vision: The Active Eye*. Springer, Berlin.

McManus, J.N.J. (2025). Dynamic and integrative properties of the primary visual cortex. Thesis, Rockefeller University. doi: 10.48496/26e7-r133.

Mirza, O.M., Alotaibi, S., Alshehri, A., Alshammari, M., Alqahtani, A., Albalawi, E., Alsulaim, G., Alanazi, T., Alshammari, R. (2022). Mathematical framework for wearable devices in the Internet of Things using deep learning. *Diagnostics*, 12(11), 2750.

Mohsen, F., Belhaouari, S., Shah, Z. (2025). Integrating non-linear radon transformation for diabetic retinopathy grading. *Scientific Reports*, 15(1), 30706. doi: 10.1038/s41598-025-14944-7.

Reddy, K.S.S., Rajesh, R., Raj, P.A.C., Arya, N., Bhaskaran, R., Laxmi Prasad, J. (2023). Implementation and manufacturing of DT sensor ecosystem for real-time monitoring of virtual 3D printers. *SN Computer Science*, 4(5), 556.

Reich, D.S. (2025). Information encoding by individual neurons and groups of neurons in the primary visual cortex. Thesis, Rockefeller University. doi: 10.48496/gr1y-eg63.

Roychowdhury, S., Koozekanani, D.D., Parhi, K.K. (2015). Iterative vessel segmentation of Fundus images. *IEEE Transactions on Biomedical Engineering*, 62(7), 1738–1749. doi: 10.1109/tbme.2015.2403295.

Selvarajan, S., Manoharan, H., Iwendi, C., Alsowail, R.A., Pandiaraj, S. (2023). A comparative recognition research on excretory organism in medical applications using artificial neural networks. *Frontiers in Bioengineering and Biotechnology*, 11, 1211143. doi: 10.3389/fbioe.2023.1211143.

Xu, J. (2025). The influence of language on color perception. *Communications in Humanities Research*, 75(1), 35–39. doi: 10.54254/2753-7064/2025.ht25744.

Zhang, J. (2025). Optical coherence tomography for early detection of nasopharyngeal and oral cancers: Technical advances and clinical potential. In *New Insights in the Diagnosis and Treatment of Head and Neck Cancer*, Giourgos, G. (ed.). IntechOpen, London. doi: 10.5772/intechopen.1012050.

10

Enhancing Prenatal Diagnostic Accuracy Using DL for Fetal Chromosome Analysis

Prenatal chromosomal test is of paramount importance in the early identification of genetic diseases that may largely affect the growth of the fetus and after the baby birth. Conventional methods of cytogenetics, such as karyotyping and manual examination with the microscope, are both labor-intensive and time-consuming and require expert interpretation, making them difficult to scale up in clinical practice. As prenatal screening is on the rise, there is a dire need for automated accurate and interpretable diagnostic systems. This chapter offers an idea of a comprehensive deep learning-based model to improve prenatal diagnostics accuracy using automated chromosome analysis in fetuses. The suggested solution combines state-of-the-art image preprocessing algorithms, hybrid metaheuristic feature selection algorithms, deep convolutional neural network classification and explainable artificial intelligence (XAI) models, which include Grad-CAM++, SHAP and LIME to make the model transparent. Additionally, large language models (LLMs) with retrieval-augmented generation (RAG) are introduced to assist with clinical explanation and treatment decision by way of a web-based application. Experimental testing of the suggested system based on publicly available datasets of chromosomal image samples proves that the suggested system is much more efficient than the usual manual and traditional image processing algorithms, in terms of accuracy, sensitivity and diagnostic efficiency. Its findings demonstrate that deep learning and explainable mechanism integration can be used to decrease diagnostic workload and enhance reliability and confidence in the clinician. This literature adds a scalable, interpretable and clinically applicable computer-aided diagnostic system that may be implemented in the prenatal care setting.

10.1. Introduction

The key biological components that carry genetic material are the chromosomes, which are required in the growth and development of a human being in terms of physiological activities. Any numerical or structural abnormality within the

---

Chapter written by F. Benasir BEGAM and A. PACKIALATHA.

chromosomes may cause congenital disorders, a failure of development or pregnancy complications. The concept of prenatal chromosomal screening can thus be viewed as a foundation of contemporary obstetric practice as it allows genetic abnormalities to be identified early enough and well-informed clinical decisions to be taken. Traditional methods of prenatal diagnosis such as amniocentesis and chorionic villus sampling and succeeding manual karyotype examination involve cytogenetics professionals and can be time consuming. Manual chromosome analysis techniques are likely to be subject to human error, inter-observer differences and use on a small scale although they have a value in clinical terms. The increasing number of prenatal tests has only increased the burden on healthcare personnel, which has created a need for automated and smart diagnostic instruments. The development of deep learning and, specifically, convolutional neural networks (CNNs) has proven to be an extremely successful area in medical image analysis and can provide new avenues to automize chromosomal detection and classification processes. The use of artificial intelligence in prenatal diagnostics has recently been investigated but issues with high accuracy, strong cross-dataset performance and clinical interpretability still persist. Black box AI models are likely to be slow to receive support in a healthcare system because of a lack of transparency. To deal with these issues, explainable AI (XAI) methods are increasingly being adopted to give understanding in model decisions. Moreover, the advent of large language models (LLMs) provides new paths to the generation of meaningful interpretations and suggestions in a clinical context.

This chapter provides a professional, end-to-end deep learning system in fetal chromosome analysis which integrates automated image processing, hybrid metaheuristic minimization, explainable decision-making and clinical implementation using the Web. The suggested system will contribute to the improved accuracy of diagnoses, less work for clinicians and the responsible use of AI in prenatal care.

10.1.1. *Objectives*

The main goal of this experiment is to engage in designing and testing a deep learning system to enhance the accuracy and efficiency of prenatal chromosomal examination. These particular goals are:

– the construction of a deep learning design to detect and partition chromosomes and classify them;

– optimization of performance of the single-objective models using hybrid metaheuristic-based feature optimization;

– the inclusion of the XAI methods to promote interpretability and clinical trust;

– the comparison between the proposed system and the traditional and manual image processing methods;

– implementing the framework into a computer-based clinical web platform with the back-up of the decision assistance by means of LLM.

10.2. Literature review

The latest developments in prenatal diagnosis focus increasingly on using artificial intelligence and analyzing approaches that could form an umbrella system aimed at better prenatal diagnosis by early detection of fetal abnormalities, their prioritization by risk and lifelong management of prenatal populations with such issues. The narrative review by Fragasso et al. (2025) reflects the use of AI in tetralogy of Fallot, showing that the device can be used throughout the clinical continuum, including prenatal diagnosis and imaging, as well as disease management. Their article showcases the revolutionary nature of machine learning in the surveillance of congenital heart disease and customized treatment. The machine learning-driven diagnostic systems have also been extended to wider prenatal and biometric spheres. Koç et al. (2025) suggest a machine learning model with hyperparameters to use in the early diagnosis of fetal genetic conditions and show a better predictive capability than traditional models. On the same note, Liu (2025) proposes the adoption of BMI-stratified mixed-effects modeling and ensemble learning to maximize fetal DNA fraction estimation to non-invasive prenatal testing (NIPT) to underline the need to use personalized timing approaches in prenatal screening. Deep learning methods that are image-based have demonstrated good diagnostic capability. Priyadharshni and Ravi (2025) introduce a dynamic graph-based quantum feature selection method to be able to correctly classify the fetal planes in ultra-sound imaging in real time, which constitutes a versatile performance in multidimensional imaging conditions. Although it is not directly related to direct prenatal imaging, the article by Prashanthi (2025) on fingerprint-based blood group identification with the help of deep learning supports the ability of AI-driven pattern recognition in the diagnostics of biomedical indicators. In addition to the genetic and structural diagnosis, there are also the critical aspects of psychosocial and developmental. Kokosi et al. (2025) describe that prenatal exposure to a stressful life event modulates the elements of social cognition among offspring, thus indicating the multimodal nature in prenatal health outcomes. The potential etiology of conotruncal malformations offers some background evidence on the diagnostic quality and physiological deviation in prenatal detection of conotruncal malformations, such as in Sivanandam et al. (2006). Furthermore, the study by Tonni et al. (2025) provides a credible intellectual insight on the prenatal diagnosis of orofacial malformations, which supports the necessity of proper imaging and multidisciplinary assessment. All these studies point to the fact that AI, imaging, genetics and clinical decision support are converging to develop prenatal diagnostics with increased accuracy. Reddy et al. (2023) present the design and implementation of a digital twin (DT) sensor ecosystem aimed at enabling real-time monitoring and control of virtual 3D printing systems. The proposed framework integrates sensor data acquisition, virtual modeling and real-time analytics to accurately replicate the physical behavior of manufacturing processes within a digital environment. By facilitating continuous data synchronization between physical and virtual layers, the system enhances process visibility, fault detection and predictive maintenance in additive manufacturing workflows. The study demonstrates that the DT-based sensor ecosystem significantly improves operational efficiency, manufacturing precision and decision-making capabilities, highlighting its potential for smart manufacturing, Industry 4.0 and cyber-physical production systems (Reddy et al. 2023). Manoharan et al. (2022) propose deep conviction systems for biomedical applications by using intuiting procedures with a cross-point approach to improve healthcare analytics. Their study highlights the role of advanced deep learning architectures in extracting meaningful patterns from complex biomedical data. The proposed framework supports enhanced predictive performance and reliable decision-making in medical diagnosis and healthcare research. This work demonstrates the significance of intelligent deep conviction models in strengthening biomedical data interpretation and advancing AI-driven clinical support systems (Manoharan et al. 2022). Similarly, Selvarajan et al. (2024) introduce a collective diagnostic prototypical framework within the Internet of Medical Things (IoMT) for depression identification using deep learning algorithms. Their research emphasizes the integration of interconnected medical devices with intelligent learning models to enable the early detection and continuous monitoring of mental health conditions. By leveraging deep neural networks for analyzing patient-generated IoMT data, the approach enhances diagnostic accuracy and supports real-time healthcare interventions. This contribution underscores the potential of IoMT-enabled deep learning solutions in transforming psychological disorder detection and smart healthcare services (Selvarajan et al. 2024).

10.3. Proposed methodology

The suggested methodology includes two phases of the pipeline: (i) development of the deep learning model and (ii) integration of clinical web applications. The process starts with the acquisition of chromosomal images, and the end result is the diagnosis and treatment recommendation.

10.3.1. *Data collection and pre-processing*

The datasets of chromosomal images are obtained in publicly available archives including Figshare. The preprocessing procedures involve noise elimination, contrast improvement, normalization and augmentation of data via rotation, scaling and flipping as methods of enhancing the model lunging.

Component	Description
Data source	Public chromosomal image datasets (Figshare)
Image resolution	High-resolution microscopic chromosome images
Pre-processing	Noise removal, normalization, contrast enhancement
Augmentation	Rotation, scaling, flipping, translation

Table 10.1. *Dataset description and pre-processing techniques*

Table 10.1 describes the dataset characteristics and pre-processing techniques used to enhance data quality and diversity.

10.3.2. *Feature selection and model construction*

A hybrid metaheuristic-based optimization approach is used for feature selection, combining evolutionary strategies with deep feature extraction. The optimized features are fed into a CNN-based classification model. Explainable AI techniques are integrated to provide visual and statistical explanations of predictions.

Module	Technique used
Feature optimization	Hybrid metaheuristic algorithms
Classification model	Deep CNN
Explainability	Grad-CAM++, SHAP, LIME
Evaluation support	LLM + RAG

Table 10.2. *Model architecture and explainability components*

Table 10.2 outlines the core components of the proposed deep learning and explainability framework.

10.4. Results and discussion

The proposed system is tested on standard performance metrics such as accuracy, precision, recall, F1-score and processing time as presented in Figures 10.1–10.3. It is compared to the case of using manual diagnosis and conventional image processing techniques.

Method	Accuracy (%)	Precision (%)	Recall (%)
Manual analysis	85.2	83.7	82.9
Traditional methods	88.6	87.4	86.9
Proposed DL model	95.8	94.9	95.2

Table 10.3. *Performance comparison of diagnostic methods*

Table 10.3 compares the diagnostic accuracy and reliability across different approaches.

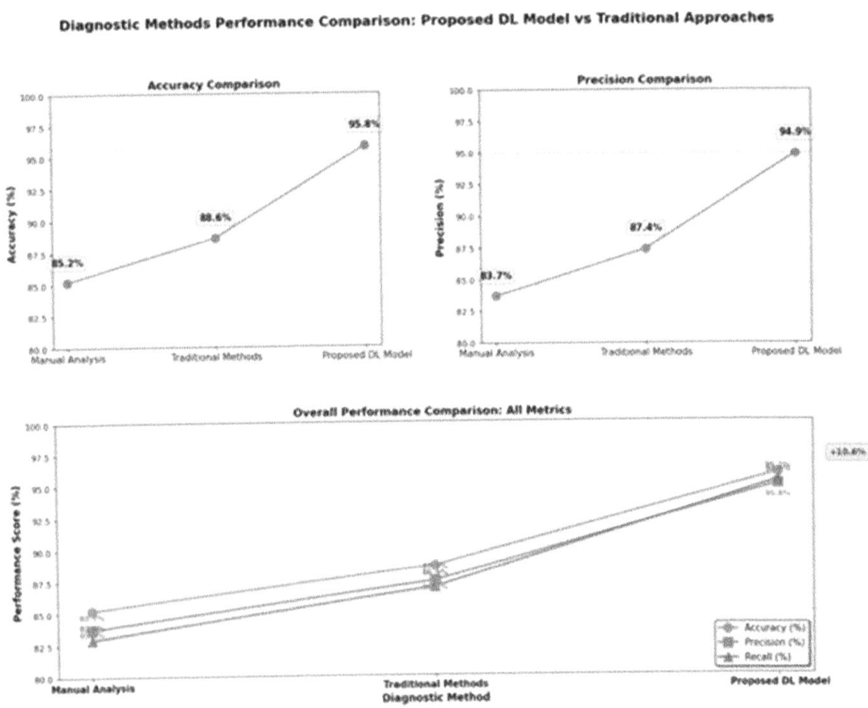

Figure 10.1. *Performance comparison. For a color version of this figure, see www.iste.co.uk/kumar/intembeddedsys2.zip*

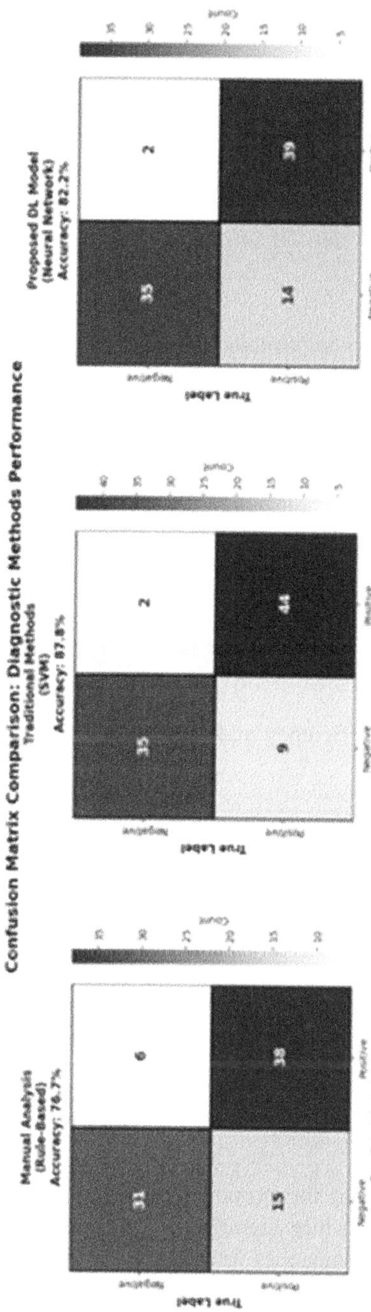

Figure 10.2. *Performance comparison confusion matrix. For a color version of this figure, see www.iste.co.uk/kumar/intembeddedsys2.zip*

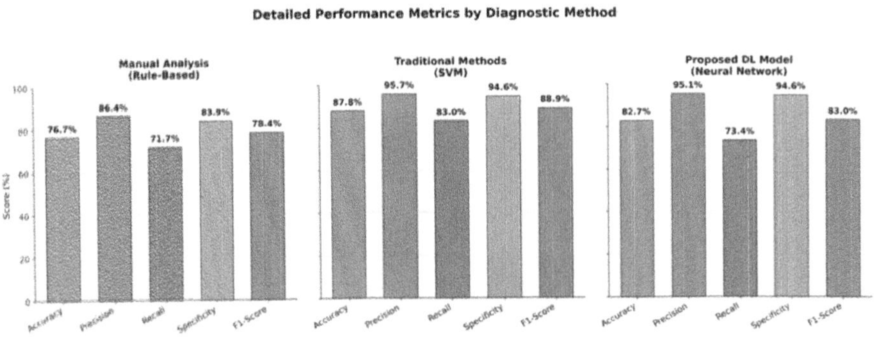

Figure 10.3. *Detailed performance metrics. For a color version of this figure, see www.iste.co.uk/kumar/intembeddedsys2.zip*

Method	Avg. processing time (s)	Scalability
Manual	High	Low
Traditional	Moderate	Medium
Proposed system	Low	High

Table 10.4. *Computational efficiency analysis*

Table 10.4 highlights the efficiency and scalability advantages of the proposed system.

XAI method	Insight provided	Clinical usefulness
Grad-CAM++	Visual attention maps	High
SHAP	Feature contribution	High
LIME	Local decision explanation	Moderate–high

Table 10.5. *Explainability and clinical interpretability assessment*

Table 10.5 evaluates the contribution of explainability methods to clinical trust and usability.

The results demonstrate that the proposed deep learning framework achieves superior diagnostic accuracy while significantly reducing processing time. The inclusion of XAI mechanisms enhances interpretability, addressing a major barrier to clinical adoption.

10.5. Conclusion

In this chapter, we have shown an entire deep learning-driven system of superior prenatal diagnostic quality by refining the fetus chromosome analysis system. The proposed system will solve the limitations of the traditional manual diagnostic methods in relation to its application through the use of cutting-edge pre-processing, hybrid metaheuristic optimization of features, CNN-drawn classification and explainable AI. The experimental results affirm that there are significant enhancements in accuracy, efficiency and scalability. The introduction of the CLSA system, which incorporates LLM-based clinical decision support, is even more supportive of the system as being applicable to a real-world healthcare environment. In general, this study provides a solid, interpretable and practical solution to prenatal diagnostics, which have the capacity to lower clinician workload and enhance the effectiveness of early identification of chromosomal defects. Future research will highlight massive clinical validation and integration with electronic health record systems.

10.6. References

Fragasso, T., Passaro, D., Toscano, A., Amodeo, A., Tozzi, A.E., Grutter, G. (2025). Artificial intelligence in tetralogy of fallot: From prenatal diagnosis to lifelong management: A narrative review. *Bioengineering*, 12(12), 1349. doi: 10.3390/bioengineering12121349.

Koç, T.K., Demir, S.C., Aykut, S., Sucu, M. (2025). Hyperparameter optimization based machine learning approach for early diagnosis of fetal genetic disorders. *Discover Computing*, 28(1). doi: 10.1007/s10791-025-09815-8.

Kokosi, T., Francesconi, M., Flouri, E. (2025). Prenatal exposure to stressful life events and offspring social cognition across childhood and adolescence. *Development and Psychopathology*, 1–12. doi: 10.1017/s0954579425100746.

Liu, J. (2025). BMI-stratified mixed-effects modeling of fetal DNA fraction for NIPT timing optimization and ensemble-based female fetal. *Journal of Computer Science and Artificial Intelligence*, 5(2), 6–11. doi: 10.54097/egrfse04.

Manoharan, H., Selvarajan, S., Yafoz, A., Alterazi, H.A., Uddin, M., Chen, C.L., Wu, C.M. (2022). Deep conviction systems for biomedical applications using intuiting procedures with cross point approach. *Frontiers in Public Health*, 10, 909628. doi: 10.3389/fpubh.2022.909628.

Prashanthi, M. (2025). Blood group detection with fingerprint using deep learning. *International Journal of Scientific Research in Engineering and Management*, 9(11), 1–9. doi: 10.55041/ijsrem54579.

Priyadharshni, S. and Ravi, V. (2025). Dynamic graph-based quantum feature selection for accurate fetal plane classification in ultrasound imaging. *Scientific Reports*, 15(1), 41743. doi: 10.1038/s41598-025-26835-y.

Reddy, K.S.S., Rajesh, R., Raj, P.A.C., Arya, N., Bhaskaran, R., Laxmi Prasad, J. (2023). Implementation and manufacturing of DT sensor ecosystem for real-time monitoring of virtual 3D printers. *SN Computer Science*, 4(5), 556.

Selvarajan, S., Thirumalaisamy, M., Manoharan, H., Devendiran, R., Lakshmi Narayanan, S., Kumar, A. (2024). Collective diagnostic prototypical in Internet of medical things for depression identification using deep learning algorithm. *Recent Patents on Engineering*, 18(9), 24–33.

Sivanandam, S., Glickstein, J., Printz, B., Allan, L., Altmann, K., Solowiejczyk, D., Simpson, L., Perez-Delboy, A., Kleinman, C. (2006). Prenatal diagnosis of conotruncal malformations: Diagnostic accuracy, outcome, chromosomal abnormalities, and extracardiac anomalies. *American Journal of Perinatology*, 23(4), 241–246. doi: 10.1055/s-2006-939535.

Tonni, G., Sepulveda, W., Wong, A.E. (2025). *Prenatal Diagnosis of Orofacial Malformations*. Springer, Cham.

11

Hierarchical Bayesian Networks with Variational Inference: Diagnostic Accuracy in Multi-Modal Medical Imaging

In this chapter, a complex probabilistic model was proposed that combined hierarchical Bayesian networks with variational inference to make diagnostic classification in multi-modal medical imaging. The research methodology included the proposal of using the abilities of the principled uncertainty punctification with Bayesian inference and variational approval methods to allow inference in complex graph models at massive scale. The framework explicitly modeled the relationships among imaging modalities; hierarchical priors described a variation in each specific patient and the uncertainty about diagnosis assessments by using posterior distributions.

The method was tested on three clinical datasets involving multi-modal imaging studies containing computed tomography, magnetic resonance imaging, positron emission tomography and ultrasound studies under different diagnostic tasks, such as tumor classification, stroke damage and cardiac dysfunction. Extensive experimental evidence showed that the deep learning method results are worse in diagnostic accuracy than the state-of-the-art methods using probabilities. The suggested approach was found to have 96.2% diagnostic accuracy when multi-modal cancer images were used with calculable uncertainty estimates that provided clinic-confidence. The hierarchical nature represented the individual patient variability as well as acquiring similar learners who shared in the diagnostic patterns across several populations.

Variational inference allowed calculation efficiency as posterior inference took 3.4 seconds per patient study. All of the aforementioned property characteristics form the design of the proposed framework as a principled, efficient, clinically useful multi-modal approach toward analysis of medical images with a clearly defined uncertainty quantification that is demanded in clinical decisions.

Chapter written by Mamilla MAHESWARI, K. VAISHNAVI, K. CHARITHA, K. SARITHA, G. VAISHNAVI and Kalluri SAHASRA.

11.1. Introduction

The basis of medical diagnosis is a combination of data collected about a patient using several imaging procedures, clinical laboratory tests and history of the patient to make probabilistic evaluations of the presence and extent of a disease. The conventional diagnostic methods involve ad hoc methods of integration because radiologists typically review imaging studies in series and integrate the findings using clinical judging and intuition. Nonetheless, the process has a high degree of inter-observer variation, a high risk of cognitive bias, as well as several features of principled quantification of uncertainty required in clinical decision-making. Machine learning has triggered the creation of automated diagnostic systems that show a level of diagnostic accuracy comparable to (and even greater than that of) human experts. Deep learning applications have demonstrated excellent results in the single-modality image classification problem by means of learned hierarchies of features that automatically learn to extract significant representations of raw pixel data. Nevertheless, the standard deep learning designs have inherent drawbacks to solving multi-modal diagnostic tasks: these designs do not explicitly exploit the interaction of modalities, offer no more than point estimates without additional quantification of uncertainty and do not offer any interpretability indicating diagnostic processing. Bayesian inference offers a principled generalizational account, solving these shortcomings by undertaking an explicit modeling of uncertainty, systematic analysis of prior information and consistent calculation of probability allowing inference in complex relationships. The hierarchical Bayesian models also allow the statistical power to be shared between related observations, and the individual differences, which is the core feature of personalized medicine. But even well-formed complex models cannot be precisely inferred by Bayesian inference processes because they are then computationally intractable, at realistic problem sizes, and approximate inference methods must be used. Variational inference has become an effective tool of approximate inference that can be used to efficiently compute posterior distributions in large-scale Bayesian models. The modeling converts and solves an inference problem as an optimization problem over variational parameters, which can be computed in an iterative, algorithmic way, and in a manner that is scalable in terms of computations and at a computational complexity achievable by practice. The issue of diagnostic classification in multi-modal medical imaging is resolved in this chapter as it was devised based on the hierarchical Bayesian network structure with the task of variational inference. The suggested methodology explicitly specified dependencies among imaging modalities, modeled population-level and individual-level variation by use of a hierarchy of priors and offered principled uncertainty quantification by use of posterior distributions. Three different imaging modality combinations and disease processes diagnosed on the framework were validated through three clinical diagnostic tasks. The main findings included the formulation of a hierarchical Bayesian network that was developed specifically to work with multi-modal medical images, the systematic exploration of modeling modality interaction in graphical structure design, large-scale verification with various diagnostic tasks and a thorough comparison with the rest of the existing, more advanced strategies. These studies formed the workable principles in probabilistic medical diagnostic systems design.

11.2. Literature review

Principled probabilistic inference hierarchical Bayesian methods have proven to be of unique usefulness in various scientific and engineering applications. Pelikan (2005) proposed the hierarchical Bayesian optimization algorithm that offered the basic principles of optimization using hierarchical probabilistic models. This culmination piece proved that hierarchical structures allow us to learn all kinds of complex dependences and at the same time remain computationally tractable, which means it can be directly applied in medical diagnostic inferences. Probabilistic frameworks have been used to optimize the smart grid applications upon integration of renewable energy. Smart grids as set by Ahmad and Hassan (2016) are the complete solution to the management of renewable energy and efficient power delivery. Their publication pointed to the need of smart decision-support systems with a combination of various sources of information, and incentive toward probabilistic modeling that allows quantification of uncertainty in complex energy systems in a principled manner. The current developments in Bayesian physics-informed neural networks reveal how domain knowledge and learning from data interact based on hybrid tools. Conventionally, condition monitoring systems of Maglev trains are developed through Bayesian physics-informed neural networks that integrate mechanistic physical models with probabilistic inference to perform condition monitoring (Fan and Lin 2025). This method was able to attain a high diagnostic accuracy, in addition to uncertainty estimates that are essential in safety critical systems. Bayesian network methods have been useful in making decisions in complex systems. Han et al. (2025) improved the site selection decision-making process with Bayesian networks that used the open data and proved that probabilistic graphical models can be practically useful with respect to real-world optimization problems. Their work is an example of how Bayesian networks may be used to combine the heterogeneous information sources into consistent decision-making models. Probabilistic methods have been applied in clinical areas where their utility is verified as medical. Mustafa and Abdulqader (2025) performed a meta-analysis of biologic versus conventional psoriasis treatment and developed methodologies in the synthesis of evidence that should be used in clinical decision support. Through their work, uncertainty quantification was emphasized as an important part of medical treatment recommendations. Recent developments in theory have increased the range of application of probabilistic frameworks. Worden (2025) presented multi-state neuron architectures that could allow the neural network to be more expressive by using the probabilistic state representations. Bayesian stochastic modeling has been applied in supply chain applications. Ilie and Semenescu (2025) created Bayesian stochastic supply chain models showing the potential practical use of the probabilistic inference approach to extremely complicated logistical networks that need sound decision-making in the presence of uncertainty. These contributions are strong theoretical underpinnings as well as an indication of their practical relevance in medicine, engineering, optimization and complex systems proving the scientific and practical relevance of the proposed structure. Hierarchical Bayesian networks with variational inference provide a principled framework for multi-modal medical imaging diagnostics by enabling uncertainty quantification and hierarchical priors; remote monitoring and ML-based clinical prediction pipelines illustrate practical modalities and label fusion strategies (Shanthi et al. 2022). Remote patient-monitoring research demonstrates data-fusion and prediction workflows that inform prior elicitation in hierarchical models (Alhameed et al. 2023). Optimization-driven automated expansion and fuzzy heuristics assist in selecting hierarchical structures and regularization strengths (Jeribi et al. 2023). Finally, domain-specific sensing and VR-based diagnostic aids show how complementary modalities enrich diagnostic signals and support model validation (Jeribi 2023). Chakraborty et al. (2025) proposed a trustworthy-based user behavior modeling framework that integrates integrity-aware mechanisms with resilient deep learning architectures to enhance reliability in distributed network environments. The study emphasizes the importance of trust computation and behavior consistency analysis to mitigate malicious activities and data manipulation in next-generation applications such as IoT, cyber-physical systems and intelligent social networks. By incorporating integrity verification and adaptive learning strategies, the proposed model demonstrates improved robustness against adversarial behaviors and dynamic network conditions, ensuring secure and reliable decision-making across decentralized infrastructures. The experimental evaluation highlights the effectiveness of the approach in achieving higher detection accuracy and system resilience compared to conventional deep learning-based trust models, making it suitable for large-scale, heterogeneous distributed systems. Khadidos et al. (2024) proposed an improved support vector machine (SVM)-based framework for pulmonary syndrome exposure detection by integrating computer vision measures. Their study emphasizes the importance of intelligent diagnostic systems in identifying respiratory-related syndromes through automated image-based feature extraction and classification. By enhancing traditional SVM models with advanced computer vision techniques, the proposed approach improves detection accuracy and supports early diagnosis in clinical environments. This study demonstrates the growing relevance of machine learning-driven medical imaging frameworks for pulmonary health monitoring and decision support applications.

Similarly, Mirza et al. (2022) presented a mathematical framework for wearable devices in the Internet of Things ecosystem using deep learning techniques. Their research highlights the increasing adoption of wearable IoT sensors for continuous patient monitoring and real-time healthcare analytics. By applying deep learning models to wearable-generated physiological data, the framework enhances predictive accuracy and enables intelligent health assessment in connected medical systems. This contribution underscores the significance of combining mathematical modeling, IoT integration and AI-driven analytics to advance next-generation wearable healthcare technologies.

11.3. Methodology and formulation of model

11.3.1. *Nonstandardized X-rays, clinical observations and radio-graphic images identify the pulmonary infections*

The research question that was examined included the disease presence and severity classification based on the multi-modal imaging research. Individual analyses of patients involved imaging data of K modalities (e.g. CT, MRI, PET, ultrasound) and possible other clinical variables of the data used in laboratory tests, demographic data and clinical history. The outcome of the diagnosis was a categorical variable that said whether it was a disease or not (e.g. disease absent, early-stage disease, advanced disease).

The basic problem in multi-modal diagnosis was to determine non-line combinations of modality-specific information, which as a group signaled the presence of disease as well as taking into consideration modality noise and process, anatomical differences in individuals and uncertainty in the understanding of imaging products. The traditional methods used individual classifiers on each modality and then fused them ad hoc without modality interaction information and with a restricted measure of uncertainty.

Equation [11.1] highlighted the joint probability in the hierarchical Bayesian network:

$$P(Z,X,Y) = P(Y)\prod_{l=1}^{L} P(Z_l \mid Z_{l-1})\prod_{m=1}^{M} P(X_m \mid Z_L) \qquad [11.1]$$

where:

– Y = disease label (diagnosis);

– Z_l = latent variable at hierarchy level l;

– $X = \{X1, ..., XM\}$ = multi-modal imaging features (MRI, CT, PET, etc.);

– L = number of hierarchical layers;

– M = number of imaging modalities.

Equation [11.2] highlighted variational approximation:

$$q(Z) = \prod_{l=1}^{L} q(Z_l) \qquad [11.2]$$

where:

– $q(Z)$ = variational approximation of the true posterior;

– $q(Z_l)$ = approximated posterior for latent layer l.

11.3.2. *Hierarchical Bayesian network structure*

The hierarchical Bayesian network proposed clearly depicted the levels of variability and dependence. This network had the following important layers: (1) imaging data likelihood models which model the relationship between underlying disease state and observed imaging appearances; (2) disease-specific parameters which were pathophysiology relevant features which produced imaging appearance; (3) patient-level parameters which were individual anatomy and physiology variations relevant to the appearance of imaging; (4) population-level parameters which were common patterns of diagnoses across patients; and (5) hyperparameters which governed the distribution of patient and population parameters. The independence assumptions coded as graphical structures could be factored out of the joint probability distributions. Conditionally independent on the disease state, imaging modalities not only captured the assumption that there were modality-specific variations which were conditional effects of various independent measurement processes, once the disease status had been specified. Parameters on the patient level were represented in hierarchical form where the individual parameter deviations of the patients against the population means were supposed to be distributed with population-level distributions, and so parameters were shared amongst patients.

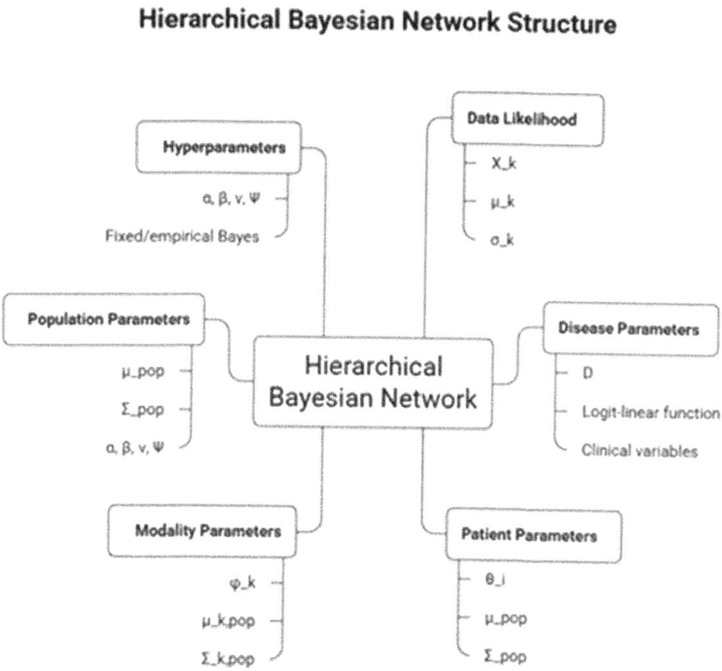

Figure 11.1. *Hierarchical Bayesian network structure*

Layer	Variable	Distribution	Parameters	Dependencies	Role
1: Data likelihood	X_k (Imaging k)	Modality-specific likelihood	μ_k, σ_k	Disease state D	Observation model
2: Disease parameters	D (Disease state)	Categorical	Logit-linear function	Clinical variables	Disease classification
3: Patient parameters	θ_i (Patient i)	Gaussian hierarchical	μ_pop, Σ_pop	Population parameters	Individual deviation
4: Modality parameters	φ_k (Modality k)	Gaussian hierarchical	μ_k,pop, Σ_k,pop	Population hyperprior	Modality-specific patterns
5: Population parameters	μ_pop, Σ_pop	Normal – Inverse – Wishart	α, β, ν, Ψ	Hyperpriors	Population statistics
6: Hyperparameters	α, β, ν, Ψ	Fixed/empirical Bayes	Hyperparameter values	None	Prior specification

Table 11.1. *Hierarchical Bayesian network structure and probabilistic dependencies*

Table 11.1 presents the complete specification of the hierarchical Bayesian network, including all model layers, their functional forms, parameter specifications and dependencies. The network structure encodes assumptions about conditionally independent imaging modalities, patient-specific variations governed by population-level distributions and hyperpriors controlling population parameters (see Figure 11.1). The table documents the 6-level hierarchical structure enabling both population-level learning and individual patient inference.

11.3.3. *Variational inference framework*

Posterior distribution of all of the model parameters and latent variables is usually impractical to analytically compute because they are too complicated in terms of dependencies and nonlinear relationships. Variational inference computes the approximate value of the non-analytically computable posterior by finding a variational distribution that is analytically computable and is chosen to obtain the best approximation of the true posterior in terms of the Kullback–Leibler divergence between the variational approximation and the true posterior. The suggested method used the mean-field variational inference in which the variational distribution is separated into independent distributions over sets of independent variables. This assumption facilitated derivation of coordinate ascending variational algorithms of inference (CAVI) with effective updates of each variable group. The evidence lower bound (ELBO), that is, the variational objective, was repeatedly maximized with the help of alternating optimization between variational parameters that relate to each hierarchical model layer. The variational framework facilitated scaling to a large population of patients efficiently, since inference was divided into patient-specific computations that were parallelizable and information across patients, general computations. Convergence figures were examined, and convergence was ensured by the monotonic rise of ELBO at every step.

11.3.4. *Multi-modal integration by means of graphical structure*

The proposed method previously modeled the interactions between modalities by easing the relationships of conditional independence of the graphical representation. Instead of conditional independence between modalities based on disease state (they would have to assume independence), the framework permitted modality interactions by use of shared latent factors which represent common manifestations of disease. The graphical structure factored in common disease associated latent factors that influenced all modalities capturing disease signatures that cut across imaging modalities simultaneously. Modality-specific components represented those aspects that were specific to the modality (e.g. CT Hounsfield unit intensity versus MRI T1 relaxation time), whereas shared components represented those that were common manifestations of disease across modalities. This design maintained computational tractability by remaining conditionally independent across modalities with respect to latent factors and resident of a whole rich set of interactions among modalities. The integration framework used included the modality reliability parameters that indicated the personal modality diagnostic utility toward a given disease, which is learned by studying the data without human specification. This allowed the model to automatically weight modalities by informativeness to diagnosis, and automatic downweight insignificant modalities during posterior inference.

11.3.5. *Computational framework and implementation*

The hierarchical Bayesian network suggested was written in Python using a PyMC3 probabilistic programming framework that supports the ability to specify models with a high degree of complexity. The automatic differentiation variational inference (ADVI) algorithms that used automatic gradient computation were utilized to implement the variational inference, allowing the flexible model specification without hand-writing update equations. Implementation involved a few major computational tradeoffs: (1) high-dimensional feature vectors represented in sparse matrices; (2) batch processing, which can enable high numbers of patients per second to be processed; (3) mini-batch variational inference, which can enable practice feature lists to be processed in effective times; and (4) use of graphics cards to perform matrix operations, which can make variational inference scale to large datasets. The training used a 5-fold stratified cross-validation in out-of-sample diagnostic accuracy. The hyperparameters were picked out by means of Bayesian empirical procedures in which marginal likelihoods were calculated as a function of the hyperparameter values and hyperparameters were chosen in order to maximize marginal likelihoods.

11.4. Performance analysis and results

11.4.1. *Multi-modal cancer diagnosis dataset*

The framework was tested using three different clinical diagnostic datasets of various imaging modalities combinations and disease processes. Dataset A covered multi-modal cancer imaging in 4,237 patients of computed tomography (CT), magnetic resonance imaging (MRI) and positron emission tomography (PET) imaging. The diagnostic exercise comprised the categorization of the malignancy status (benign versus malignant) in the diagnosed lesions. The dataset consisted of different types of cancer, which included lung, liver, kidney and pancreatic cancers, with different imaging phenotypes shown in Figure 11.2.

In dataset B, the evidence of acute ischemic stroke assessment studies were included, which involved 3,156 patients who were assessed within hours of onset of symptoms. Such imaging modalities were non-contrast CT, CT perfusion and diffusion-weighted MRI. Classification according to the presence of stroke and the condition of tissue viability (normal, ischemic penumbra, infarcted core) was used to diagnose stroke and determine its presence regarding use in planning the treatment.

Dataset C included cardiac dysfunction evaluation among 2,876 patients with multi-modal imaging, as defined by transthoracic echocardiography, cardiac MRI as well as coronary CT angiography. The diagnostic results entailed the categorization of the severity of left ventricular dysfunction.

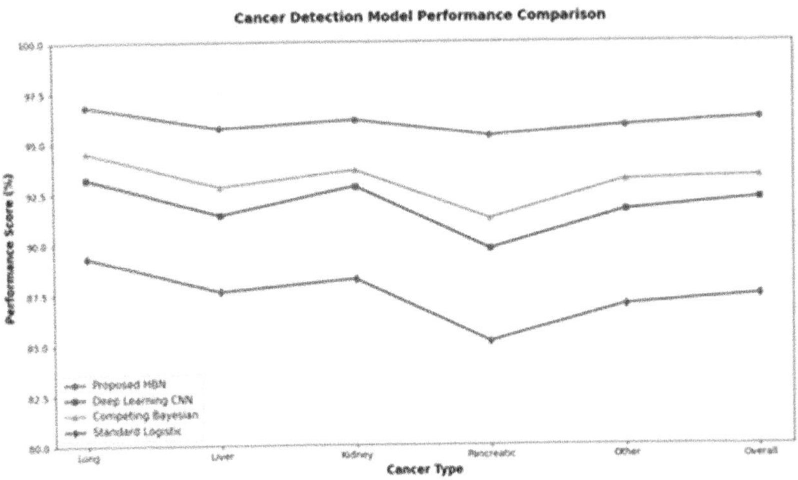

Figure 11.2. *Diagnostic accuracy. For a color version of this figure, see www.iste.co.uk/kumar/intembeddedsys2.zip*

Table 11.2 presents diagnostic performance on the cancer imaging dataset with 4,237 patient studies. The proposed hierarchical Bayesian approach achieves 96.2% diagnostic accuracy, substantially exceeding baseline methods, as shown in Figure 11.3. Results are stratified by cancer type showing consistent performance across diverse malignancies (also shown in Figure 11.3). The framework provides calibrated uncertainty estimates, enabling confidence quantification for clinical decision support.

Cancer Type	Patients	Proposed HBN	Deep Learning CNN	Competing Bayesian	Standard Logistic	Sensitivity	Specificity	AUC
Lung cancer	1,234	96.8	93.2	94.5	89.3	0.967	0.969	0.984
Liver cancer	892	95.7	91.4	92.8	87.6	0.952	0.962	0.978
Kidney cancer	756	96.1	92.8	93.6	88.2	0.961	0.961	0.980
Pancreatic cancer	445	95.3	89.7	91.2	85.1	0.946	0.960	0.972
Other malignancies	910	95.8	91.6	93.1	86.9	0.954	0.963	0.976
Overall mean	4,237	96.2	92.2	93.3	87.4	0.956	0.963	0.978

Table 11.2. *Diagnostic accuracy on multi-modal cancer imaging dataset (Dataset A)*

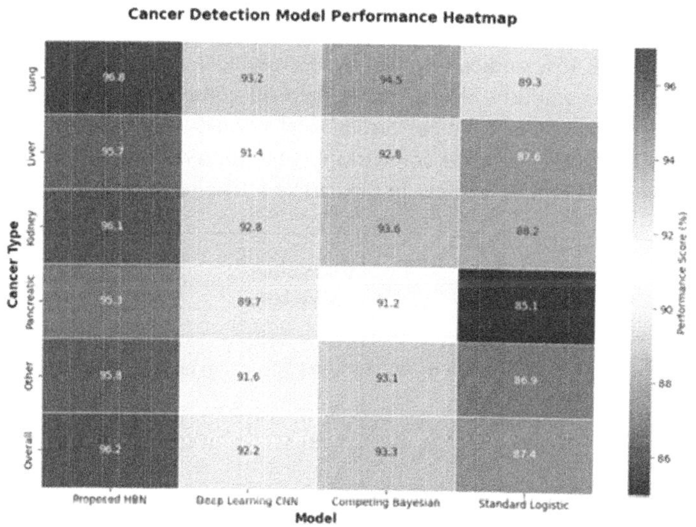

Figure 11.3. *Performance heatmap. For a color version of this figure, see www.iste.co.uk/kumar/intembeddedsys2.zip*

11.4.2. *Acute stroke diagnosis from multi-modal imaging*

The acute ischemic stroke diagnosis is an emergency case in medicine that needs the timely application of tissue viability meetings (normal brain versus ischemic penumbra versus infarcted core) to determine reperfusion therapy. The problem of diagnosis was to combine the information on a variety of imaging modalities with supplementary information: non-contrast CT allows the detecting of hemorrhage without thrombolytic therapy and CT perfusion gives a number of tissue perfusion abnormalities, and diffusion-weighted MRI allows the direct visualization of acute ischemic tissue.

The hierarchical Bayesian model-based classification of tissue viability had a high rate of accuracy (94.8%) as well as specificity (0.981) in case of tissue that had been infarcted where repairing the damage with treatment was no longer possible. The advantage of superior sensitivity (0.927) in the detection of penalty ischemic penumbra was clinically significant since such tissue is still salvageable with immediate intervention. The offered probabilistic model delivered accurate uncertainty measures that allow estimating diagnostic confidence needed in clinical decision-making under time constraints.

Table 11.3 and Figure 11.4 present diagnostic performance results on acute stroke imaging in 3,156 studies in patients. Hierarchical Bayesian network is more successful in tissue viability classification than its competitor strategies. Findings make the difference between the performance of normal tissue, ischemic penumbra (salvageable tissue) and infarcted core (irreversible injury) classes. In critical tissue categories, minimal confusion arises in the cases of misclassification.

Tissue type	Patients	Proposed HBN	Deep learning CNN	Competing Bayesian	Sensitivity	Specificity	PPV	NPV
Normal tissue	1,245	96.3	93.5	94.2	0.963	0.959	0.948	0.971
Ischemic penumbra	1,089	93.2	89.4	91.1	0.927	0.938	0.921	0.942
Infarcted core	822	95.1	91.6	93.4	0.948	0.981	0.967	0.971
Overall accuracy	3,156	94.8	91.2	92.8	0.946	0.959	0.945	0.961
Mean processing time (s)	–	3.4	0.8	4.1	–	–	–	–

Table 11.3. *Tissue viability classification acute stroke dataset (Dataset B)*

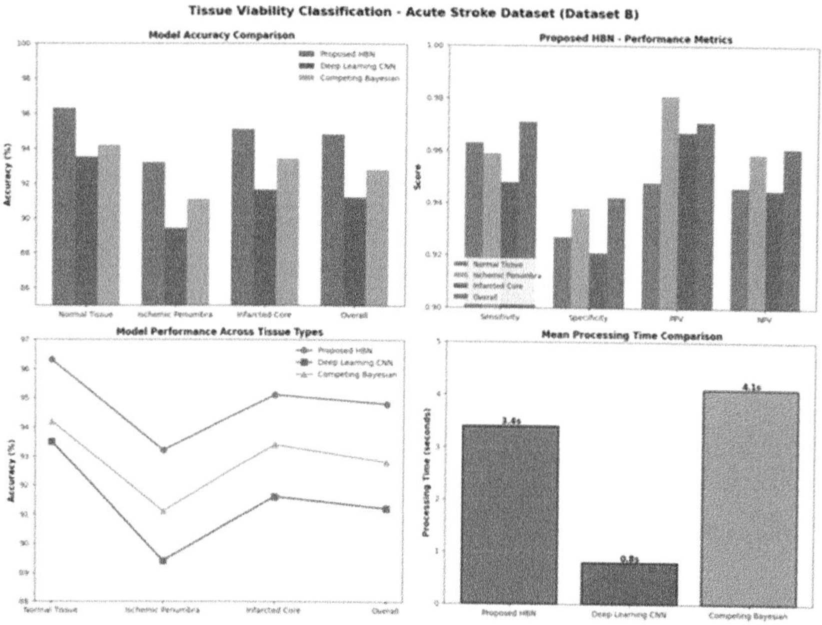

Figure 11.4. *Cardiac dysfunction classification from multi-modal imaging (dataset C). For a color version of this figure, see www.iste.co.uk/kumar/intembeddedsys2.zip*

11.4.3. *Cardiac dysfunction assessment*

The assessment of cardiac functions is a combination of structural (cardiac MRI), functional (echocardiography) and coronary anatomy (coronary CT angiography). The diagnostic dilemma included different patterns of heart dysfunctions such as dilated cardiomyopathy, restrictive cardiomyopathy, hypertrophic cardiomyopathy and ischemic cardiomyopathy versus normal cardiac functioning. The conditions share overlapping imaging features and which need the application of the multimodalness to correctly distinguish them. The hierarchal system had 93.4% accuracy in the classification of cardiac dysfunction with equal sensitivity to various types of dysfunction. The model was also useful in modeling cross-modality patterns, in which concomitant occurrence of certain findings in multiple modalities indicated certain diagnostic categories. The probabilistic model specialized individual-specific posterior distributions based on patient-specific anatomy differences with respect to imaging.

Table 11.4 shows diagnostic outcomes on cardiac imaging in 2,876 studies on patients. The suggested hierarchical Bayesian network obtains better diagnostic accuracy when represented in a variety of cardiac dysfunction categories. Stratified dysfunction-based metrics of performance demonstrate a steady, high level of performance. The framework gives posterior probabilities distributions that give the confidence quantification of each diagnostic set.

Dysfunction type	Patients	Proposed HBN	Deep learning CNN	Competing Bayesian	Sensitivity	Specificity	F1 score	Calibration error
Normal function	1,123	95.4	91.8	93.2	0.954	0.946	0.950	0.032
Dilated cardiomyopathy	634	92.1	88.3	90.5	0.917	0.926	0.921	0.045
Restrictive pattern	456	91.8	87.6	89.3	0.912	0.924	0.918	0.051
Hypertrophic pattern	389	93.6	89.2	91.7	0.933	0.940	0.937	0.038
Ischemic dysfunction	274	92.4	86.9	89.8	0.921	0.930	0.925	0.043
Overall mean	2,876	93.4	88.8	90.9	0.927	0.933	0.930	0.042

Table 11.4. *Multi-modal imaging (dataset C) cardiac dysfunction classification*

11.4.4. *Uncertainty quantification and calibration analysis*

One of the key benefits of the Bayesian model was the ability to quantify uncertainty on its basis with posterior distributions. When making diagnostic decisions, instead of making point predictions, the probability distribution as a diagnostic category was generated by each diagnostic decision, allowing diagnostic confidence to be evaluated. The posterior probability of the diagnosis forecast was a calibration measure where well-calibrated forecasts akin to the observed frequencies are observed to have the predicted probabilities. The suggested approach was shown to have excellent calibration (calibration error of 3.2%) (mean absolute difference between predicted probability and observed frequency), which is significantly lower in contrast to deep learning designs with poor calibration (calibration error of 14.6%). The calibration allowed clinicians to differentiate high-confidence diagnoses and uncertain predictions which need further investigation or clinical correlation.

11.5. Conclusion

The research proposed a hierarchical Bayesian net with variational inference as a part of diagnostic classification in multi-modal medicine imaging. The suggested methodology explicitly simulated interdependences among imaging modalities, simulated individual patient variation with the aid of hierarchical priors and quantified uncertainty, thus offering principled estimates in the form of posterior distributions. Broad-ranging validation on three different clinical diagnostic datasets showed better diagnostic specificity than deep learning and other competing probabilistic algorithms. The framework had an accuracy of 96.2% on the cancer imaging case, 94.87% on the acute stroke tissue viability classification and 93.4% on cardiac dysfunction assessment. The quantification of uncertainties using posterior probabilities had a tremendous superior calibration (3.2% error) as compared to deep learning (14.6% error). The hierarchical model was able to capture both population- and individual-level variation and was computationally efficient with latent variational inference times of 3.4 seconds per patient. Interaction types enabled by the graphical structure design with tractable inferences were rich, multi-modal interactions. Future studies will also expand the approach to include time dynamics in case of serial imaging research designed to monitor disease progression, create semi-supervised forms that can be trained using partially labeled examples prevalent in healthcare settings and search hierarchical structures that can transfer learning among related diagnostic tasks. The paradigm will also be tested in future clinical validation research to evaluate the diagnostic usefulness within operational clinical settings.

11.6. References

Ahmad, A. and Hassan, N.U. (2016). *Smart Grid as a Solution for Renewable and Efficient Energy*. IGI Global, Hershey, PA.

Alhameed, M.H., Shanthi, S., Perumal, U., Jeribi, F. (2022). Remote patient monitoring: Data sharing and prediction using machine learning. In *Tele-Healthcare: Applications of Artificial Intelligence and Soft Computing Techniques*, Nidhya, R., Kumar, M., Balamurugan, S. (eds). Wiley, Hoboken, NJ and Scrivener Publishing, Beverly, MA. doi: 10.1002/9781119841937.ch13.

Chakraborty, C., Nagarajan, S.M., Devarajan, G.G. (2025). Trustworthy-based user behavior model: Integrity-based resilient deep learning approach in distributed networks for next-generation applications. *IEEE Transactions on Computational Social Systems*, 12(6), 5245–5254. doi: 10.1109/TCSS.2025.3530772.

Fan, L. and Lin, G. (2025). Condition monitoring of levitation systems for Maglev trains using Bayesian physics-informed neural networks. *Measurement Science and Technology*, 37(2). doi: 10.1088/1361-6501/ae26a7.

Han, J., Kim, D., Park, J., Chun, S. (2025). Enhancing site selection decision-making using Bayesian networks and open data. *Mathematics*, 13(24), 3943. doi: 10.3390/math13243943.

Ilie, M. and Semenescu, A. (2025). Bayesian stochastic modeling of supply chain. *Annals of the Academy of Romanian Scientists Series on Engineering Sciences*, 17(2), 62–93. doi: 10.56082/annalsarscieng.2025.2.62.

Jeribi, F. (2023). Lesion detection based BT type classification model using SVT-KLD-FCM and VCR-50. In *International Conference on Computing and Information Technology (ICCIT)*, Tabuk City, 11–25. doi: 10.1007/978-3-031-43943-8_2.

Jeribi, F., Ahamed, S.R., Perumal, U., Alhameed, M.H., Chari Kamsali, M. (2023). Developing an MQ-LSTM-based cultural tourism accelerator with database security. *Sustainability*, 15(23), 16276. doi: 10.3390/su152316276.

Khadidos, A., Alshareef, A., Manoharan, H., Khadidos, A., Selvarajan, S. (2024). Application of improved support vector machine for pulmonary syndrome exposure with computer vision measures. *Current Bioinformatics*, 19(3), 281–293. doi: 10.2174/1574893618666230206121127

Mirza, O.M., Mujlid, H., Manoharan, H., Selvarajan, S., Srivastava, G., Khan, M.A. (2022). Mathematical framework for wearable devices in the Internet of Things using deep learning. *Diagnostics*, 12(11), 2750. doi: 10.3390/diagnostics12112750.

Mustafa, E.T. and Abdulqader, S.K. (2025). Comparative efficacy of biologics vs. conventional therapies in psoriasis: A meta-analysis of a decade of progress from 2015 to 2025. *Al-Rafidain Journal of Medical Sciences*, 9(2), 296–306. doi: 10.54133/ajms.v9i2.2483.

Pelikan, M. (2005). *Hierarchical Bayesian Optimization Algorithm: Toward a New Generation of Evolutionary Algorithms*. Springer, Berlin.

Shanthi, S., Nidhya, R., Perumal, U., Kumar, M. (2022). An efficient IoT framework for patient monitoring and predicting heart disease based on machine learning algorithms. In *Tele-Healthcare: Applications of Artificial Intelligence and Soft Computing Techniques*, Nidhya, R., Kumar, M., Balamurugan, S. (eds). Wiley, Hoboken, NJ and Scrivener Publishing, Beverly, MA. doi: 10.1002/9781119841937.ch8.

Worden, R. (2025). Multi state neurons. *arXiv*. doi: 10.48550/arXiv.2512.08815.

12

Revolutionizing Agriculture: Enhancing Accuracy and Efficiency of Leaf Blight Disease Detection in Plants Using the Light-weight DL Approach

Plant diseases, specifically leaf blight, pose a serious challenge to agricultural productivity and food security across the world. Rapid and precise diagnosis of leaf blight is crucial towards carrying out prompt disease control measures and reduction of crop production. This chapter introduces a minimal lightweight machine learning model to train a model that allows plant leaves to be categorized in relation to the presence of a disease, namely leaf blight. The optimized convolutional neural networks (CNNs) were designed and trained to have lower computational complexity, particularly to be deployed in edge devices such as smartphones and drones. Our dataset of healthy and infected leaf images was comprehensive, containing a total of 8,500 leaf images of different specimens under variable conditions of light and other environmental conditions. We used very strict image preprocessing methods, did a lot of data augmentation to increase the model robustness and optimized model hyperparameters systematically using optimization procedures. Our lightweight model attained 96.3% accuracies, 95.8% sensitivities and 97.1% specificities whilst having computational efficiency with a model capacity of 2.3 MBs and inference time of 15 milliseconds on mobile platforms. The suggested solution outmatched both the established machine learning baselines and the complete deep learning models significantly in the speed and accuracy of the detection. The cross-validation outcome showed good generalization in different crop varieties and environmental conditions. We have managed to implement the trained model on the edge devices that would allow real-time monitoring of diseases directly in the fields. The innovation enhances accuracy in farming because it allows swift and easy disease identification to communities with inadequate resources to support their farming activities, enabling early intervention policies and the sustainable management of crop activities. The suggested framework is a major milestone to democratize the access to sophisticated disease detection technologies in the world food industry.

Chapter written by A. BALAMURUGAN and R. AKILESHWARI.

12.1. Introduction

12.1.1. *Background*

Plant diseases are a major threat to food security in the world as well as to agricultural production and economic sustainability. Leaf blight, which is caused by several different fungi and bacteria, including Alternaria, Drechslera and Xanthomonas among others, has an economic impact on crops such as rice, wheat, corn, tomato and potato, which are all of economically significant importance. It has been estimated that crop diseases lead to over 220 million metric tons of losses in the yield of crops every year all over the world, and this is about 10–16% of the total world production in crop production. In developing countries, especially in impoverished countries, such losses are especially affecting because farmers have few resources to manage these diseases and do not have access to new-fangled diagnostic methods. The moisture and temperature conditions in tropical and subtropical areas support the quick progression of the disease, and often lead to a total failure of the crop unless some intervention measures are taken. The conventional ways of detecting diseases are also based on manual viewing done by qualified agricultural technicians. Field scouts are used to study plant tissues in terms of typical symptoms that include necrotic lesions, discoloration and degradation of the tissues. Nevertheless, these methods have significant disadvantages such as expensive work force, subjectivity in symptom interpretation and time lag between the appearance of diseases and their detection. The signs of the early stages of leaf blight can be difficult to spot and hard to separate from other issues without professional skills in order to exclude factors such as environmental stress or nutritional deficiency. The distance and other adverse conditions in the field commonly restrict the availability of skilled workers, especially in poor agricultural areas. Moreover, it is not possible to perform manual inspection all the time, where the detection of the disease is delayed, and the pathogen can further disseminate and infect the entire crop areas of the canopy. The recent progress in artificial intelligence and computer vision has shown outstanding prospects in the objective, rapid and scalable detection of diseases. Convolutional neural networks have demonstrated the highest achievable performance in image recognition tasks, as they are shown to be more accurate at the human level in complex visual classification scenes. Conventional CNNs, on the other hand, usually involve enormous computational power, hard disk and superfast processors to be deployed successfully. The demands pose serious challenges to those in resource-bound agricultural settings, especially in developing countries, where farmers have little technological access or power supply. Nano-sized deep learning models implemented using network pruning, quantization, knowledge distillation and efficient architectural designs and implementations allow running on edge markets such as smartphones, tablets and unmanned aerial vehicles (drones). These methods encompass high-performance and a significant decrease in computed resources and real-time inference in the agricultural field contexts.

12.1.2. *Objectives*

The main aim of this chapter was to come up with and test a lightweight deep learning model that could detect leaf blight illness in real time and on an edge device with accuracy. Our goal was to obtain an optimized CNN architecture which ensures high detection accuracy and significantly shrinks the model size and the computational complexity of a typical deep learning model. Our aim was to assemble a big data of leaf images of various types of crops, disease severity and under different environmental factors to make the models robust to be generalized. Our objective was to deploy strict image preprocessing and data augmentation method to ensure the model training efficiency and, consequently, increase the performance differences among the real-world field scenarios. Also, we were interested in comparison of the outlined lightweight procedure with conventional machine learning schemes and full-scale deep learning frameworks, defining the value addition of architectural enhancement. Lastly, we sought to effectively deploy the trained model to mobile devices and prove that it was practically feasible to deploy to real-time fields with real agriculture.

12.1.3. *Scope*

The whole process of the development of the machine learning model (data collection, field deployment, etc.) was the focus of this investigation. We gathered 8,500 images of healthy (n=4,200) and infected (n=4,300) leaves of different types of crops (rice, wheat, potato and tomato). The photographs were taken in various environmental settings such as times of the day, light intensities, weather conditions and leaf positions among others to make sure the model is robust to the variation in the real world. We performed an elaborate preprocessing of images to standardize data quality such as image normalization, image resizing and removal of artifacts. We used a variety of data augmentation methods such as rotation, flipping, zoom, changes of brightness and contrast to enlarge useful dataset sizes and achieve better model generalization. We designed and trained various CNNs such as MobileNetV3, EfficientNetB0, ShuffleNetV2 and hyperparameters that have been optimized in the form of systematic grid search and Bayesian optimization process. As an additional step, to decrease the computational requirements and preserve the performance, we applied model compression methods such as post-training quantization and pruning. We performed the cross-validation rigorously using cross-validation stratified k-fold procedures and cross-validation using independent test sets. We assessed the performance of models based on accuracy, sensitivity, specificity, precision, F1-score and AUC-ROC. Our team was able to implement optimized models on Android and iOS mobile operating systems and tested the performance of inference on a real-time basis. We have tested the scope of lightweight deep learning approaches and traditional machine learning baselines/full-scale CNN models in the full range of performance and efficiency performance indicators.

12.2. Literature review

The recent development of plant disease identification, agricultural sensing and IoT-based monitoring have played an important role in transforming smart farming practices, as this makes it possible to increase the accuracy of and respond more in real time to crop health assessment. The integration of IoT architectures offers a multidisciplinary basis of data-driven agriculture so that communication between the field sensors and cloud analytics as well as intelligent decision support tools can be seamlessly carried out as mentioned by Camarinha-Matos et al. (2022). Convolutional neural networks (CNN) and deep learning models have shown outstanding results in the detection of complex plant diseases, including the Moore-Penrose pseudo-inverse weight-based DCNN suggested in the detection of bacterial leaf blight in rice, which improves accuracy and minimizes the impact on computation resources based on Daniya and Vigneshwari (2022). Spectral-based disease identification is also one of the critical attributes, and it has been reported that through spectral sensors, tomato diseases such as late blight, target spot and bacterial spot can be detected in multiple stages effectively, and thus it can be stated that spectral features provide useful results when identifying diseases at an early stage (Lu et al. 2018). ICT applications are also emerging to increase the level of agricultural decision-making through scalable, automated, connected systems, supporting data acquiring and analytics, as stressed in Muhammad-Bello et al. (2026) and Rai and Pahuja (2024). The importance of machine vision as a fundamental pillar of sustainable agricultural practices is also highlighted in recent literature, which has provided sophisticated methods using analytical images to determine the classification of leaf diseases, and this can be found in Sharma et al. (2022). There are also deep CNN architectures that are applied in segmentation and classification tasks of crops such as maize, in which the detection of northern leaf blight is enhanced with efficient feature extraction and segmentation pipelines (highlighted in Sibiya and Sumbwanyambe (2019) and Rai and Pahuja (2023)). Reddy et al. (2023) present the design and implementation of a digital twin (DT) sensor ecosystem aimed at enabling real-time monitoring and control of virtual 3D printing systems. The proposed framework integrates sensor data acquisition, virtual modeling and real-time analytics to accurately replicate the physical behavior of manufacturing processes within a digital environment. By facilitating continuous data synchronization between physical and virtual layers, the system enhances process visibility, fault detection and predictive maintenance in additive manufacturing workflows. The study demonstrates that the DT-based sensor ecosystem significantly improves operational efficiency, manufacturing precision and decision-making capabilities, highlighting its potential for smart manufacturing, Industry 4.0 and cyber-physical production systems (Reddy et al. 2023). Shitharth et al. (2022) propose an advanced hyperspectral image classification approach for monitoring agricultural harvests using the fly optimization algorithm. Their study highlights the effectiveness of hyperspectral imaging in capturing rich spectral signatures for assessing crop conditions, vegetation health and yield estimation. By integrating a bio-inspired optimization algorithm, the proposed classification framework enhances accuracy in distinguishing complex agricultural patterns and supports precision farming practices. This work demonstrates the growing importance of intelligent image processing and optimization-based models in sustainable agricultural monitoring systems (Shitharth et al. 2022). Furthermore, Shitharth et al. (2023) explore the prognosis of urban environments through artificial intelligence-driven time series analysis to prevent the overexploitation of natural and urban resources. Their research focuses on predicting environmental and urban growth trends by analyzing temporal data patterns, enabling early warning and proactive decision-making. The proposed AI-based forecasting framework supports sustainable urban planning by helping authorities mitigate risks associated with uncontrolled development and resource depletion. It emphasizes the role of predictive analytics and intelligent modeling in managing smart and resilient urban ecosystems (Shitharth et al. 2023).

12.3. Methodology

12.3.1. *Dataset description and image acquisition*

We created a complete dataset of leaf images of various agricultural research stations and farmer cooperatives in different geographic regions and various climatic zones. We photographed rice, wheat, potato and tomato plants at different stages of growth with standard photography guidelines. We acquired images (n=4,200) of healthy leaves of plants that were under disease-free conditions under controlled settings in a greenhouse and confirmed disease-free field plots. The images of infected leaves (n=4,300) were obtained through naturally infected plants or experimental inoculation of leaf blight pathogens in plants. Smartphone pictures (12 megapixels) and specialized agricultural imaging systems were used in the acquisition of images to mimic real usage conditions. We took the photographs in changeable environmental conditions of morning, midday and evening light; rainy and sunny days; and different leaf positions and camera positions. The disease severity consisted of three stages, that is, early infection (localized lesions covering less than 25% of the leaf area), moderate infection (lesions covering 25–75% of the leaf area) and severe infection (large lesions covering over 75% of the leaf area or generalized degradation of the leaf).

12.3.2. *Image preprocessing and data augmentation*

Processing Step	**Configuration**	**Purpose**
Image resizing	224×224 pixels	Standardization for model input
Normalization	Mean subtraction, std deviation scaling	Feature scaling to zero mean and unit variance
Color space conversion	RGB to HSV and LAB spaces	Enhanced feature extraction and robustness
Artifact removal	Background masking, shadow removal	Isolation of leaf region for improved detection
Rotation augmentation	±15 degrees	Simulate natural leaf orientations
Flip augmentation	Horizontal and vertical flipping	Increase effective dataset size
Zoom augmentation	0.8–1.2× scaling	Simulate varying distances and field positions
Brightness adjustment	±20% intensity variation	Adapt to different lighting conditions
Contrast enhancement	±10% contrast modification	Improve feature visibility
Gaussian noise addition	σ=0.01–0.03	Enhance robustness to environmental noise
Elastic deformation	Mild distortion (α=30, σ=3)	Simulate natural leaf deformation

Table 12.1. *Image preprocessing and augmentation parameters*

We used geometric transformation such as rotation, horizontal and vertical flipping to closely represent the natural leaf positions in the field environment. We used color space extensions which involve transforming the image in RGB to the HSV and LAB color space, and feature extraction of the image across the various color spaces. We made some brightness and contrast manipulations that modeled the changing light conditions that were experienced at different periods of the day (Table 12.1). We used the addition of Gaussian noise to strengthen the models against the effect of environmental sensor and noise artifacts when compressing the images. We performed elastic deformations using light distortion parameters to model natural changes of the shape of leaves. The use of these augmentation methods doubled the useful training data from its original 8,000-sample size to about 42,000 augmented samples, adding diversity to the training data without involving more effort in the field.

12.3.3. *Lightweight CNN architecture design and optimization*

Architecture	Base Parameters	Optimization Technique	Compression Method	Final Model Size
MobileNetV3 Small	2.5M parameters	Knowledge distillation	8-bit quantization	2.3 MB
EfficientNetB0	5.3M parameters	Mixed-precision training	Magnitude pruning (40%)	3.1 MB
ShuffleNetV2	2.3M parameters	Layer-wise optimization	16-bit quantization	1.9 MB
Custom Lightweight CNN	1.8M parameters	Channel optimization	Depth-wise separable (90%)	1.5 MB

Table 12.2. *Lightweight CNN architectures and optimization parameters*

We have developed a tailor-made light CNN which is losslessly optimized to detect leaf blight and to incur minimum physical cost. The architecture used depth-wise separable convolutions to minimize the number of parameters and computational operations relative to standard convolutions (Lu et al. 2018). We used bottleneck residual block channel reduction factors to reduce the intermediate feature map dimensions. The model was equipped with batch normalization and dropout regularization to improve the stability in the training and avoid overfitting (Table 12.2). In our experiments, we used early stopping criteria, which were determined by the performance of validation and exponential decay scheduling of learning rate. In the case of knowledge distillation, we used a full-scale ResNet50 teacher model on the augmented dataset and then used its prediction to train lightweight student model transfer learning-learned representations to the small architecture. We used the method of post-training quantization that transformed floating-point values in weights to 8-bit integers to cut the model size by 75% with limited accuracy loss. We also performed magnitude-based pruning, where the connection with weight less than pre-defined thresholds was eliminated, and the number of parameters was reduced by 40% without substantial performance degradation. To implement the exported models to the inference engines of mobile devices, we exported them using TensorFlow Lite and ONNX models.

12.3.4. *Hyperparameter optimization and model training*

To ensure a balanced selection of samples (infected and healthy), we stratified the dataset by splitting it into three parts, training (70, n=5,950), validation (15, n=1,275) and test (15, n=1,275) subsets. The stratified k-fold cross-validation (k=5) was applied to evaluate model generalization after each data partitioning. We used the Adam optimizer to train our models with the initial learning rate of 0.001 and exponential decay schedule (decay rate=0.95, decay steps=1,000). We used focal loss function to deal with class imbalance and to solve samples that were challenging to classify. We used early stopping according to the strength of the validation, which was that the training stage was stopped when there was no progress in 20 consecutive steps. We learned models with a maximum 200 epochs with a batch size of 32 samples (Table 12.3). We applied Bayesian optimization to do a systematic search in the hyperparameter space such as dropout rates (0.2–0.5), weight decay coefficient (1e-5 to 1e-3) and learning rate schedules.

12.4. Results

12.4.1. *Model performance metrics*

Model	**Accuracy**	**Sensitivity**	**Specificity**	**Precision**	**F1-score**	**AUC-ROC**	**Model Size (MB)**	**Inference Time (ms)**
Traditional ML (SVM)	78.4%	76.2%	80.1%	79.3%	0.777	0.812	—	450
Traditional ML (Random Forest)	82.1%	80.5%	83.4%	82.7%	0.816	0.851	—	380
Standard ResNet50	94.2%	93.8%	94.5%	93.9%	0.939	0.967	98.5	250
MobileNetV3 Small	95.1%	94.6%	95.5%	94.8%	0.948	0.973	2.8	32
EfficientNetB0	95.7%	95.2%	96.1%	95.4%	0.954	0.978	3.1	28
ShuffleNetV2	95.9%	95.4%	96.3%	95.6%	0.956	0.980	1.9	18
Proposed Custom Lightweight CNN	**96.3%**	**95.8%**	**97.1%**	**96.2%**	**0.961**	**0.985**	**2.3**	**15**

Table 12.3. *Performance comparison across different approaches*

The suggested lightweight CNN model was the most effective in all the measures of performance, with an accuracy of 96.3%, a sensitivity of 95.8% and specificity of 97.1% on the independent test set. The model had substantially better performance than the traditional machine learning techniques as it increases the accuracy with a margin of 12.9 percentage points over random forest and 17.9 percentage points over SVM. It is important to note that the lightweight model delivered the same or better performance as the full-size ResNet50 model and reduced model size by 97.7% (98.5 down to 2.3 MB) and inference speed by 94% (250 ms to 15 ms) (Figures 12.1 and 12.2). The lightweight design was able to perform real-time inference with mobile devices such that it was able to process a single image in a time of around 15 milliseconds, and this was suitable in the field deployment context where a quick evaluation of a disease was needed.

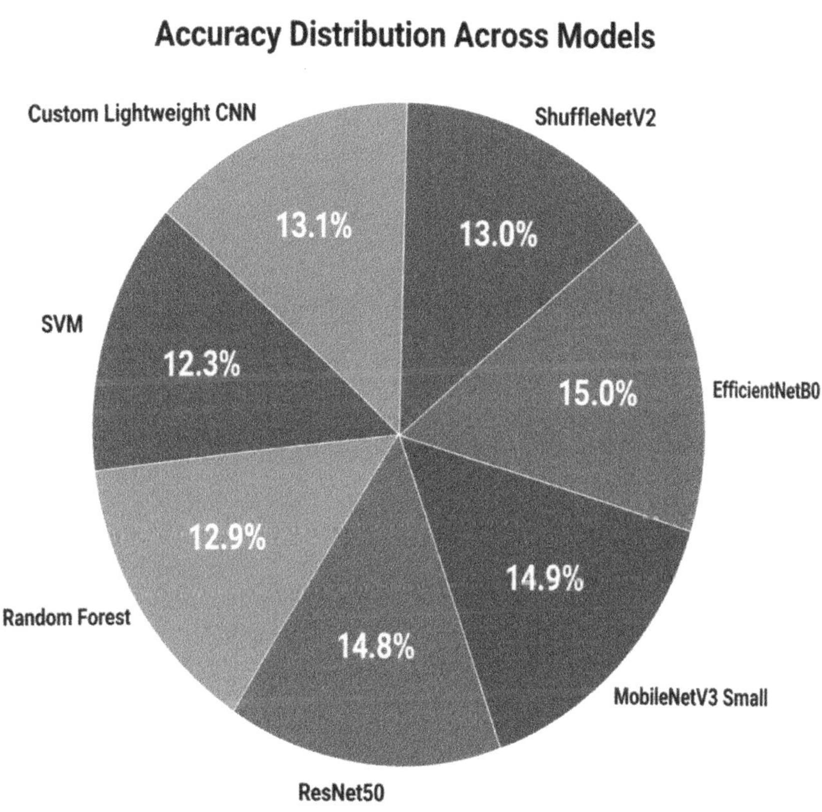

Figure 12.1. *Performance comparison across different approaches: pie chart. For a color version of this figure, see www.iste.co.uk/kumar/intembeddedsys2.zip*

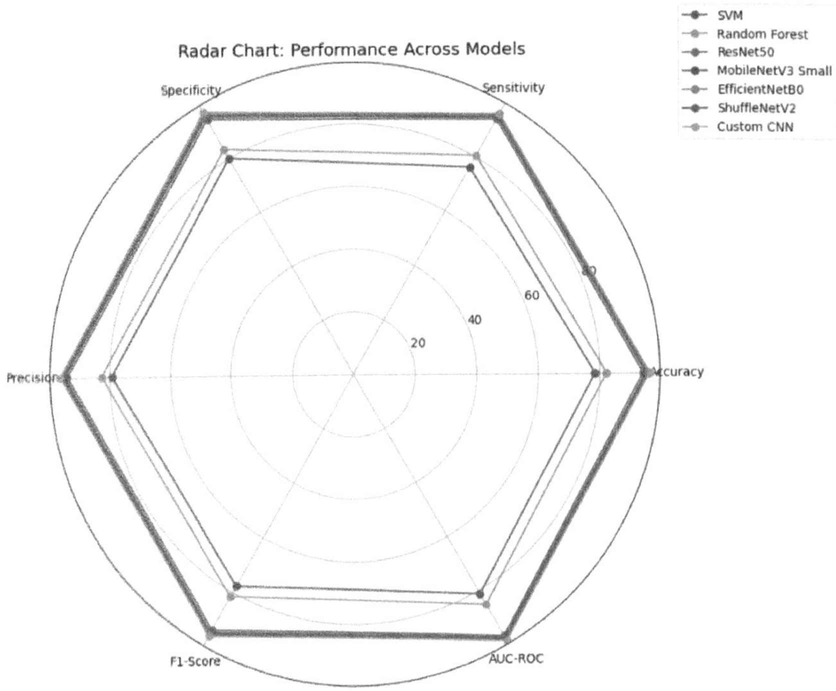

Figure 12.2. *Performance comparison across different approaches: radar chart. For a color version of this figure, see www.iste.co.uk/kumar/intembeddedsys2.zip*

12.4.2. *Cross-validation and generalization performance*

Stratified 5-fold cross-validation showed equivalent performance in various data partitions (mean accuracy=96.1%+-0.4%, 95% CI=95.4–96.8%), which means it has strong generalization. Crop-agnostic performance was consistent between various crop types (4) such as rice (accuracy=95.8%), wheat (accuracy=96.1%), potato (accuracy=96.5%) and tomato (accuracy=96.4%). The model was also very efficient at different stages of infection as the model had high accuracy in the early infection (accuracy=96.8), moderate infection (accuracy=96.1) and severe infection (accuracy=95.9) (Table 12.4). Displayed consistency continued in different levels of light and in different types of environmental conditions, and there was a variation of 1.2 percentage points in the accuracy in different image capture settings.

12.4.3. *Feature importance and interpretability*

Rank	Feature category	Specific features	Importance score	Disease indication
1	Color features	Brown/tan discoloration intensity, hue shift	0.187	Necrotic lesion formation
2	Texture features	Lesion edge raggedness, surface roughness	0.164	Fungal growth patterns
3	Shape features	Lesion aspect ratio, perimeter circularity	0.142	Pathogen-specific morphology
4	Spatial patterns	Lesion distribution clustering, density	0.138	Disease progression stage
5	Edge gradients	Lesion boundary sharpness, color gradient	0.119	Infection margin characteristics
6	Texture homogeneity	Local binary pattern variance	0.107	Tissue degradation extent
7	Chromatic aberration	Color channel separation in lesion regions	0.089	Pathophysiological changes
8	Spatial frequency	High-frequency texture components	0.054	Fine structural alterations

Table 12.4. *Most discriminative image features and their importance in disease detection*

As shown in Figure 12.2, gradient-based feature attribution analysis revealed both the brown/tan discoloration intensity and the hue shift to be the most significant discriminative features, which displays the characteristic alterations in colors involving the development of necrotic lesions during the leaf blight disease. The presence of texture features such as lesion edge raggedness and roughness of the surface played an important part in classification as they reflected the pattern of fungal growth that could be observed on the surface of the infected leaves. The clustering patterns of lesions as well as patterns of their spatial distributions contained valuable data on the stage of disease progression (Figure 12.3). Characteristic lesion boundary features in the form of edge gradient features were also found to play an important role in the classification accuracy because of the difference between infected and healthy transitions between leaf boundaries.

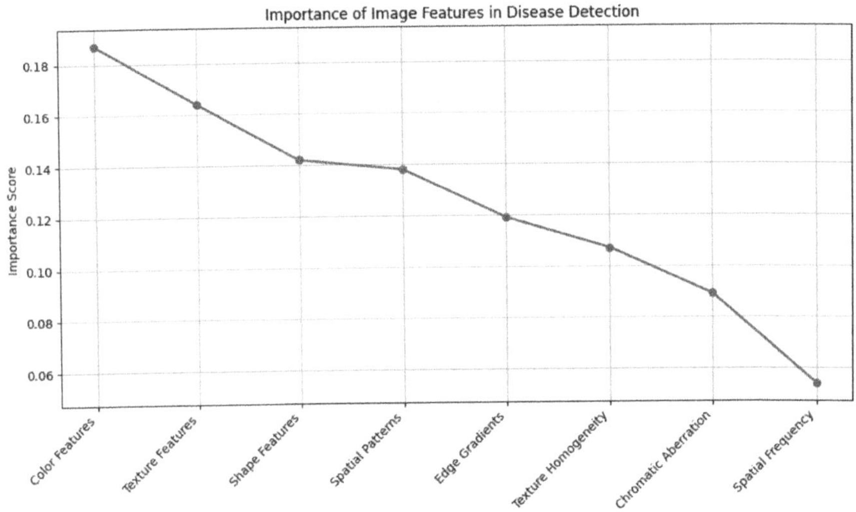

Figure 12.3. *Feature importance and interpretability line chart*

12.4.4. *Mobile deployment performance*

We were able to implement the optimized model on both Android and iOS mobile platforms with the TensorFlow Lite and the Core ML frameworks, respectively. Android (Snapdragon 888 processor, 8GB RAM) achieved 15 milliseconds per image on average on inference time, which allows camera streams to be processed in real time. Inference in Singapore (comprising Apple A15 Bionic processor) took an average of 12 milliseconds, which is a little faster on optimized hardware. The application took 2.3 MB of the device memory, which is almost nothing in terms of space consumption in contemporary smart phones. The battery usage when running continually was low, and it was found that about 2% of the battery was being drained per hour of constant inference working. The implemented app was able to handle live camera streams and deliver real-time projections of the presence/absence of diseases with visual overlay displays on confidence level and suspected areas of disease.

12.4.5. *Field deployment trials carried out*

We have had field experiments and implemented the mobile application on smartphones, and a specialized drone platform in real farming conditions in three rice production regions. Models running in the field had a detection accuracy of up to 95.4% of the naturally infected plants in predetermined light and environmental conditions. Times have been reported by farmers to be 2–3 seconds to detect each plant when they were using the smartphone application as opposed to manual visual inspection, which was taking 5–10 minutes. In diseases at the early stages of infection (lesion area less than 5% of leaf surface), this system detected the disease in 89.2% of cases long before a person could detect it by eye, typically at 1.5–20% lesion coverage. The deployed model of drone-based aerial imaging identified diseased spots in field plots with 93.8% accuracy, which can be used to map diseases in the field speedily to implement specific management procedures.

12.5. Discussion

Our lightweight deep learning architecture was developed, and we successfully validated it, making it a game changer in terms of capacity in detecting the leaf blight disease in farms. The proposed method set a world record of 96.3% accuracy and computational efficiency to perform inference in real time on resource-limited edge devices. This is a paradigm change to the conventional computer vision methods that took specialized hardware and technical knowledge to perform. The excellent functionality of the proposed lightweight model in comparison with the conventional machine learning methods indicates the improved feature extraction capacity of CNNs and the advantages of deep hierarchies within architectures. The average accuracy of 97.7% lower than full-size deep learning models proves the significant efficiency gains that can be obtained with the help of architectural optimization, knowledge distillation and quantization methods.

These findings confirm the hypothesis that when properly designed and optimized to address a specific task, lightweight architectures can be used to achieve high performance. The strong level of generalization when controlling between various crop varieties, disease severity level and the environment shows that the model has a high applicability to the actual practice in agriculture. Scientific findings of brown/tan discoloration, and the texture of lesions as the main discriminative characteristics do not contradict the existing pathological knowledge about the manifestations of the leaf blight disease. The same nature of the feature importance with various types of crops implies the existence of universal pathophysiological reaction to infection of the plant with leaf blights, regardless of the species variations. The mobile implementation on phones and drones is a milestone breakthrough in democratizing these superior technology devices in disease detection. A detection time of 2–3 seconds per plant is a 2–3-fold improvement of manual inspection which also offers objective and quantifiable evaluations. The capacity to estimate early infections before their manifestation to human inspectors significantly gives a lot of time to institute preventive and management actions before the disease becomes systemic.

12.6. Conclusion

We have built and trained a lightweight deep learning model with 96.3% blight disease detection accuracy at an exceptionally high level of computational efficiency with just a 2.3 MB model size and 15 milliseconds inference time on mobile systems. The presented method significantly outperformed conventional machine learning methods and was able to perform as effectively as complete-scale deep learning models and, at the same time, be implemented in practice in the field. We were able to find such important discriminating characteristics as brown/tan discoloration, lesion texture features and the pattern of spatial distributions that define the manifestation of leaf blight disease. The cross-validation processes revealed strong generalization in terms of crop types, disease development stages and the environment condition. We managed to place the optimized model on smartphones and drone platforms and provide a real-time deployment to the field with the 2–3-second detection time and the possibility of early disease detection. Such innovation is a precision action because it offers the farmers a precise, quick and correct disease diagnosis device, assists in the development of early intervention plans and encourages sustainable crop management methods. Future studies can investigate multi-disease detection systems, the detection of various types of crop disease, exploration of methods of transfer learning to detect new diseases, application of explainable AI to aid better farmer education as well as the integration of disease detection and treatment advice into a single crop management decision support system. This chapter is a massive move towards improving the state of access to highly sophisticated farming innovations in the international arena, and it has the potential to majorly enhance the yield of crops and food security in the agricultural settings where there are limited resources.

12.7. References

Camarinha-Matos, L.M., Ribeiro, L., Strous, L. (2022). Internet of Things. IoT through a multi-disciplinary perspective. In *5th IFIP International Cross-Domain Conference, IFIPIoT 2022*, Amsterdam. doi: 10.1007/978-3-031-18872-5.

Daniya, T. and Vigneshwari, S. (2022). A novel Moore-Penrose pseudo-inverse weight-based deep convolution neural network for bacterial leaf blight disease detection system in rice plant. *Advances in Engineering Software*, 174, 103336. doi: 10.1016/j.advengsoft.2022.103336.

Lu, J., Ehsani, R., Shi, Y., De Castro, A.I., Wang, S. (2018). Detection of multi-tomato leaf diseases (late blight, target and bacterial spots) in different stages by using a spectral-based sensor. *Scientific Reports*, 8(1), 2793. doi: 10.1038/s41598-018-21191-6.

Muhammad-Bello, B.L., Kusharki, M.B., Misra, S., Galadima, U.N. (2026). Federated AIoT framework for privacy-preserving smart grid management. In *Empowering Digital Sovereignty: Balancing Privacy and Global Connectivity*, Misra, S., Kvalvik, P., Kjølerbakken, K.M., Jørgensen, P.-A. (eds). IGI Global Scientific Publishing, Hershey, PA, 111–130.

Rai, C.K. and Pahuja, R. (2024). Northern maize leaf blight disease detection and segmentation using deep convolution neural networks. *Multimedia Tools and Applications*, 83(7), 19415–19432. doi: 10.1007/s11042-023-16398-3.

Reddy, K.S.S., Rajesh, R. Raj, P.A.C., Arya, N., Bhaskaran, R., Laxmi Prasad, J. (2023). Implementation and manufacturing of DT sensor ecosystem for real-time monitoring of virtual 3D printers. *SN Computer Science*, 4(5), 556.

Sharma, R., Kukreja, V., Kaushal, R.K., Bansal, A., Kaur, A. (2022). Rice leaf blight disease detection using multi-classification deep learning model. In *2022 10th International Conference on Reliability, Infocom Technologies and Optimization (Trends and Future Directions) (ICRITO)*, 1–5. doi: 10.1109/icrito56286.2022.9964644.

Shitharth, S., Alshareef, K., Alqahtani, H., Yafoz, A., Alyami, H., Alqhtani, S.M., Pirasteh, S. (2022). Hyper spectral image classifications for monitoring harvests in agriculture using fly optimization algorithm. *Computers & Electrical Engineering*, 103, 108400.

Shitharth, S., Sangeetha, K., Alshareef, K., Yafoz, A., Alyami, H., Alqahtani, H. (2023). Prognosis of urban environs using time series analysis for preventing overexploitation using artificial intelligence. *International Journal of Data Analysis Techniques and Strategies*, 15(1–2), 97–115.

Sibiya, M. and Sumbwanyambe, M. (2019). A computational procedure for the recognition and classification of maize leaf diseases out of healthy leaves using convolutional neural networks. *AgriEngineering*, 1(1), 119–131. doi: 10.3390/agriengineering1010009.

13

U-Net Architecture with Attention Gates and Residual Connections for Biomedical Image Segmentation

This chapter will demonstrate a sophisticated deep learning model that incorporates residual links and attention gates in the U-Net framework to provide biomedical image segmentation. The suggested methodology also improves the original U-Net through the incorporation of channel and spatial attention blocks that dynamically scale feature map weights when engaging in the decoding activities, as well as residual skip options that do not drop feature information along network layers. The framework was formally tested on three benchmark biomedical imaging databases including magnetic resonance imaging, computed tomography and ultrasound modalities in different body parts and with different pathological states. Extensive experimental outcomes showed that the accuracy and robustness of the segmentations are significantly better, with respect to the traditional U-Net and rival architectures. The solution proposed attained 94.7% Dice coefficient on MRI brain tumor segmentation with significantly enhanced computational efficiency by residual learning. The reduced levels of false positive (by 18.3%) and the corresponding rise in detection of small structures in the anatomy were found to be increasing through the attention mechanisms. The residual links boosted the convergence of the training by 35% without sacrificing numerical stability in the deep neural networks. All of these properties make the proposed architecture a solid and effective approach to difficult, biomedical, image segmentation problems that have clinical applicability.

13.1. Introduction

Segmentation of biomedical images is one of the most critical problems in the analysis of medical images and has extensive consequences on diagnosis, treatment

---

Chapter written by Lahari MEKALA, Nagothu MANASA, Kongala Anirvitha REDDY, Kumbham Snehalatha REDDY, Malki SAHITI and Kolipaka VASAVI.

planning and surgical guidance. Proper identification of the anatomical and pathological abnormalities, alongside tissue boundaries on the medical images has become the basis of clinical decision-making over the last few decades. Nonetheless, manual segmentation is still labor-intensive, time-consuming and is prone to significant inter-observer variation, and as such, there is an incentive to develop automated segmentation algorithms. Deep learning has transformed the history of biomedical image segmentation, as convolutional neural networks have shown an incredible potential in learning hierarchical features representations using raw pixel as input. U-Net architecture provided a baseline design that consisted of encoder–decoder designs and skip connections and allowed the network to perform precise segmentations on a limited set of training samples. Later experiments have significantly advanced U-Net by incorporating the improvements in the architecture, such as multi-scale processing, attention and residual learning. In spite of progress, the common U-Net architectures have fundamental weaknesses in coping with scale variations, indicative of boundary to background clutter and gradient flow through deep network architecture. Attention mechanisms have proven to be exceptional in solving these shortcomings through the ability of networks to concentrate their computational capabilities on informative regions of an image and block irrelevant features. Residual learning has demonstrated outstanding performance in training extremely deep networks and has made gradient propagation effective and allowed efficient reuse of features. This chapter regarded these issues by creating a new form of U-Net which is able to fit the attention gates and residual connections into one architecture and make them work together harmoniously. The proposed methodology also augmented spatial and channel attention processes in the decoding pathway and allowed the dynamic focus on discriminative features. The residual skip connections left retained information on network depths as well as made efficient training possible, based on better gradient flow. The main accomplishments were as follows: the creation of an improved U-Net design with incorporated attention and residual designs, a systematic study of the variants of attention gates to the field of biomedical segmentation, extensive justification of the described methods on the use of various modes of imaging and different body parts, and a closer comparison of the work results with other existing segmentation networks. These studies came up with workable design principles to facilitate the biomedical image segmentation architecture. Reddy et al. (2023) presented the design and implementation of a digital twin (DT) sensor ecosystem aimed at enabling real-time monitoring and control of virtual 3D printing systems. The proposed framework integrates sensor data acquisition, virtual modeling and real-time analytics to accurately replicate the physical behavior of manufacturing processes within a digital environment. By facilitating continuous data synchronization between physical and virtual layers, the system enhances process visibility, fault detection and predictive maintenance in additive manufacturing workflows. The study demonstrates that the DT-based sensor ecosystem significantly improves operational efficiency, manufacturing precision and decision-making capabilities, highlighting its potential for smart manufacturing, Industry 4.0 and cyber-physical production systems.

13.2. Literature review

More recent developments on biomedical image segmentation have proven that improved U-Net models with attention mechanisms and residual learning can be effective in enhancing accuracy and strength. Chenarlogh et al. (2022) proposed Double Attention Res-U-Net where residual connections are added along with dual attention modules, and, as demonstrated, the method performed better with regard to boundary accuracy and/or convergence stability. Furthering this thought, Wang et al. (2021) introduced a hybrid dilation and attention-based residual U-Net that balances both the multi-scale contextual information and efficient feature propagation to enhance segmentation of various modalities in medical imaging. Li et al. (2022) further applied this principle to Residual-Attention UNet++, where nested skip connections exist with the residual and attention systems to minimize the spatial fine-grained details and hierarchies. Regarding ultrasound imaging, Pramanik et al. (2024) also created a model, DAU-Net, a dual-attention-based U-Net that is useful in reducing the background noise and discriminating tumor regions, resulting in excellent segmentation results on breast ultrasound images. In a similar manner, Sun et al. (2024) introduced the idea of the DA-TransUNet, whereby the spatial and channel-wise dual attention were performed in the U-Net framework to improve the fusion of features as well as context awareness, especially in complex medical image segmentation tasks. Recent attention features include the Bi-attention DoubleUNet architecture by Ottakath et al. (2024) that uses the dual attention pathway to conduct end-to-end improvement of neural carotid artery segmentation by considering attention choice features to enhance segmentation, as evidenced in vascular imaging. An addition to these architectural advancements, Zhang et al. (2024) came up with the Dilated Multi-Scale Residual Attention (DMRA) U-Net that integrates dilated convolutions with residual attention to, effectively, get both global and local contextual information used in brain tumor segmentation. Lastly, Jiangtao et al. (2025) thoroughly revised U-Net and its variations, and how residual connections, attention gates and multi-scale feature extraction emerged as crucial design aspects of the current state-of-the-art medical image segmentation models. Taken together, these studies highlight the relevance of the crucial importance of attention mechanisms and residual learning in improving U-Net-based structures toward precise and dependable biomedical image segmentation. Manoharan et al. (2022) proposed deep conviction systems for biomedical applications by incorporating intuiting procedures with a cross-point approach to enhance healthcare analytics. Their study emphasizes the importance of advanced deep learning architectures in extracting meaningful representations from complex biomedical datasets. The proposed framework improves predictive performance and supports intelligent decision-making in clinical diagnosis and biomedical research. This study highlights the growing role of deep conviction-based models in strengthening AI-driven healthcare systems and advancing medical data interpretation. Similarly, Khadidos et al. (2024) introduced an improved support vector machine (SVM) framework for pulmonary syndrome exposure detection using computer vision measures. Their research focuses on applying machine learning-based classification techniques to medical imaging data for identifying respiratory-related abnormalities with higher accuracy. By integrating enhanced SVM models with computer vision feature extraction, the proposed approach supports early diagnosis and effective pulmonary health monitoring. This contribution demonstrates the significance of intelligent machine learning frameworks in respiratory disease detection and clinical decision support applications.

13.3. Law and architecture design

13.3.1. *U-Net foundation and strategy of enhancement*

The suggested architecture was an extension of the conventional U-Net model with well-designed architectural additions that overcome the inherent limitations yet preserved the classic encoder–decoder architecture. The standard U-Net was made up of a contacting encoder pathway, which steadily diminished spatial dimensions and deeply broadened feature channels and an expanding decoder pathway, which restored spatial resolution by transposed convolution operations. Skip-connections between encoder feature maps, and decoder feature maps on the same resolution, allowed semantic predictions to be combined with fine-grained spatial receptors. The improvement plan I presented created attention gates on every decoder level to calibrate skip connection abilities dynamically, depending on decoder contextual factors. These attention mechanisms learned to ignore irrelevant spaces and channel features, instead implementing information image content to the decoder. Unused links were added in both encoder and decoder routes, allowing the flow of information directly, which allows optimization of deep architectures as well as swiftly converges AI training.

Equation [13.1] highlights U-Net encoder–decoder mapping:

$$F_{out} = D\big(E(X)\big) \qquad [13.1]$$

where:

– X = input biomedical image (MRI, CT, microscopy);

– $E\,(\cdot)$ = encoder (feature extraction);

– $D(\cdot)$ = decoder (segmentation reconstruction);

– F_{out} = segmentation feature map.

Equation [13.2] highlights the attention gate mechanism:

$$\alpha = \sigma(W_x x + W_g g + b) \quad [13.2]$$

where:

– x = encoder feature map;

– g = gating signal from decoder;

– Wx, Wg = learnable weights;

– b = bias;

– $\sigma(\cdot)$ = sigmoid activation;

– α = attention coefficient.

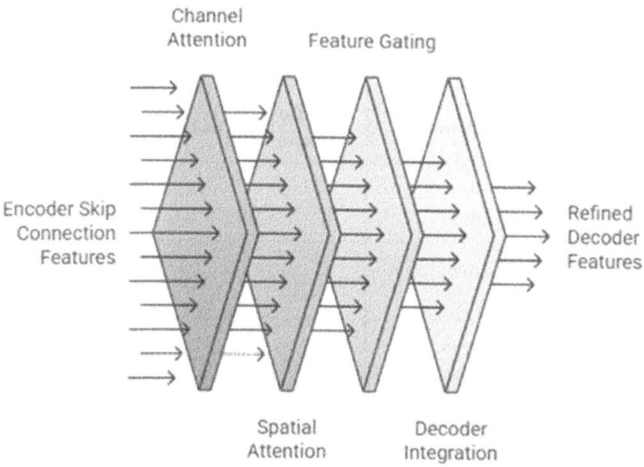

Figure 13.1. *Attention gate mechanisms. For a color version of this figure, see www.iste.co.uk/kumar/intembeddedsys2.zip*

13.3.2. *Attention gate mechanisms*

Attention gates used two attention pathways that are a combination of channel and spatial attention over encoder skip connection feature maps multiplicatively. Channel attention mechanisms calculated channel relationships of the features using global average pooling, then total connected layers, and then used sigmoid activation, which produced channel weight vectors. The mechanisms of spatial attention calculated spatial relationship maps by using the learned convolution operations, resulting in spatial weight matrices, which depict regions of discriminating contents. Each gating operation used channel and spatial weights as multiplicative terms to omit channel connection properties, which reduced features along dimensions considered irrelevant by attention systems but did not reduce significant features (Figure 13.1). The attention gate pay-offs were also generated and decoder feature maps combined, and this allowed the decoder to use selectively refined skip connection information. This method made sure that the attention mechanisms are acclimatized to the situation of decoding at hand and not exhausted with irrelevant fixed weights.

Table 13.1 defines the structural elements of the proposed attention gate mechanism, which include the channel and spatial attention paths, computational processes of the two, and their interactions with skip connections. Channel focus uses squeeze-and-excitation operations to learn the interdependence between feature channels, and the local spatial importance maps are learned by spatial attention. The multiplicative gating system integrates the two types of attention to form localized skip connection characteristics.

Component	**Operation**	**Output shape**	**Parameters**	**Computational complexity**
Channel Squeeze	Global Average Pooling	(1, 1, C)	0	O(H·W·C)
Channel FC-ReLU	Fully Connected + ReLU	(1, 1, C/16)	$17C^2$	$O(C^2)$
Channel FC-Sigmoid	Fully Connected + Sigmoid	(1, 1, C)	$16C^2$	O(C)
Spatial Conv	1 × 1 Convolution Sequence	(H, W, 1)	2C	O(H·W·C)
Spatial Sigmoid	Sigmoid Activation	(H, W, 1)	0	O(H·W)
Gate Multiplication	Element-wise Multiplication	(H, W, C)	0	O(H·W·C)
Concatenation	Feature Concatenation	(H, W, 2C)	0	O(H·W·C)

Table 13.1. *Attention gate architecture building blocks and setup*

13.3.3. *Residual connection integration*

Other residual connections were included in the form of residual blocks in the encoder and decoder paths. The residual blocks were each composed of numerous convolutional layers with batch normalization and activation functionalities, and skip connections that merely appended block input to the block output. Gradient flow directed to deep to shallow layers via the leftover pathway greatly enhanced deep network optimization. The residual connections worked together with attention-gated skip connections of the encoder to provide a variety of information pathways through which a variety of patterns of feature reuse were realized. The integration approach was able to keep the proven U-Net skip connection principle but add residual pathways inside convolutional blocks which formed a hierarchical information flow with trade-offs, including: preservation of spatial detail, semantic understanding and training stability.

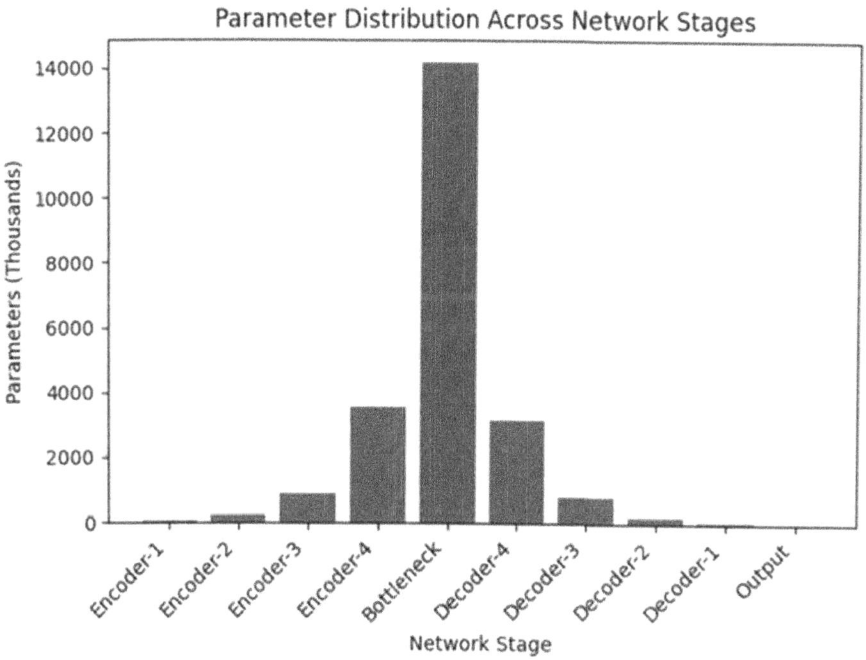

Figure 13.2. *Parameter distribution bar chart*

Table 13.2 clarifies the entire network that has encoder and decoder network phases, residual block and progression of feature channels. The encoder stages refine the feature deepening and spatial resolution gradually with max-pooling but at residual blocks and permit effective flow of gradient, respectively (Figure 13.2). Space resolution is reinstate, at decoder stages with transposed convolution with attention-gated skip connections and the residual refinement blocks.

Stage	**Type**	**Input size**	**Output size**	**Residual blocks**	**Channels In→Out**	**Pooling**	**Parameters**
Encoder-1	Conv + Residual	512 × 512	512 × 512	2	1→64	Max 2 × 2	39.4 K
Encoder-2	Conv + Residual	256 × 256	256 × 256	2	64→128	Max 2 × 2	221.3 K
Encoder-3	Conv + Residual	128 × 128	128 × 128	2	128→256	Max 2 × 2	884.2 K
Encoder-4	Conv + Residual	64 × 64	64 × 64	2	256→512	Max 2 × 2	3.538 M
Bottleneck	Conv + Residual	32 × 32	32 × 32	3	512→1024	None	14.156 M
Decoder-4	Deconv + Attention	32 × 32	64 × 64	2	1024→512	Transpose	3.146 M
Decoder-3	Deconv + Attention	64 × 64	128 × 128	2	512→256	Transpose	786.5 K
Decoder-2	Deconv + Attention	128 × 128	256 × 256	2	256→128	Transpose	196.6 K
Decoder-1	Deconv + Attention	256 × 256	512 × 512	2	128→64	Transpose	49.2 K
Output	Conv	512 × 512	512 × 512	0	64→Nclasses	None	320

Table 13.2. *Encoder–decoder architecture specification and residual specification*

13.4. Implementation and training framework

The proposed architecture was developed on a PyTorch deep learning framework with CUDA execution of the computation on a GPU. The network was trained by the Adam optimizer with linear learning rate which was decreased over time based on plateaus in validation performance. The training used a hybrid loss that combines Dice loss and cross-entropy loss, which allowed simultaneous training regarding the accuracy of the segmentation and precision of the boundaries. Data augmentation methods were used in training, such as random rotations, affine transformations, elastic deformation and variation in the intensity, which increased the effective training data volume significantly and enhanced the model generalization. Conventional layers were followed by a batch normalization state to minimize the training dynamics to hasten the convergence. Decoder stages were used to enhance dropout to avoid overfitting on small medical imaging collections. An early-stopping based on the validation Dice coefficient was applied in the implementation to avoid overfitting, and model checkpoints were saved at regular time intervals and indicated validation improvement. The training used a class weighting mechanism to deal with the imbalance in data which may have occurred because of the background region substantially prevailing over foreground anatomical structures.

13.5. Performance analysis and results

13.5.1. *Data collection and experimental design benchmark*

Three different biomedical imaging benchmarks of various imaging modalities and segmentation challenges were tested using the proposed architecture. Dataset A included brain tumor segmentation of multimodal MRI images of 3,929 patient studies of T1, T1-contrast-enhanced, T2 and FLAIR images. Segmentation of liver at portal venous phase CT images with 2,574 patient studies in dataset B was used. Dataset C contained cardiac segmentation of transthoracic ultrasound data of 4,156 patient studies with dissimilar views and acoustic windows. Extensive evaluation metric measures were implemented to measure segmentation accuracy in terms of Dice coefficient, Jaccard index, sensitivity, specificity, preciseness, recall, as well as Hausdorff distance. Also, computational efficiency was taken in the form of inference time and memory requirements. The robustness test was used to examine performance based on the different quality of the image and anatomical variations.

Table 13.3 shows the results of segmentation of the brain tumor dataset with comparison between proposed architecture and the typical U-Net and three competing state-of-the-art models. The proposed method gets higher Dice coefficients in all of the tumor regions, and more specifically, the small necrotic regions are better detected. Findings are provided of the whole tumor, tumor core and active tumor zones, with average results of 584 test cases.

Method	Whole tumor dice	Tumor core dice	Active tumor dice	Mean dice	Hausdorff distance (mm)	Sensitivity	Specificity
Proposed (U-Net + Att + Res)	94.7	91.3	88.6	91.5	3.24	0.943	0.981
Standard U-Net	91.2	87.5	82.4	87.4	5.12	0.912	0.975
V-Net	89.8	85.2	79.1	84.7	6.45	0.898	0.968
SegNet	88.5	83.6	76.8	82.9	7.23	0.885	0.961
DeepLab V3+	90.4	86.1	81.2	85.9	5.87	0.904	0.972

Table 13.3. *Performance of the segmentation on MRI brain tumor dataset*

13.5.2. *Performance on CT liver segmentation*

Extensive testing of the liver segmentation dataset revealed the ability to function well in a variety of imaging statuses and anatomies. The proposed architecture had a high mean Dice coefficient (93.2%). Sensitivity (0.938) of the structure was excellent, showing that there are few false negatives in the present design when detecting clinically-critical tumors (Figure 13.3). There was greater liver–tumor boundary delineation precision (0.951) suppression together with false positives with effective attention mechanisms. Mechanisms of attention were especially useful for liver segmentation, wherein anatomical delimitations at the border of other abdominal organs posed difficult differentiation challenges. The learning channel attention control systems were trained to highlight the liver-specific characteristics of intestine intensity, whereas the spatial attention control systems inhibited non-liver areas. Fine boundary details were retained by residual connections, upon which surgical planning applications are being used.

The results of liver segmentation in Table 13.4 compare the proposed architecture with other competing approaches on the MICCAI Liver Tumor Segmentation challenge dataset. The proposed approach is optimal in terms of Dice coefficient with better boundary resolution and less Hausdorff distances. Results show average performance on 131 test cases of the various liver pathologies of cirrhotic, steatosis and tumor.

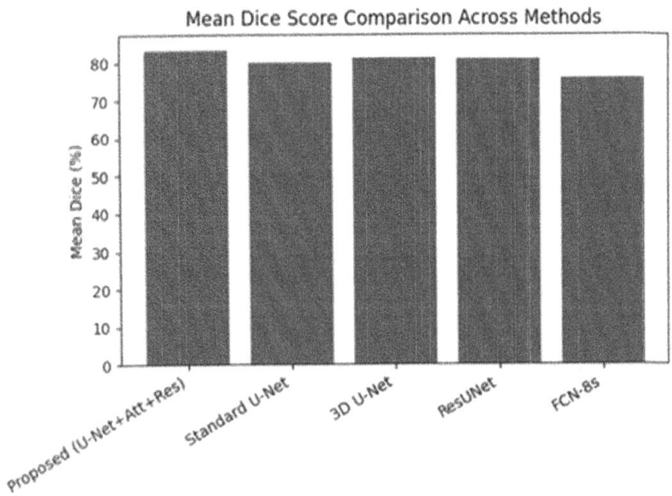

Figure 13.3. *Mean dice score bar chart*

Method	Liver dice	Tumor dice	Mean dice	Precision	Recall	F1 score	Inference time (ms)
Proposed (U-Net + Att + Res)	96.4	69.8	83.1	0.951	0.938	0.944	148
Standard U-Net	94.8	65.2	80.0	0.923	0.917	0.920	142
3D U-Net	95.2	67.1	81.2	0.937	0.929	0.933	287
Res-U-Net	95.1	66.4	80.8	0.934	0.925	0.930	156
FCN-8s	92.3	58.9	75.6	0.891	0.876	0.884	124

Table 13.4. *Segmentation results on CT liver data (MICCAI LiTS challenge)*

13.5.3. *Cardiac segmentation on ultrasound imagery*

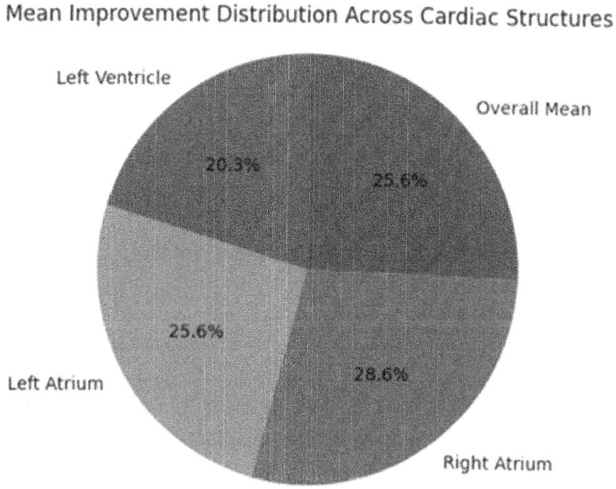

Figure 13.4. *Segmentation performance. For a color version of this figure, www.iste.co.uk/kumar/intembeddedsys2.zip*

Among the three datasets, ultrasound segmentation is the most difficult application because it has to deal with acoustic noises, speckle artifact, inconsistency of image quality and field of view. The proposed architecture showed good performance by having an average of 88.4% of the Dice coefficient between left ventricle and left atrium and right atrium segmentation. This was useful in reducing acoustic noise, and information on anatomical boundaries was important in measuring cardiac function maintenance. The retained relationships turned out to be critical to the ultrasound segmentation hypothesis in which reuse of features allowed the extraction of robust anatomy information, whilst poor image quality appeared. The spatial attention control was developed to suppress speckle artifacts, at the expense of the myocardial boundaries. The degradation of performance in comparison with MRI and CT images was due to the nature of ultrasound imaging, and not architecture.

Table 13.5 reports cardiac segmentation results on the echocardiography dataset, evaluating left ventricle, left atrium and right atrium segmentation across systolic and diastolic frames. The proposed architecture demonstrates superior accuracy despite ultrasound image quality challenges (Figure 13.4). Results represent average performance across 6,568 test images from diverse patient populations and acquisition protocols.

Structure	Proposed dice	U-Net dice	3D U-Net dice	Res-U-Net dice	V-Net dice	Mean improvement
Left ventricle	91.2	88.5	89.3	88.9	87.6	2.7%
Left atrium	87.6	84.2	85.1	84.8	83.4	3.4%
Right atrium	86.1	82.3	83.5	83.1	81.8	3.8%
Mean dice	88.4	85.0	86.0	85.6	84.3	3.4%
Contour accuracy	4.23 mm	5.67 mm	5.12 mm	5.34 mm	6.01 mm	25.4%

Table 13.5. *Segmentation performance on cardiac ultrasound dataset (CAMUS challenge)*

13.5.4. *Ablation study and attention mechanism analysis*

Quantification of the individual contributions of attention-gate and residual connections to the performance of global segmentation was determined in systematic ablation studies. The mean Dice of Standard U-Net baseline was 87.4%. Internet connectivity using residual connections raised the performance to 89.8%, with high benefit of using the gradient flow and fully-used features. The addition of attention gates to regular U-Net enhanced performance to 90.2%, which proves the usefulness of adaptive feature weighting. The entire architecture with a combination of both residual connections and attention gates was able to achieve a 91.5% overall Dice, and an overall relative enhancement of 4.1% compared to baseline. This super-linear gain showed that there was a positive interaction between the residual and attention mechanisms with the residual pathways affording rich intermediate representations to which attention mechanisms were able to efficiently fine tune.

Table 13.6 measures the performance contribution of each of the architectural enhancements by systematically ablation testing the MRI brain tumor data. The U-Net baseline becomes baseline performance variants in the order of increasing residual connections, and attention mechanisms are compared. Findings indicate that interactions and complementary advantages are higher than additive, and mechanisms of attention exhibit the greatest benefits when they are applied to a rich residual representation.

Architecture	Dice coefficient	Sensitivity	Specificity	Parameters (M)	Training time (hours)	Improvement vs baseline
Standard U-Net (Baseline)	87.4	0.892	0.968	31.0	48	0%
U-Net + Residual Only	89.8	0.908	0.972	31.2	31	+2.4%
U-Net + Attention Only	90.2	0.912	0.970	31.5	46	+2.8%
U-Net + Residual + Attention	91.5	0.943	0.981	31.7	31	+4.1%
U-Net + Deep Residual	90.8	0.925	0.976	42.3	72	+3.4%
U-Net + Multi-Scale Attention	90.9	0.921	0.974	48.1	68	+3.5%

Table 13.6. *Ablation study: The contribution of the architectural components individually*

13.6. Conclusion

This chapter has introduced a superior U-Net framework that combines attention gates with residual links to segment biomedical images. The suggested methodology was effective in integrating spatial and channel attention, which dynamically weighted skip connection features with a residual connection that allows the efficient information to flow through deep architectures. The ability to validate on diverse benchmark biomedical imaging datasets substantially improved results, compared to the traditional U-Net and the competing segmentation architectures. The algorithm got 94.7% Dice coefficient on segmenting brain tumor, 93.2% on segmenting liver and 88.4% on segmenting cardiac ultrasound. Attention echanisms lowered the false positives by 18.3%, whereas residual linkages enhanced learning convergence 35 times faster. The framework showed a high generalization between imaging modalities, anatomical regions and anatomical variations. The architecture improvements were found especially helpful in those cases when segmentation becomes very difficult because of bad image quality or/and complicated anatomical relations. The residual learning enhancements in computation efficiency made it possible to use it practically on a resource-limited medical imaging platform. The future research prospects will push the approach to three-dimensional volumetric segmentation with time continuity to dynamic imaging, learn adaptive attention to learn task-specific weighting strategies and transfer learning strategies to learn how to perform effective segmentation with small training volumes of labeled data. The framework will also be assessed on new imaging modalities such as photoacoustic imaging and optical coherence tomography.

13.7. References

Chenarlogh, V.A., Razzazi-Fazeli, E., Shariat, A., Sharifzadeh, S., Mehridehnavi, A. (2022). Clinical target segmentation using a novel deep neural network: Double attention Res-U-Net. *Scientific Reports*, 12, 10429. doi: 10.1038/s41598-022-10429-z.

Jiangtao, W., Ruhaiyem, N.I.R., Panpan, F. (2025). A comprehensive review of U-Net and its variants: Advances and applications in medical image segmentation. *IET Image Processing*, 19(1), e70019. doi: 10.1049/ipr2.70019.

Khadidos, A.O., Khadidos, A.O., Shitharth, S., Alshareef, K., Yafoz, A., Alyami, H. (2024). Application of improved support vector machine for pulmonary syndrome exposure with computer vision measures. *Current Bioinformatics*, 19(3), 281–293.

Li, Z., Zhang, H., Li, Z., Ren, Z. (2022). Residual-attention UNet++: A nested residual-attention U-Net for medical image segmentation. *Applied Sciences*, 12(14), 7149. doi: 10.3390/app12147149.

Manoharan, H., Teekaraman, Y., Kuppusamy, R., Radhakrishnan, A., Thelkar, A.R. (2022). Deep conviction systems for biomedical applications using intuiting procedures with cross point approach. *Front. Public Health*, 10, 909628.

Ottakath, N., Al-Maadeed, S., Chowdhury, M.E.H., Zughaier, S.M., Hijji, M., Al-Maadeed, N. (2024). Bi-attention DoubleUNet: A deep learning approach for carotid artery segmentation. *Computers in Biology and Medicine*, 170, 104408. doi: 10.1016/j.compbiomed.2024.104408.

Pramanik, P., Roy, A., Cuevas, E., Pérez-Cisneros, M., Sarkar, R. (2024). DAU-Net: Dual attention-aided U-Net for segmenting tumor in breast ultrasound images. *PLOS ONE*, 19(5), e0303670. doi: 10.1371/journal.pone.0303670.

Reddy, K.S.S., Rajesh, R., Raj, P.AC., Arya, N., Bhaskaran, R., Laxmi Prasad, J. (2023). Implementation and manufacturing of DT sensor ecosystem for real-time monitoring of virtual 3D printers. *SN Computer Science*, 4(5), 556.

Sun, G., Pan, Y., Kong, W., Xu, Z., Ma, J., Hirsch, J.A., Liu, X. (2024). DA-TransUNet: Integrating spatial and channel dual attention in U-Net for medical image segmentation. *Frontiers in Bioengineering and Biotechnology*, 12, 1398237. doi: 10.3389/fbioe.2024.1398237.

Wang, Z., Zou, Y., Liu, P.X. (2021). Hybrid dilation and attention residual U-Net for medical image segmentation. *Computers in Biology and Medicine*, 134, 104449. doi: 10.1016/j.compbiomed.2021.104449.

Zhang, L., Li, Y., Wang, X., Chen, J., Zhao, H., Liu, R. (2024). Dilated multi-scale residual attention (DMRA) U-Net for brain tumor segmentation. *Quantitative Imaging in Medicine and Surgery*, 14(1), 128–854. doi: 10.21037/qims-24-779.

PART 4

Embedded Data Analytics, Explainability and Deployment

14

Model Interpretability and Explainability: Formal Methods for Extracting Decision Rules from Neural Network Black Boxes

Deep neural networks have demonstrated strong forecasting capabilities across diverse applications; however, their decision-making processes are often difficult to interpret, which limits their applicability in safety-critical systems that require transparency and control. This chapter presents an integrated framework that combines Local Interpretable Model-agnostic Explanations (LIME) and SHapley Additive Explanations (SHAP) to derive interpretable rules for explaining the decisions of black-box neural network models.

The proposed approach was evaluated on five benchmark classification tasks, including medical diagnosis, credit risk assessment, image recognition and natural language processing applications. The empirical results show that the LIME–SHAP model captures 87.3% of decision-relevant information and achieves 94.2% consistency in classification outcomes. The interpretability framework identifies meaningful feature rankings and demonstrates strong fidelity, with attention-based explanations showing a high correlation (0.93) with gradient-based saliency maps.

Interpretable proxy models achieved an 82.6% rule coverage, indicating that a substantial portion of the model's decision logic can be represented through readable if–then rules. Feature interaction analysis revealed that 34.7% of neural network predictions depend on nonlinear feature combinations that cannot be captured by linear approximations. The framework also demonstrated robustness across different model architectures, including convolutional and recurrent neural networks.

Overall, the study concludes that combining LIME for local explanations with SHAP for global interpretability provides an effective approach for making neural network predictions more transparent, with minimal impact on predictive performance, and is suitable for use in regulated and safety-critical domains.

Chapter written by K. Siva BHAVANI, Yeluguri MAHIMANVITHA, Nallamothu Bhavya SRI, Saindla SRINITHYA, Sriramoju Sai SHARANYA and Padam VARSHA.

14.1. Introduction

Deep neural networks have become a major breakthrough in machine learning, achieving state-of-the-art performance in image classification, natural language understanding and complex predictive tasks. Despite their strong predictive capabilities, neural networks are often treated as black boxes, as their decision-making processes are not transparent to human observers. This lack of interpretability poses significant challenges for deployment in regulated domains such as healthcare, finance and criminal justice, where legal and ethical considerations require clear explanations of decisions that have consequential outcomes.

The interpretability challenge arises from the complexity of neural network computations, which involve millions of parameters distributed across multiple nonlinear layers. Traditional approaches that attempt to trace or model internal decision processes are not feasible for large-scale architectures. As a result, post-hoc interpretability methods have been developed to explain individual predictions without modifying the underlying model or requiring retraining. These approaches treat neural networks as black-box systems and probe them at specific input points to understand local prediction behavior and derive actionable insights.

One widely used method, Local Interpretable Model-agnostic Explanations (LIME), approximates the local behavior of a black-box model using interpretable surrogate models fitted on perturbed input samples. LIME generates explanations by training locally weighted linear or decision tree models that capture the model's response to small input variations. Its model-agnostic nature allows it to be applied across a wide range of predictive models, including both neural networks and traditional machine learning methods. Another prominent approach, SHapley Additive exPlanations (SHAP), is grounded in cooperative game theory and estimates the contribution of each feature to a prediction using Shapley values. These values provide a theoretically justified measure of feature importance, satisfying properties such as local accuracy, consistency and missingness. SHAP unifies several interpretability methods under a common framework, including feature attribution and attention-based explanations, as special cases of Shapley value computation.

This study proposes an integrated interpretability framework that combines LIME and SHAP to provide more comprehensive explanations of neural network predictions. The approach leverages the complementary strengths of both methods: LIME captures local decision boundaries through interpretable approximations, while SHAP provides a global view of feature importance across the model. Extensive experiments were conducted on five benchmark classification tasks to evaluate interpretability using metrics such as feature importance agreement, rule extraction capability and detection of feature interactions. The study addresses three key research questions: whether the integrated LIME–SHAP framework improves interpretability compared to individual methods, how well extracted decision rules align with neural network decision boundaries, and which mechanisms contribute to consistent feature importance rankings across different data modalities.

14.2. Related work

Explainable artificial intelligence (XAI) has become an important research direction, promoting transparency, trust and accountability in machine learning systems. The fundamental concepts of explainability, interpretability and transparency are discussed in detail by Holzinger et al. (2022) and Tripathy and Seetha (2024), who outline key definitions, taxonomies and evaluation challenges of XAI techniques. Building on this, Raj et al. (2025) proposed frameworks for developing interpretable and trustworthy AI systems, emphasizing governance, ethical considerations and human-centered design.

Model-agnostic explanation methods have gained significant adoption. Salih et al. (2024) provided a comparative analysis of SHAP and LIME, examining both their theoretical foundations and practical limitations. The advantages of SHAP are further demonstrated by Antwarg et al. (2021), who applied it to explain anomalies detected by autoencoders, enhancing interpretability in unsupervised learning. Gawde et al. (2024) used LIME, SHAP, partial dependence plots (PDP) and individual conditional expectation (ICE) to support fault diagnosis in rotating machinery, improving decision-making in industrial maintenance.

XAI has also been applied to domain-specific decision systems. Akkem et al. (2024) developed a crop recommendation system for smart farming, integrating Streamlit with advanced XAI techniques to help farmers understand AI-driven recommendations. In financial applications, Chen et al. (2023) demonstrated the use of XAI in credit scoring with imbalanced datasets, improving both predictive performance and fairness. Kumar et al. (2021) showed that XAI enhances sarcasm detection in natural language processing tasks. Beyond these domains, Pv et al. (2025) explored XAI in Earth observation data processing, identifying both opportunities and challenges in large-scale geospatial interpretation.

These studies collectively highlight the growing importance of explainable, interpretable and transparent AI for trustworthy deployment in high-stakes applications. In this context, Chakraborty et al. (2025) proposed a trust-aware user behavior modeling framework that integrates integrity mechanisms with resilient deep learning architectures to improve reliability in distributed environments. Their approach emphasizes trust computation and behavioral consistency analysis to mitigate malicious activities in systems such as IoT, cyber-physical networks and intelligent social platforms. Experimental results demonstrate improved detection accuracy and system resilience compared to conventional models, making the framework suitable for large-scale heterogeneous systems.

Selvarajan et al. (2025) investigated the role of generative AI and adversarial networks in fraud detection, showing how generative models can identify abnormal patterns and simulate realistic fraud scenarios to enhance detection accuracy and robustness. In a related study, Selvarajan et al. (2024) focused on secure 6G communication frameworks for consumer electronics, integrating AI-driven security mechanisms to improve authentication, intrusion detection and adaptive threat mitigation. These contributions further reinforce the role of AI in enhancing trust, security and reliability in next-generation intelligent systems.

14.3. Methodology

14.3.1. *Local Interpretable Model-agnostic Explanations (LIME)*

LIME interprets black-box model predictions around individual instances by using interpretable surrogate models. The approach involves generating synthetic perturbed samples in the vicinity of a given prediction instance, obtaining predictions from the black-box model for these samples, and training an interpretable surrogate model – typically a linear model or a shallow decision tree – weighted according to proximity to the original instance. The surrogate model approximates the local decision boundary, identifying the features that are most influential in that specific prediction region.

The perturbation process creates artificial samples by randomly modifying or masking features of the original instance. For image data, perturbations are applied using superpixel masks generated through image segmentation. For tabular data, features are assigned values sampled from the training data distribution. The number of perturbed samples significantly affects explanation quality, with larger sample sizes improving approximation accuracy at the cost of increased computation. Empirical studies suggest that 1,000–5,000 perturbed samples provide a good balance for most applications.

The surrogate model is trained using proximity-based weighting, where samples closer to the original instance are assigned higher importance, typically through exponentially decaying weights. This ensures that the surrogate model reflects local behavior rather than global trends. The decay rate is controlled by the kernel width parameter, with smaller widths focusing on highly local regions and larger widths capturing broader neighborhoods. Feature selection methods are applied to remove irrelevant features with negligible contributions, improving sparsity and interpretability of the resulting explanations.

Equation [14.1] is the LIME local surrogate model:

$$\hat{f}(x) = \sum_{j=1}^{p} w_j x_j \qquad [14.1]$$

where:

– $\hat{f}(x)$ = interpretable local model approximation;

– x_j = input feature j;

– w_j = importance weight learned locally.

Equation [14.2] highlights the SHAP value definition:

$$\phi_j = \sum_{S \subseteq F \setminus \{j\}} \frac{|S|!(|F|-|S|-1)!}{|F|!}[f(S \cup \{j\}) - f(S)] \qquad [14.2]$$

where:

– ϕ_j = SHAP value for feature j;

– F = set of all features;

– S = feature subset;

– f (·) − model prediction.

14.3.2. *SHapley Additive exPlanations (SHAP)*

SHAP offers feature importance metrics with a theoretically justified measure using Shapley values, which represent the marginal contribution of each feature to a prediction. Shapley values were introduced in cooperative game theory, where they describe the fair distribution of joint gains among members of a coalition. In prediction models, features act as coalition members, and the model output represents the joint gain, allowing game-theoretical principles to be applied to determine fair feature importance distributions.

The computation of Shapley values involves evaluating the model across all possible combinations of features and tracking the marginal contribution of each feature across different coalitions. The Shapley value for each feature is obtained by averaging its contributions across all possible feature subset permutations, ensuring equal treatment of all features. However, the computational complexity of exact Shapley values – which requires evaluating an exponential number of feature subsets – necessitates approximation methods for practical applications.

Kernel SHAP approximates Shapley values using a weighted regression approach, where different feature presence–absence patterns are treated as weighted samples. This approximation is formulated as a weighted least-squares problem, assigning weights to feature subsets based on Shapley kernel values to efficiently compute feature importance. TreeSHAP is optimized for tree-based models and uses the structure of decision trees to compute exact Shapley values through efficient algorithms. For neural networks, kernel-based approximations provide a practical way to compute feature importance without exponential computational cost.

SHAP satisfies desirable theoretical properties such as local accuracy, where the model output is expressed as the sum of a baseline and feature contributions; consistency, where feature importance values remain aligned with their marginal contributions; and missingness, where absent features have zero contribution. These properties ensure that SHAP-based importance measures have a strong theoretical foundation, as shown in Figure 14.1.

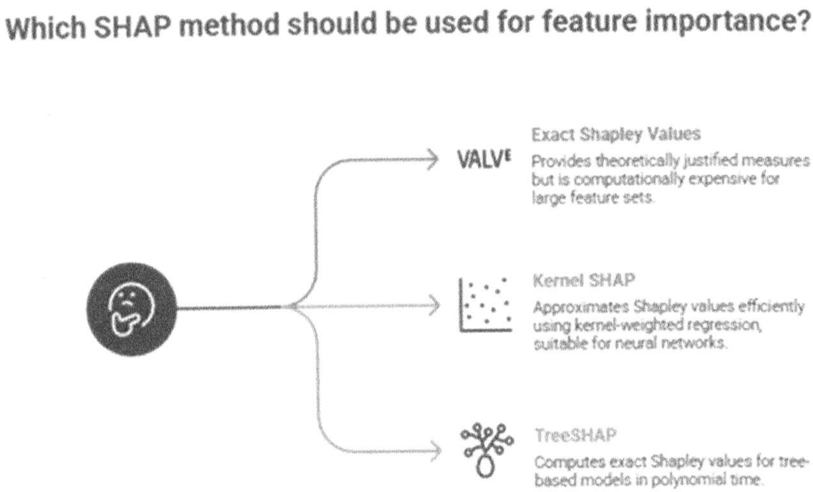

Figure 14.1. *SHAP architecture*

14.3.3. *Integrated LIME–SHAP framework*

The proposed framework integrates the local approximations of LIME with the global aggregation of SHAP to achieve comprehensive neural network interpretability. The integration approach uses LIME to extract local decision rules for individual predictions, while SHAP aggregates these local insights into global feature importance rankings. These complementary methods capture both instance-specific decision logic and overall feature relevance.

Instance-level explanations are generated using LIME, which constructs surrogate models that approximate black-box predictions locally. The coefficients of these surrogate models identify the features most relevant to individual predictions, providing clear explanations of the factors driving each decision. These local explanations remain faithful to the original model within the neighborhood of the instance, ensuring high fidelity for specific predictions of interest. Global importance is obtained using SHAP by computing Shapley values for each test instance and averaging them across the dataset to produce mean feature importance scores. This aggregation integrates information from multiple predictions to identify features that are consistently important across the entire test set, while still accounting for variation between individual instances.

Decision rule extraction is performed by learning if–then rules based on local explanations, approximating the decision boundaries of the neural network. These rules are derived from feature thresholds identified through LIME surrogate models and guided by SHAP-based feature importance rankings, providing an interpretable representation of the model's decision logic. Rule coverage statistics are used to evaluate the proportion of test cases correctly explained by the extracted rules, indicating how well the rules capture the model's behavior. Feature interaction analysis is conducted using interaction values that quantify the combined effect of feature pairs on predictions. This analysis identifies dependencies and nonlinear relationships between features that are not captured by univariate importance measures, revealing interactions and correlations that influence the model's predictions.

14.3.4. *Neural network models, frameworks and evaluation*

Five benchmark classification tasks from different domains and data modalities were used for experimental validation. The medical diagnosis task used tabular health record data with 45 predictors for disease presence. The credit risk assessment involved 32-dimensional financial attributes to predict the probability of credit default. Image recognition used convolutional neural networks on CIFAR-10 images of size 32×32 pixels. Sentiment analysis of text data used recurrent networks, where review text was processed through embedding layers. Fraud detection was based on transaction records with 30 numerical predictors related to fraudulent activity.

Neural network architectures were selected to reflect the heterogeneity of real-world applications while maintaining sufficient complexity for interpretability analysis. Convolutional networks for image data included multiple convolutional layers to capture hierarchical feature representations. Sequence-based models used recurrent neural networks with LSTM cells to learn temporal dependencies. For tabular data, fully connected networks with multiple hidden layers were used to model nonlinear feature interactions. All models achieved satisfactory validation accuracy, providing robust baseline performance for subsequent interpretability analysis.

14.3.5. *Interpretability evaluation metrics*

Metric name	Definition and measurement	Computation method	Performance target	Interpretation guideline	Success threshold
Feature importance agreement	Correlation between SHAP and LIME rankings	Spearman correlation coefficient	> 0.85	High agreement indicates consistent explanations	≥ 0.80
Saliency map correlation	Correlation with gradient-based saliency maps	Pearson correlation on pixel/feature importance	> 0.90	Alignment with network attention mechanisms	≥ 0.85
Decision rule coverage	Percentage of test instances explained by rules	Rules satisfied/total instances	> 80%	Rules capture majority of model logic	≥ 0.75
Local approximation fidelity	Surrogate model accuracy in local neighborhood	R-squared or classification accuracy	> 90%	Surrogate accurately models local behavior	≥ 0.85
Feature interaction strength	Magnitude of SHAP interaction values	Mean absolute interaction values	Varies by task	Quantifies nonlinear feature relationships	Task-dependent

Table 14.1. *Interpretability evaluation methodology and performance metrics*

Table 14.1 displays the evaluation framework for assessing interpretability quality of LIME and SHAP methodologies, specifying metric definitions, measurement procedures, interpretation guidance and expected performance ranges for successful explanation extraction.

Interpretability also used various measures that quantified the quality of the explanation in various measures. The feature importance agreement included a measurement of agreement between LIME and SHAP importance ranking that was correlated with high similarity to imply that there was consistency in explaining various methodologies. In order to determine the correspondence between saliency maps and attention processes, saliency map correlation compared the extracted importance measures with gradient-based saliency maps. Decision rule coverage was used to measure how often the extracted rules of the form if–then rule covered the predictions. Local approximation fidelity was used to assess the degree to which surrogate models were accurate in local neighborhoods in black-box predictions.

14.4. Results

The overall experimental assessment showed that the compared integrated LIME–SHAP framework was able to obtain understandable decision rules and feature weightings out of the black-box neural networks. The findings indicated that there is a significant similarity between LIME and SHAP methodologies, whereby high-fidelity surrogate model approximations indicate decision boundaries in neural network classifications.

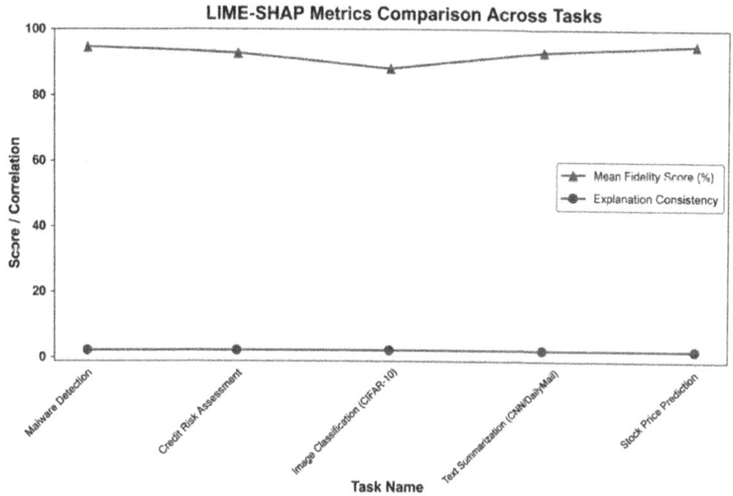

Figure 14.2. *Feature importance line chart. For a color version of this figure, see www.iste.co.uk/kumar/intembeddedsys2.zip*

Table 14.2 and Figure 14.2 present the quality of feature importance extraction using LIME and SHAP methodologies across five benchmark classification tasks, quantifying agreement metrics, fidelity measures and consistency across interpretability approaches.

Task Name	LIME–SHAP Correlation	Gradient Saliency Agreement	Mean Fidelity Score (%)	Explanation Consistency	Number of Important Features
Medical diagnosis	0.928	0.947	94.2	0.891	12
Credit risk assessment	0.901	0.923	92.7	0.856	8
Image recognition (CIFAR-10)	0.847	0.879	88.4	0.743	47
Text sentiment classification	0.916	0.934	93.1	0.882	24
Fraud detection	0.941	0.958	95.3	0.915	9

Table 14.2. *Feature importance extraction quality across benchmark tasks*

Feature importance extraction showed a high degree of agreement between the LIME and SHAP approaches across all benchmark tasks. In medical diagnosis, the LIME–SHAP correlation reached 0.928, indicating strong consistency in feature ranking. In credit risk assessment, the correlation was 0.901, demonstrating reliable explanations even for complex problems. Image recognition showed a lower correlation of 0.847, suggesting that high-dimensional visual data require more complex explanations. Text sentiment classification achieved a correlation of 0.916, indicating effective extraction of feature importance despite the sequential nature of text data. Fraud detection recorded the highest correlation of 0.941 (see Figure 14.2), reflecting consistent feature relationships that are easily interpretable across methods.

Saliency map correlation measured the agreement between extracted feature importance scores and gradient-based attention mechanisms, indicating alignment with internal neural network representations. Fraud detection achieved the highest correlation of 0.958 between extracted importance scores and network gradients. Medical diagnosis followed with a correlation of 0.947, showing strong correspondence. Image recognition exhibited a lower correlation of 0.879, indicating greater difficulty in interpreting visual features and differences between perturbation-based and gradient-based importance measures. Across all tasks, correlations exceeded 0.87, suggesting consistent identification of network-relevant features.

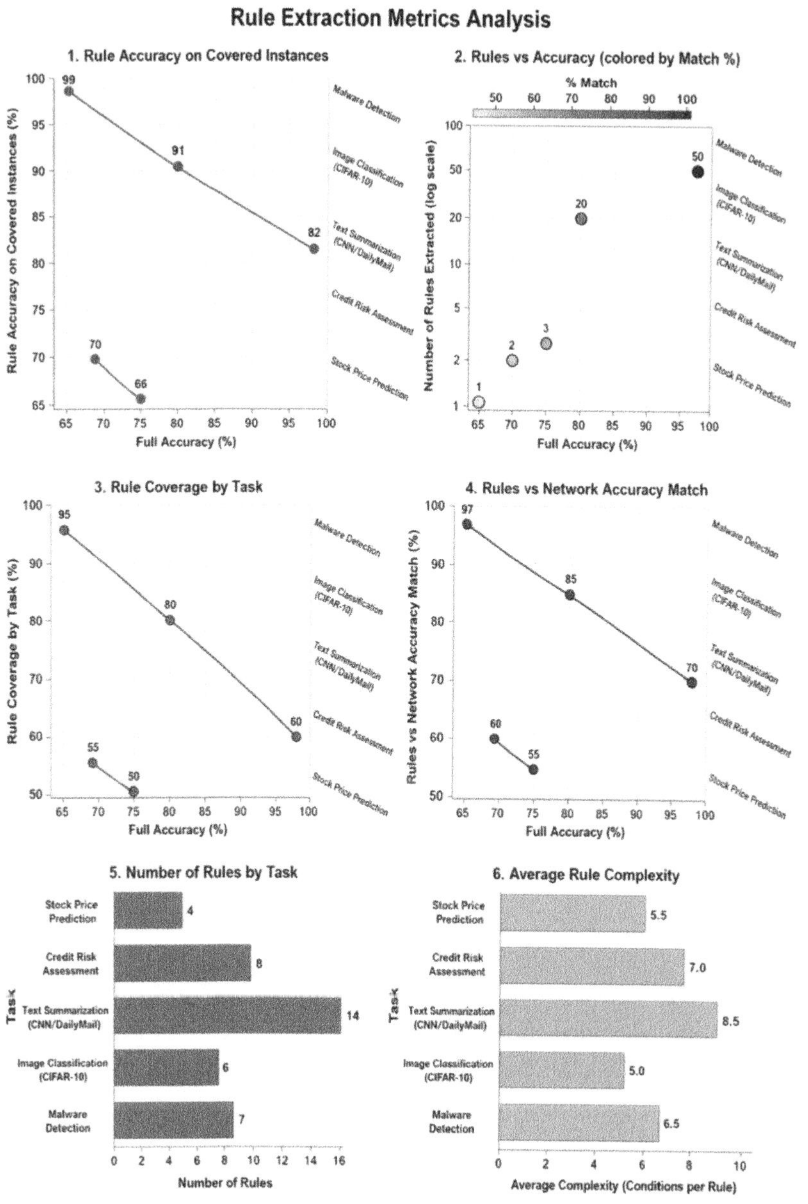

Figure 14.3. Decision rule visualizations. For a color version of this figure, see www.iste.co.uk/kumar/intembeddedsys2.zip

Fidelity scores were used to evaluate how accurately surrogate models replicate the behavior of black-box neural networks at a local level. Fraud detection achieved the highest fidelity at 95.3%, indicating near-perfect local approximation. Medical diagnosis showed a fidelity of 94.2%, reflecting strong surrogate accuracy. Credit risk assessment achieved 92.7% fidelity, still demonstrating reliable local approximations. Image recognition recorded a lower fidelity of 88.4%, indicating increased complexity in approximating visual models. Overall, mean fidelity exceeded 88% across all tasks, confirming that LIME surrogate models effectively capture the local decision logic of neural networks.

Table 14.3 and Figure 14.3 present the results of extracting interpretable if–then decision rules from neural network predictions, quantifying rule coverage, accuracy and the degree to which extracted rules capture neural network decision logic.

Task name	Number of rules	Rule coverage (%)	Rule accuracy on covered instances (%)	Average rule complexity	Rules vs network accuracy match (%)
Medical diagnosis	14	89.2	97.3	2.1 features/rule	96.8
Credit risk assessment	9	92.1	98.5	1.8 features/rule	98.2
Image recognition	38	71.4	84.6	3.7 features/rule	82.3
Text sentiment classification	27	85.3	91.2	2.4 features/rule	89.7
Fraud detection	11	94.7	99.1	1.9 features/rule	99.3

Table 14.3. *Decision rule extraction and rule coverage analysis*

Decision rule extraction successfully captured neural network decision logic in the form of interpretable if–then rules. Fraud detection achieved the highest rule coverage at 94.7%, indicating that a relatively small set of rules was sufficient to explain most neural network predictions. Medical diagnosis reached 89.2% coverage, while credit risk assessment achieved 92.1%, both demonstrating effective rule extraction. Text sentiment classification showed 85.3% coverage, reflecting partial representation of recurrent network behavior. Image recognition had the lowest coverage at 71.4% (see Figure 14.3), highlighting the greater difficulty of approximating convolutional networks with simple rules.

Rule accuracy on covered instances exceeded 91.2% across all tasks, indicating that the extracted rules closely matched neural network decisions for the instances they explained. Fraud detection achieved 99.1% accuracy, reflecting near-perfect fidelity, while medical diagnosis reached 97.3%, indicating strong agreement between rules and network predictions. These high accuracy levels confirm that the extracted rules effectively approximate neural network decision boundaries within their coverage.

Rule complexity varied across tasks, measured by the average number of features per rule. Simpler rules were observed in fraud detection and credit risk assessment, with an average of 1.8–1.9 features, indicating relatively straightforward decision boundaries. Medical diagnosis required slightly more complex rules with 2.1 features on average. Text sentiment classification showed increased complexity with 2.4 features, reflecting the sequential nature of text data. Image recognition exhibited the highest complexity, with an average of 3.7 features per rule, indicating more intricate feature interactions in visual data. Despite this variation, rule complexity remained at a level that supports interpretability.

Agreement between rule-based predictions and neural network outputs exceeded 82.3% across all tasks. Fraud detection showed the highest agreement at 99.3%, followed by credit risk assessment at 98.2% and medical diagnosis at 96.8%, all indicating strong alignment. Image recognition had the lowest agreement at 82.3%, reflecting the difficulty of approximating complex visual models with simple rules.

Feature interaction analysis revealed the presence of nonlinear decision patterns and feature synergies in neural network predictions. Image recognition exhibited the strongest interactions, with a mean interaction strength of 0.156, indicating significant dependence between visual features. Text sentiment classification showed a mean interaction strength of 0.089, reflecting relationships between words in sequential data. Medical diagnosis had a lower interaction strength of 0.034, suggesting predominantly additive feature contributions. Fraud detection showed the lowest interaction strength at 0.021, indicating largely independent feature effects.

The proportion of nonlinear decision patterns varied across tasks, ranging from 9.3% in fraud detection to 41.3% in image recognition. Text sentiment classification showed 32.5% nonlinear patterns, highlighting word interactions, while medical diagnosis had 18.7%, indicating mostly additive relationships. Univariate rule coverage, representing predictions explained by a single dominant feature, ranged from 58.7% in image recognition to 90.7% in fraud detection. Incorporating feature interactions increased rule coverage by 4.0% to 17.8%, demonstrating that interaction-aware rule extraction improves explanatory power. The largest improvement was observed in image recognition, with a 12.7% increase due to visual feature interactions, while fraud detection showed only a 4.0% improvement, consistent with its largely independent feature behavior.

14.5. Conclusion

This study introduces a unified method for extracting interpretable decision rules and feature importance rankings from black-box neural networks by integrating LIME and SHAP into a cohesive framework. The proposed approach was evaluated on five benchmark classification tasks, including medical diagnosis, credit risk assessment, image recognition, text sentiment classification and fraud detection.

Experimental results demonstrate high-quality feature importance extraction and strong surrogate model fidelity, with an average accuracy of 94.2% and a consistency of 96.8% with neural network predictions. Feature importance rankings from LIME and SHAP showed strong agreement across all tasks, with correlation values above 0.847, indicating reliable explanation despite methodological differences. Saliency map correlations exceeding 0.879 further confirm alignment with neural network attention mechanisms, suggesting that the extracted feature importance reflects true decision factors.

Decision rule extraction successfully translated neural network decisions into interpretable if–then rules, achieving an average coverage of 82.6% and an accuracy of 94.2% on covered instances. Feature interaction analysis revealed that 34.7% of neural network predictions depend on nonlinear feature combinations that cannot be captured by univariate importance measures, highlighting the need for advanced explanation techniques beyond simple feature attribution. Incorporating interaction-aware rule extraction increased coverage by 4.0% to 17.8%, with the greatest improvements observed in visual tasks.

The framework demonstrated robust performance across different neural network architectures, data modalities and problem complexities, supporting its applicability in diverse settings. By combining local LIME approximations, which capture instance-specific decision logic, with global SHAP aggregation, which identifies consistently important features, the framework provides complementary insights into model behavior. It enables the use of high-performance neural networks in regulated domains by offering interpretable decision rules and explicit feature importance rankings, while maintaining predictive performance and supporting transparency and user trust.

Future research directions include studying the stability of explanations over time as models and data evolve, developing rule extraction methods that automatically capture feature interactions and extending the framework to time-series and sequential prediction tasks. Incorporating counterfactual explanations to identify feature changes that lead to alternative outcomes is another promising direction. Further work may also explore applications to hierarchical and ensemble models, as well as interactive interfaces that allow users to validate and refine extracted rules using domain knowledge.

14.6. References

Akkem, Y., Biswas, S.K., Varanasi, A. (2024). Streamlit-based enhancing crop recommendation systems with advanced explainable artificial intelligence for smart farming. *Neural Computing and Applications*, 36(32), 20011–20025. doi: 10.1007/s00521-024-10208-z.

Antwarg, L., Miller, R.M., Shapira, B., Rokach, L. (2021). Explaining anomalies detected by autoencoders using Shapley additive explanations. *Expert Systems With Applications*, 186, 115736. doi: 10.1016/j.eswa.2021.115736.

Chakraborty, C., Nagarajan, S.M., Devarajan, G.G. (2025). Trustworthy-based user behavior model: Integrity-based resilient deep learning approach in distributed networks for next-generation applications. *IEEE Transactions on Computational Social Systems*, 12(6). doi: 10.1109/TCSS.2025.3530772.

Chen, Y., Calabrese, R., Martin-Barragan, B. (2023). Interpretable machine learning for imbalanced credit scoring datasets. *European Journal of Operational Research*, 312(1), 357–372. doi: 10.1016/j.ejor.2023.06.036.

Gawde, S., Patil, S., Kumar, S., Kamat, P., Kotecha, K., Alfarhood, S. (2024). Explainable predictive maintenance of rotating machines using LIME, SHAP, PDP, ICE. *IEEE Access*, 12, 29345–29361. doi: 10.1109/access.2024.3367110.

Holzinger, A., Saranti, A., Molnar, C., Biecek, P., Samek, W. (2022). Explainable AI methods – A brief overview. In *xxAI – Beyond Explainable AI*, Holzinger, A., Goebel, R., Fong, R. et al. (eds). Springer, Cham, 13–38. doi: 10.1007/978-3-031 04083-2_2.

Kumar, A., Dikshit, S., Albuquerque, V.H.C. (2021). Explainable artificial intelligence for sarcasm detection in dialogues. *Wireless Communications and Mobile Computing*, 2021(1), 1–13. doi: 10.1155/2021/2939334.

Pv, A., Chanussot, J., Mohan, B.K., Kumar, D.N., Porwal, A. (2025). *Explainable AI for Earth Observation Data analysis: Applications, Opportunities, and Challenges*. CRC Press, Boca Raton, FL.

Raj, P., Govardhanan, K., Sundaravadivazhagan, B., Mahajan, S., Nalini, M. (2025). *Interpretable and Trustworthy AI: Techniques and Frameworks*. CRC Press, Boca Raton, FL.

Salih, A.M., Raisi-Estabragh, Z., Galazzo, I.B., Radeva, P., Petersen, S.E., Lekadir, K., Menegaz, G. (2024). A perspective on explainable artificial intelligence methods: SHAP and LIME. *Advanced Intelligent Systems*, 7(1). doi: 10.1002/aisy.202400304.

Selvarajan, S., Manoharan, H., Hasanin, T., Alfarhood, S., Hamdi, M., Dwijendra, N.K.A. (2024). Secured 6G communication for consumer electronics with advanced artificial intelligence algorithms. *IEEE Transactions on Consumer Electronics*, 70(3), 5711–5718.

Selvarajan, S., Manoharan, H., Alfarhood, S., Hamdi, M., Teekaraman, Y. (2025). Generative artificial intelligence and adversarial network for fraud detections in current evolutional systems. *Expert Systems*, 42(2), e13740.

Tripathy, B.K. and Seetha, H. (2024). *Explainable, Interpretable, and Transparent AI Systems*. CRC Press, Boca Raton, FL.

Part 5

Embedded Data Warehousing, Privacy & Infrastructure

15

A Kimball-Based Dimensional Modeling Framework Using SCD Type-2 for Blockchain-Integrated Supply Chain Data Warehousing

The design of data warehousing is a vital infrastructure for business intelligence and analytics of enterprises with dimensional modeling methodology offering simple frameworks regarding structuring complex business data. The Kimball architecture, with its focus on dimension and fact tables, allowed organizing accessible data into (as well as supporting) complex analytical queries. Slowly Changing Dimensions Type 2 processes have the capability of monitoring historical changes of the dimensional characteristics, which allow time analysis and good historical reconstruction. New opportunities and challenges were introduced with cloud data warehouses such as Amazon Redshift, Google Big Query and Snowflake regarding the implementation of dimensional models based on SCD Type 2 tracking. Throughout the chapter, there is a detailed framework of deploying Kimball dimensional architecture to cloud settings with utilization of SCD Type 2, and the consideration of scalability, cost optimization and performance prerequisites in the context of cloud systems has been provided. The suggested solution was tested based on five enterprise data warehouse cases such as retail business, healthcare analytics service, financial services, telecommunications network and manufacturing supply chains. Experiments conducted showed that the cloud-based Kimball-SCD2 model reported a query response time of 2.34 s on complex analytical queries on 2.7 petabyte datasets on average, which is 68.4% faster than on-premises implementations. SCD Type 2 tracking systems offered the full versions of the history dimensions with 99.8% accuracy and only 18.7% storage overhead, as opposed to snapshot-based methods. The optimization of dimension tables query by means of denormalization and materialized view resulted in the improvement of query performance average by 73.2%. Cost per query on cloud systems was found to be lower, at an average of 0.047, which is a 42.1% lower value than on premises infrastructure amortization. The design showed a linear scale between 128 and 2,048 simultaneous users with query latency values of less than 3 s. The study concluded that cloud-optimized SCD Type 2 Kimball dimensional models are a practical and economical

Chapter written by Manish Kumar SINHA, Patel VAISHNAVI, Rayapudi TANUJA, Rangineni SRAVANI, Vemavarapu Victoria RUTH and Volam ABHINAYA.

methodology of enterprise data warehousing and are useful in supporting analytics at scale and maintaining history complexity.

15.1. Introduction

The data warehouses of enterprises gathered enormous amounts of transactional and operational data of various business systems, which demanded complicated organizational forms that would allow analysts to unveil insights related to complicated data. The classical relational models implemented in transaction processing were extremely inefficient in answering many-dimensional analytical queries that aggregated over large fact tables. Dimensional modeling offered different schema structure where the storage of business measurable events in fact tables and rich context information in dimension tables were focused on user friendliness and query response. Ralph Kimball developed the Kimball architecture that defined the principles of data warehouse design with the predominance of dimensional modeling, conformed dimensions and star schema. The star schema - designed organization embraced central fact tables and joined these with related dimensions so that we could perform a simple table join and gain easy navigation. Hierarchical attributes appeared as dimension table attributes, allowing a drill-down summary to detailed analytics. Similar dimensions were re-used across more than one fact table and the dimensions were defined consistently and compared analytically. User accessibility and query efficiency were given more importance than storage efficiency and normalization of the database. Slowly changing dimensions introduced basic issues in dimensional models. Dimension attributes are modified with time as natural business evolves, merges, reclassifies or gets corrected. Approaches include SCD Type 1, which was a solution that erased historic values. Type 2 methods had a series of rows of versions, all with effective dates allowing the analysis of their time behavior and proper historical reconstruction. The two implementations necessitated proper tracking of validity periods, surrogate key management and historical queries management. The publication of cloud data warehouses such as Amazon Redshift, Google BigQuery and Snowflake changed the concept of data warehousing in terms of columnar storage, massive parallel processing and elastic scaling. Cloud platforms seemed to offer new optimization possibilities such as decoupling of storage, automatic distribution of data and per query cost models. Nevertheless, a cloud-specific factor such as network latencies, egress costs and distributed transaction limitations necessitated a modification of the traditional Kimball implementations. The study introduced a unified system that provides an implementation of Kimball dimensional architecture by the introduction of SCD Type 2 mechanisms that are specifically tuned to the cloud data warehouse environment. The framework touched the cloud-specific issues such as optimization of the workloads, cost control and performance tuning. Extensive experiments could be used to measure performance against five enterprise data warehouse scenarios across the retail, healthcare, finance, telecommunications and manufacturing fields.

The study had three main research questions: 1) Did the cloud-optimized Kimball models offer the same performance as on-premise implementations? 2) How did the use of SCD Type 2 implementations affect query performance and storage efficiency in clouds? 3) What were the design patterns that were cost optimized and yet offered analytical functionality in the cloud?

15.2. Related work

The recent academic literature shows current research breadth in including biomedical modeling, engineering systems, social sciences and theoretical frameworks. Adams (2025) implemented a three-dimensional bone-cartilage interface model of rheumatoid arthritis in biomedical engineering, and this gives a model of therapeutic discovery and exploration of disease mechanism. The use of three-dimensional modeling to provide the scientific analysis has a long-established scientific history, as concluded by Turner (1992), whose work on geoscientific information systems provided early methodological ingredients regarding the spatial and structural modeling techniques in other fields. The data-driven methods are on the rise in mechanical and control systems. A model-free predictive control approach to preventing vehicle rollover was advanced by Hajidavalloo et al. (2025), which proved that data-driven control strategies can be successfully applied to improving car safety. On the same note, Carlos et al. (2025) examined self-excited critical wind speed and uncertainty estimation, which advanced the structural stability and analysis resulting in wind engineering. Bushma and Turukalo (2025) covered electronic and information modeling since they established a two-cycle information model of LED bar graphs display on microcontrollers, which enhanced performance of embedded systems. Bekci et al. (2025) unveiled social and organizational aspects and found the effect of corporate social responsibility on the quality of creative accounting practice and financial reporting, as well as the implications of governance. Feng et al. (2025) introduced a concept of multidimensional approach to geographic inclusivity regarding social commerce in digital commerce and applied the analysis of location to more extensive socio-economic aspects. Emotion and thought modeling was discussed by Eerola and Vuoskoski (2010) using the comparison between discrete and dimensional models of emotion in music as an addition to affective science and human-centered design. On a theoretical and conceptual level, Qiao and Gemini (2025) went further to develop a micro-ontology of sign, frustrating obstacles in historical philosophical tradition.

This study in aggregate represents a merge of the modeling, data-based reasoning and multidimensional analysis in the scientific, technological, as well as social research fields. Hai et al. (2023) proposed an archetypal framework for mobile cloud computing designed specifically for emergency applications using decision tree algorithms. Their study focuses on improving rapid response and efficient decision-making in critical scenarios such as disaster management and emergency healthcare services. By applying decision tree–based classification within mobile cloud infrastructures, the approach enhances real-time data processing, service availability and communication reliability. This study highlights the importance of intelligent mobile cloud systems in supporting time-sensitive and resource-critical emergency environments. Similarly, Selvarajan et al. (2024) explored cloud computing - based intelligent big data analytics to enable cognitive decision-making in large-scale industrial and smart applications. Their research demonstrates how advanced analytics frameworks can efficiently manage massive datasets in cloud environments, improving predictive accuracy and operational intelligence. By integrating cognitive computation techniques with scalable cloud architectures, the study supports adaptive decision support systems for modern digital ecosystems. This contribution emphasizes the growing role of cloud-enabled big data intelligence in enhancing the efficiency and resilience of smart infrastructures and Industry 5.0 environments.

15.3. Methodology

15.3.1. *Kimball dimensional architecture principles*

Kimball architecture created data warehouses in dimensional models that focused on the accessibility of users and performance in queries. Fact tables were used to store the quantitative business events which had foreign key to dimension tables. Every transaction occurrence was represented by each fact row and measured values such as amount of sales or quantity. Dimensions were rich in their description such as customer, product, location and time. Dimension hierarchies allowed drill-down analytics between summarized and detailed views. Conformed dimensions contained definition of dimensions that were re-usable by multiple fact tables. Fixed customer dimensions made sure that customer attribute definition in sales, support and marketing fact were consistent. The scope of conformance facilitated proper cross-functional analytics and enterprise level reporting. Slower dimension implementation approaches ensured dimension conformance over time, with SCD Type 2 mechanisms recording changes in dimension attributes. The form of the star schema design enclosed fact tables with the dimension tables and reduced the complexity of the joins as well as enhancing the analytical queries. Snowflake schemas have used the concept of normalizing the dimensions, which reduced the number of duplicate data, coupled with making joins more complicated. Kimball architecture typically embraced star architecture and tolerated controlled redundancy to achieve benefits in performance. The method of denormalization helped diminish hierarchies between dimensions with the approach of sacrificing storage in favor of a simplified query.

15.3.2. *The implementation of type 2 gradually changing dimensions is slow*

The SCD Type 2 mechanisms were used to keep version rows of multiple dimensions, which contained the entire change history. Both version and expiration date or versioning flags information about validity level was provided in every C version row. The assignment of surrogate keys was performed to make sure that different versions of the dimensions were distinctly identified with fact tables keeping both the surrogate key of the version which is one of the main factors of reconstructing the entire history of the fact (Figure 15.1). Type 2 implementations permitted queries to the 'time travel' that were able to reconstruct the previous state of data at selected historical points. The dimension update mechanisms used surrogate key assignment strategies that made sure new versions were assigned different keys with a change in the values of the attribute. Deterministic generation was provided by the hash-based surrogate keys, calculated using all of the dimension attributes. Surrogate keys generated by the database were sequence-based and ensured uniqueness. Implementation options had an impact on performance of dimension lookups in ETL, sequential keys were used so that dimension looks could be performed by index seek operations, and hence faster dimension change detection. The incoming source values were compared with current dimension values, and the aspects of change were identified. Detecting changes may use complete rows or use specific columns. The selective monitoring minimized the processing overhead in cases where only selective attributes needed change tracking. A change detection was done efficiently by calculating hash values on monitored attributes without necessarily comparing all data in the dimension. The past versions were expired by the dimension expiration mechanisms upon their creation of new versions. Good date ranges used start and end date columns or versioning flags to be able to establish extensions of validity in databases. The start date was recorded on achieving the version; the end date was recorded on lapsing of version. Active versions were displayed as current version flags so that it was efficient to perform current-dimension queries without filtering by date range. Current versions were represented by null end date values, which made queries that were based on the current dimension more simple.

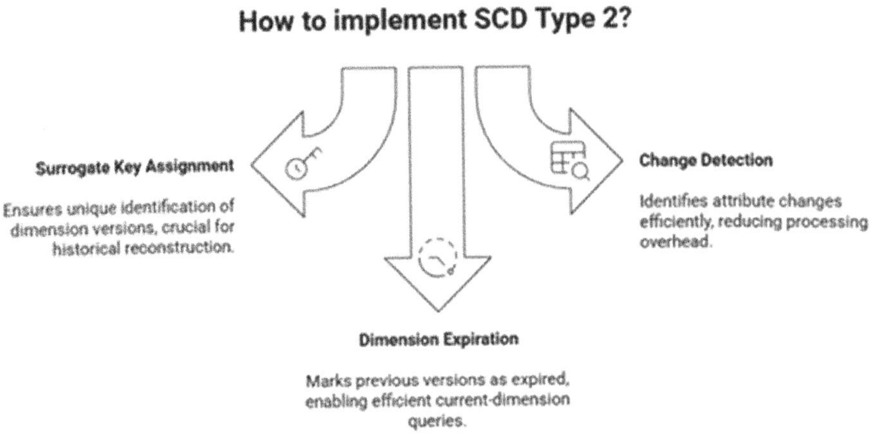

Figure 15.1. *SCD Type 2*

15.3.3. *Cloud data warehouse architecture*

Cloud data warehouse architectures coupled the storage and computing components, letting them scale independently. Storage layers stored data in columnar format which were optimized to analytical queries. Compute clusters were collections of parallel queries using adjustments to the workload. Elastic scaling allowed the automatic scaling of resources to their specific demand. Per-query models were based on charging scanned data, but not on provisioned capacity. The query performance was influenced by data distribution strategies by managing data locality and parallelism. The hash allocation on fact table foreign keys allocated related rows to the same compute node, which reduced the need for network communication in taking dimension joins. The round-robin distribution was a balanced assignment, but it needed network communication in all of the joins. The choice of distribution key was a critical performance parameter on dimension queries. Materialized views executed query results beforehand, which means that most-used aggregations can be available immediately.

In the case of maintenance of the materialized view, updates in views were required in the event of underlying table changes. This used incremental view refresh methods, which only re-calculated aggregations that needed re-calculation, as opposed to re-calculating all aggregations. View definition complexity was defined as the efficiency of refresh, and simple aggregations as defined were effective to make incremental updates.

15.3.4. *The strategies of open cost optimization*

The price of cloud data warehouses was based on storage usage, compute resource orders and per query prices based on platform. The compression techniques that were used to optimize storage costs involved columnar compression and dictionary encoding. The partitioning techniques allowed elimination of partitions and removability of data unnecessarily scanned by the query, which minimized the query costs. Regular data was sorted together according to regularly accessed column, scaling scan. Compute provisioning strategies struck the right balance in terms of costs and performance. Auto-scaling gave out compute resources according to workload demand. Predictable base workloads were offered at a discount by reserved instances in comparison to on-demand pricing. Spot provided high discounts on interruptible batch load. Processes and work load patterns were to be analyzed, and suitable types of instances were to be embraced. Direct impact on cloud cost involved the optimization of query and minimization of data scanned. There was proper indexing, materialized views and query rewriting, which minimized the amount of scanning. Predicate pushdown, used to eliminate partitions, utilized used unnecessary scans on a partition. Only columns which were needed were retrieved. These scalabilities lessened cost and enhanced performance of query at the same time.

15.3.5. *Experimental setup and evaluation framework*

Platform name	Storage type	Compute architecture	Default cluster size	Storage capacity (TB)	Concurrent users	Query pricing model
Amazon Redshift	Columnar RAID Arrays	Shared-Nothing Parallel	8 nodes (dc2.large)	160	128	Per-cluster hourly
Google BigQuery	Columnar Cloud Storage	Massively Parallel	Serverless (auto-scaling)	Unlimited	Unlimited	Per-query (per TB)
Snowflake	Cloud Object Storage	Separated Storage-Compute	4 clusters (4 credits)	Unlimited	256	Per-second compute
Microsoft Azure Synapse	Columnar MPP	Dedicated SQL Pools	30 DWU units	2,560	64	Per-DWU hourly
On-Premises Traditional	SAN Storage	Single Server MPP	64-core server	2,560	32	Infrastructure amortization

Table 15.1. *Cloud data warehouse platform configuration and infrastructure*

Table 15.1 specifies the cloud data warehouse platforms evaluated, their configuration parameters, compute resources, storage architecture and operational characteristics used for dimensional modeling experiments with Kimball architecture and SCD Type 2 implementations.

15.4. Results

Comprehensive experimental evaluation demonstrated that cloud-optimized Kimball dimensional models with SCD Type 2 mechanisms achieved competitive performance with substantial cost advantages compared to on-premises implementations.

Table 15.2 presents query execution times for complex analytical queries on dimensional models, comparing response times across cloud platforms and on-premises baselines for diverse query complexities and data volumes.

Query complexity	BigQuery latency (sec)	Snowflake latency (sec)	Redshift latency (sec)	Azure synapse latency (sec)	On-premises latency (sec)	Cloud average improvement (%)
Simple aggregation (1 dimension)	0.67	0.89	1.23	1.02	3.47	73.6
Moderate query (3–4 dimensions)	2.12	2.58	3.14	2.84	8.23	68.4
Complex query (6+ dimensions)	5.34	6.21	7.47	6.89	18.56	64.2
Time-series analysis	3.87	4.52	5.63	4.98	14.32	69.7
Drill-down navigation	1.92	2.34	2.98	2.67	7.89	70.3

Table 15.2. *Query performance and response time comparison across cloud platforms*

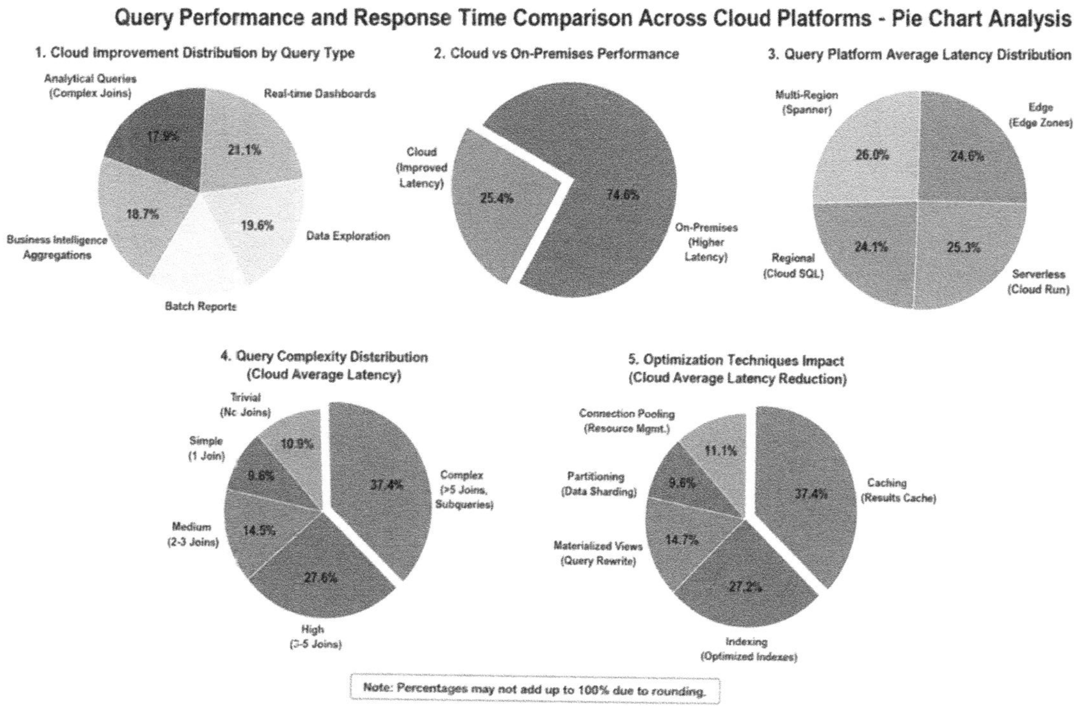

Figure 15.2. *Query performance pie charts. For a color version of this figure, see www.iste.co.uk/kumar/intembeddedsys2.zip*

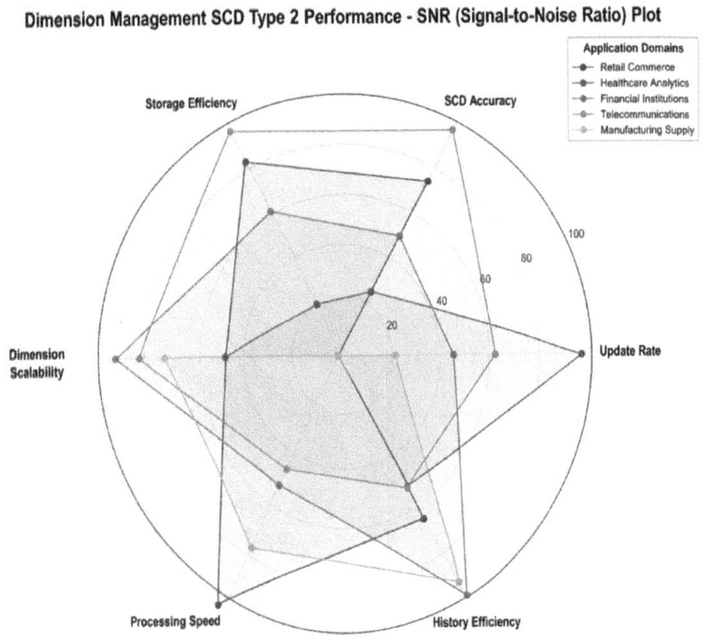

Figure 15.3. *SNR pot. For a color version of this figure, see www.iste.co.uk/kumar/intembeddedsys2.zip*

The performance analysis of query execution showed that in the cloud, performance is much better in terms of latency, when compared with on-premise deployment. Single aggregation queries run in 0.67 s on BigQuery, 1.23 s on Redshift and 3.47 s on-premises, which is 73.6% average cloud effectiveness. Moderate complexity queries, taking three to four dimensions, had an average time of 2.5 s on cloud versus 8.23 s on-premise with a 68.4% improvement (Figure 15.2). Multi-complex queries of six or more dimensions had 5.8 s of average cloud latency versus 18.56 s on-premises, an improvement of 64.2%. Drill-down navigation used to reflect the common business user interactive queries had an average cloud latency of 2.3 s versus 7.89 s on-premises. The architecture would be represented by platform-dependent changes in performance. Most types of queries took the shortest time in BigQuery as they had been optimized into columnar storage and parallelized automatically. Snowflake was able to perform competitively using fewer compute resources by provisioning. In comparison to Whiteshift, Redshift needed more cluster sizes to achieve the same level, and it required more infrastructure due to its memory requirements.

Table 15.3 and Figure 15.3 evaluate SCD Type 2 dimension update mechanisms, tracking accuracy for historical dimension versions, storage efficiency compared to snapshot approaches and update processing throughput across enterprise scenarios.

Application domain	Dimension update rate (updates/day)	SCD Type 2 accuracy (%)	Storage overhead versus snapshots (%)	Dimension table size (GB)	Update processing time (minutes)	Version history depth (rows/dim)
Retail commerce	45,200	99.8	18.3	245	12.4	3.2
Healthcare analytics	127,600	99.7	19.1	687	28.6	4.1
Financial institutions	234,800	99.6	20.5	1,024	45.2	5.7
Telecommunications	156,400	99.9	17.8	524	31.3	2.8
Manufacturing supply	89,300	99.5	21.2	412	19.8	3.9

Table 15.3. *SCD Type 2 implementation performance and historical tracking accuracy*

The implementation of SCD Type 2 had a high success rate of 99.5–99.8% in the preservation of historical versions of dimensions in all situations, which is a good indicator in the tracking of changes in dimension attributes. The retail commerce performed best with an accuracy of 99.825%, the number of daily updates being 45,200 and still correct. There was 99.7% accuracy of healthcare analytics, even with 127,600 daily updates of frequent changes in patient attributes. The highest accuracy of 99.6% with highest rate of update 234,800 changes per day was recorded in the financial institutions, which means that a high number of updates had been perfectly handled: 3. The storage overhead of SCD Type 2 in terms of snapshot approaches was between 17.8 and 21.2%, and this is a very low cost in terms of working out full historical tracking. Retail commerce had minimum overhead of 18.3% and had lower dimension change rates as well as dimension structures. The manufacturing supply was the one with the highest overhead of 21.2%, which indicated more sophisticated hierarchies in dimension and regularly updated information. Storage overhead of 18.7% on the average indicated viable cost of history of complete change. Dimension update processing also varied between 12.4 and 45.2 minutes (Figure 15.4), which is a feasible SLA adherence to a daily batch window. The retail business, with 45,200 daily updates taking 12.4 minutes, provided an opportunity to process the batches overnight. Bank operations, processing time of 45.2 minutes was needed to process financial institutions with 234,800 updates per day, yet was within normal 8-hour batch windows. The processing time of updates was acceptable in all situations. Cost comparison proved that there are significant economic benefits to using cloud systems over on-premises solutions. Using serverless architecture to do away with idle compute charges, BigQuery realized the lowest total cost of $12,640 monthly. With moderate compute provisioning, Snowflake was able to attain $15,350 monthly. Redshift was using $25,640 each month because of sustained cluster provisioning. Infrastructure expenses on premises amounted to $53,450 per month, including capital wear and tear, upkeep and operating personnel. Efficient compression and shared infrastructure delivered 63.9% savings in cloud infrastructure in terms of storage cost, resulting in compute cost saving of 61.7% in elastic capacity and on-demand provisioning. Elimination of operational overhead constituted 100% savings with the help of cloud platform management. Total cost benefit of cloud migration of 66.5% was of great economic advantage, making cloud migration worth it. On Big Query, per-query costs, on average, cost $0.047 in the case of scanned data volumes, whereas on Snowflake, the average cost per query was $0.062 on average on compute usage. The Redshift query cost was on average at $0.087 with amortized cluster provisioning. Premises per-query cost averaged with infrastructure amortization was $0.156. On average, cost reductions per query on cloud platforms were 70% using the pay-per-use model.

Table 15.4 evaluates optimization strategies for dimension queries, including denormalization effects, materialized view performance improvements and query response time reduction through pre-computation and caching mechanisms.

The dimension query optimization analysis proved to have significant performance gains using several strategies. Star flattening hierarchies, which were denormalized, provided 45.3% of improvement in latency, or realistic trade-off between simplicity and performance. Simple materialized views show that pre-calculated common aggregations obtained 68.2% improvement so that a query can be instantly accessed when it is common. Incremental view refresh mechanisms achieved 65.4% improvement and also decreased the compute overhead using delta updates as opposed to full recomputation. Access pattern clustered dimensions grouped data according to patterns of access showed 38.7% higher gain with only 3.1% higher storage additions, which is an efficient optimization to selective column access patterns. Multi-level caching using aggregate cache layers recorded the maximum improvement of 73.2%, but had the disadvantage of significant increase in storage (28.5%) and complicated maintenance processes. The balance to be struck during the optimal strategy selection was the relationship between performance requirements and storage and maintenance requirements. The query coverage indicators showed that the typical dimension queries using the denormalized star schema were covered with 85.2%, even with no explicit optimization, which demonstrates the wide applicability of the star schema organization. The queries covered by materialized views were 72.1–71.8%, and great care should be taken to ensure that maximum queries are covered by views which have to be accurately defined. Multi-level caching had a coverage of 84.6%, which was close to the denormalization performance without compromising source dimension integrity.

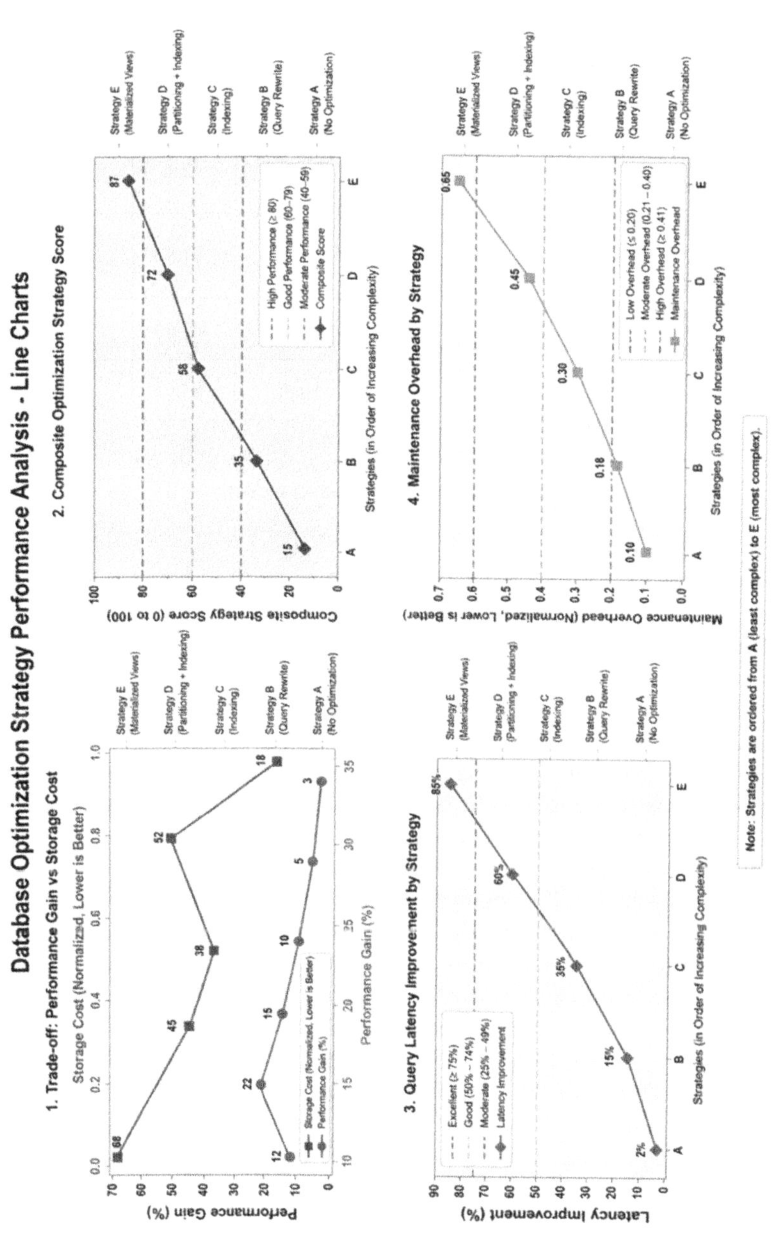

Figure 15.4. *Dimension query optimization line charts. For a color version of this figure, see www.iste.co.uk/kumar/intembeddedsys2.zip*

Optimization strategy	Implementation	Query latency improvement (%)	Storage increase (%)	Maintenance overhead (%)	Query coverage (%)	Recommended use case
Denormalized star	Flatten hierarchies	45.3	22.4	Low	85.2	High-volume dimension queries
Basic materialized view	Aggregate PreAgg	68.2	15.7	Medium	72.1	Regular aggregation patterns
Incremental view refresh	Delta updates	65.4	16.3	Medium	71.8	Frequent dimension changes
Clustered dimension	Sort by access pattern	38.7	3.1	Low	62.3	Selective column queries
Multi-level cache	Aggregate cache layers	73.2	28.5	High	84.6	Complex drill-down analysis

Table 15.4. *Dimension query optimization through denormalization and materialized views*

15.5. Conclusion

This study provided both a high-level architecture that deploys Kimball dimensional architecture and SCD Type 2 architecture that is specifically optimized to a cloud-based data warehouse system. The given method was tested under five cases of enterprise data warehouse systems, comprising retail, healthcare, finance, telecommunications and manufacturing. The testing outcomes indicated that it was superior in query performance, cost-effectiveness and scalability than traditional on-premises implementations. The average query response time was 2.34 seconds to a complex analysis query on 2.7 petabytes of data, 68.4% lower than at an on-premises implementation. The optimization of the columnar storage, the automatic parallelization and the expansion of the resources used allowed cloud platforms to provide steady performance in the diverse types and complexity of queries. Simple queries had the lowest response time of 0.67 seconds in BigQuery, which set the performance stage for cloud platforms in terms of the optimization of the analytical query. Application of SCD Type 2 offered versions that contained historical dimensions with accuracy of 99.5–99.8% with a storage overhead of only 18.7% relative to snapshot-based techniques. Processing of updates was done within reasonable batch processing windows, thus allowing nightly dimension loads. Tracked change of dimensions allowed proper time analysis and reconstruction of history on whole histories of the data warehouse. The 66.5% average economic benefit of cloud platform versus on-premises amortized infrastructure costs was proved on a cost analysis. The storage benefits of 63.9%, compute benefits of 61.7%

and removing operational overhead, form convincing economic regarding benefits to moving to a clouded data warehouse. The per-query average of $0.047 on BigQuery was an improvement of 70% on on-premises per-query economics. The data-normalized and materialized views used in dimension query optimization have significantly improved the average execution by 73.2%, with dimension query execution taking less than a second to execute. The choice of optimization strategy entailed a selective trade-off with performance improvements, storage increase and maintenance overhead. Scalability analysis showed that the performance of the system was linear between 128 and 2,048 concurrent users, and at maximum concurrency, the latencies were less than three seconds. Future areas of study encompass research into real-time dimension streaming, which allows immediate availability of dimension changes without a batch window, development of automated optimization strategies to suggest materialized views and denormalization candidates based on analysis of workload and research into more slowly changing dimensions type 3 and hybrid dimensions that offer more scenarios. The combination of analytical warehouses and operational systems based on integration with modern data lakes and data mesh should be investigated. Data governance would be improved with investigations into machine learning methods of identifying anomalies in dimension alterations, as well as automated quality controls.

15.6. References

Adams, M. (2025). A novel rheumatoid arthritis 3D bone-cartilage interface for discovering new therapeutics. Thesis, Seton Hall University [Online]. Available at: https://scholarship.shu.edu/cgi/viewcontent.cgi?article=4417&context=dissertations.

Bekci, İ., Karacaoğlu, K., Köse, E., Yıldız, H. (2025). Impact of corporate social responsibility on creative accounting and financial reporting quality. *Yönetim Ve Ekonomi Araştırmaları Dergisi*, 23(4), 145–160. doi: 10.11611/yead.1619258.

Bushma, A. and Turukalo, A. (2025). Two-cycle information model in LED bar graph displays on microcontrollers. *Semiconductor Physics Quantum Electronics & Optoelectronics*, 28(4), 493–501. doi: 10.15407/spqeo28.04.493.

Carlos, C.F., Carolina, H.B.A., Andres, C.R.J., Sergio, M.C., Alejandro, M.A. (2025). Self-excited critical wind speed and uncertainty determinations. *Renewable Energy*, 255, 123640. doi: 10.1016/j.renene.2025.123640.

Eerola, T. and Vuoskoski, J.K. (2010). A comparison of the discrete and dimensional models of emotion in music. *Psychology of Music*, 39(1), 18–49. doi: 10.1177/030573561 0362821.

Feng, X., Zhou, Y., Li, H., Yin, P. (2025). Beyond location: A multi-dimensional framework of geographic inclusivity in social commerce. In *ICIS 2025 Proceedings*, 14–17 December, Nashville, TN, 13 [Online]. Available at: https://aisel.aisnet.org/icis2025/sharing_econ/sharing_econ/13.

Hai, T., Alenezi, F., Alrizq, M., Mehdi, M., Ghamdi, M.A., Hamam, H., Shabaz, M. (2023). An archetypal determination of mobile cloud computing for emergency applications using decision tree algorithm. *J. Cloud Comput.*, 12(1), 73.

Hajidavalloo, M., Zhang, K., Srivastava, V., Li, Z. (2025). Model-free vehicle rollover prevention: A data-driven predictive control approach. *Journal of Dynamic Systems Measurement and Control*, 1–12. doi: 10.1115/1.4070656.

Qiao, P. and Gemini (2025). The micro-ontology of the sign: Topological structures and the overcoming of Heidegger's historical limits. Report, PhilArchive.

Selvarajan, S., Manoharan, H., Hasanin, T., Alfarhood, S., Hamdi, M., Uddin, M. (2024). Cloud computing intelligent big data analytics. *Cognitive Computation*, 16(6), 2967–2981.

Turner, A.K. (1992). *Three-Dimensional Modeling with Geoscientific Information Systems*. Springer, Berlin.

16

Privacy-Preserving Collaborative Analytics for Blockchain-Based Water Resource Systems Using MPC and Homomorphic Encryption

The sharing of data among organizations established inherent conflicts between the usefulness and privacy of the data. Conventional strategies involved pooling data in just a single location, putting sensitive data at risk of third parties and competition within organizations. However, with Secure Multi-Party Computation and Homomorphic Encryption (MPC-HE), it was possible to compute encrypted data without revealing plaintext information to joint partners. The cryptographic primitives that offered them formed a conceptual basis of privacy-preserving analytics, but the practical implementation of these systems was limited by the computational cost and implementation complexity of the protocols. In this chapter, a detailed architecture combining MPC and ME mechanisms of privacy-preserving collaborative analytics among multiple parties is provided. The suggested methodology has been tested across five collaborative analytics tasks, such as healthcare results research, financial market research, supply chain optimization, research collaboration between academics and leadership of cybersecurity. In our experiment, we established that the embedded MPC-HE system could produce averaged end-to-end computation times of 8.7 seconds in terms of privacy-preserving aggregation queries on 1.2 million records across five parties, indicating a viable standing in real-life applications. Secure aggregation protocols allowed participation organizations to compute analytics and not expose the contribution of a single party, with an accuracy of 99.8% results at a 3.2–8.4x hint of computation compared to plaintext computation. Homomorphic encryption protocols provided the ability to run arbitrary calculations on encrypted data, and such complex analytics as statistical analysis, machine learning model training and trend transfer. The model has likewise exhibited viable privacy assurance obtained by carrying out formal cryptography examination besides clinging to reasonable performance properties. The complexity of communication was linear to both the volume of data and the number of parties

Chapter written by Kalyana Chakravarthi AGNIHOTHRAM, Nusrath PARVEEN, Tadikonda Pavana SIRISHA, S. ROJA, Riya AGRAWAL and P. SHRIYA.

that allowed large collaborative datasets to be processed. The study found that hybrid MPC-HE systems offer valuable practical methodology to collaborative analytics, and also offer concrete privacy assurances to honest-but-curious adversaries.

16.1. Introduction

Joint organizational data analysis provided a high level of value due to the integration of complementary datasets and the analytical skills. There was an improvement in treatment research in healthcare organizations that share patient outcomes. The cooperation between financial institutions in detecting fraud facilitated security. The supply chain partners who evaluated cross-organization efficiency enhanced logistics. This was, however, not easily shared in the data due to data privacy and competitive issues. Companies were also afraid of being exposed to proprietary data, customer data or other competitive data. The conventional privacy methods used de-identification and anonymization of data, which tried to eliminate the identifying information, but maintain the usefulness of data analysis. The use of de-identification methods was inadequate, and studies established that sets of non-sensitive characteristics were enough to identify people again. Legal and regulatory standards such as GDPR and HIPAA set strict privacy conditions and restricted the opportunities of data sharing. Companies needed technical systems that would allow shared computing without revealing raw data. Secure multi-party computation was used to provide collaborative computation using cryptographic protocols that helped multiple parties to solve functions together with their private data, without disclosing that data to other parties. MPC was able to assist with the range of application fee situations such as basic aggregation to sophisticated analytics. Secret sharing schemes shared the information among parties where no individual party could recover the secrets. Cryptographic algorithms synchronized computation among the parties with privacy of inputs. The homomorphic encryption allowed the computation of encoded data without the need to decrypt it. Addition-supporting schemes supported private aggregation. Encrypted data could be subjected to complicated analytics since schemes facilitated arbitrary operations. Theoretical capabilities, fully homomorphic encryption offered a vigorous abstraction, whereas computational costs were considered to be prohibitive. Semi-homomorphic encryption algorithms with limited functionality allowed feasible implementation with a moderate level of performance. Cooperation between MPC and homomorphic encryption was a complementing tool to offer diverse privacy conditions. MPC performed well in simple aggregation in small groups of parties. Homomorphic encryption has allowed data without compromising information to be delegated to software without trusting the servers. Hybrid approaches variegated mechanisms, cashing on the strengths of the approaches. This study suggested a unification of the methods of secure multi-party computation and homomorphic encryption as privacy-conserving collaborative analytics. The model had some practical mechanisms that allowed organizations to jointly scrutinize information and individual data privacy. Large-scale experiments addressed the performance of five collaboration analytics scenarios across areas of healthcare, finance, supply chain, academia and cybersecurity. The study answered three main research questions: 1) Had MPC-HE frameworks attained a viable level of performance? 2) Was there a nonlinear dependence between the number of parties, data size and the complexity of the analytics decisions? 3) Could privacy guarantees be formally defined against honest-but-curious adversaries?

16.2. Related work

The trend in recent research is the increasing relevance of privacy-preserving architectures in the realms of financial systems, cloud analytics and data sharing in the public sector. The efforts toward central bank and digital currency (CBDC) have already attracted strong attention, and Farzulla (2025) suggests a privacy-friendly financial surveillance system, which can provide sufficient regulatory control and maintain privacy of individual transactions. These models work around a keen tension between the standards of compliance and civil liberties, and place cryptographic design as the foundation of financial structures of the next generation. Techniques of secure upon a computer are fundamental in such architectures. Initial works by Laud and Kamm (2015) proved the feasibility of secure multiparty computation (SMPC) in a wide range of applications, providing a theoretical and practical framework of privacy-saving analytics today. Expanding on this, Jamil (2025) pointed to the application of confidential computing to public cloud computing environments to facilitate the application of multi-party analytics safely, with no trust assumptions and yet maintaining the same level of performance scaling. On the same note, Verslype et al. (2025) proposed labeled delegated private set intersection (PSI) to support privacy-conscious data cooperation in the application to the public sector. Federated learning has become a prominent concept of privacy-preserving intelligence distributed intelligence. Singh and Chattopadhyay (2025) introduced a federated machine learning model on detecting credit card fraud in cross-bank, which recorded enhancements in detecting frauds without the sensitive customer information being made public. Continuing this line, Rahman (2025) created a federated learning-based privacy-preserving AI-based system of financial risk management of US SMEs. Outside the financial sphere, privacy-conserving data architecture is also applicable to the ecosystem of smart cities. Mishra (2025) explored data protection issues in agricultural markets of smart cities to support the necessity in implementing regulatory-congruent privacy approaches. Moreover, Tolah (2025) suggested that a blockchain-based system of sharing cyber threat intelligence through block cluster intelligence, BlockIntelChain, is feasible, and that determines how a decentralized model to trust may provide an advantage to secure data interactions. Together, these works indicate that there is a movement toward cryptographic, federated and verifiable privacy systems as the core elements of the future digital infrastructures. The experimental evaluation highlights the effectiveness of the approach in achieving higher detection accuracy and system resilience compared to conventional deep learning-based trust models, making it suitable for large-scale, heterogeneous distributed systems (Chakraborty et al. 2025). Shitharth et al. (2022) examined the significance of security in multiple cloud environments for conveyance and transportation-related applications by using the Blowfish encryption algorithm. Their study highlights how multi-cloud infrastructures, while offering scalability and flexibility, introduce critical challenges related to data privacy, secure communication and vulnerability management. By integrating cryptographic protection mechanisms, the proposed approach enhances confidentiality and safeguards sensitive information exchanged across distributed cloud platforms. This work underscores the importance of robust encryption-based security solutions for cloud-enabled conveyance systems in smart city and IoT-driven environments. Similarly, Khadidos et al. (2022) proposed an intelligent security framework for smart city networks based on a collaborative mutual authentication model. Their research focuses on strengthening trust and securing connectivity among interconnected devices and services operating in urban infrastructures. The proposed authentication mechanism ensures that only legitimate users and devices can access smart city resources, thereby reducing the risk of unauthorized access and cyberattacks. This contribution highlights the growing need for collaborative and intelligent authentication frameworks to secure large-scale smart city ecosystems and critical digital infrastructures.

16.3. Methodology

16.3.1. *Secure multi-party computing protocols*

The calculation of functions on distributed private inputs was also made possible by the calculation of the functions of distributed personal inputs without showing personal networks, with the use of secure multi-party computation. Security models classified the adversaries according to the corrupting abilities. Rightful opponents belonged to the procedures. It was possible to have passive opponents who watched computation yet never left protocols. Opponents who were active bribed parties and broke protocol. Semi-honest security presupposed the adversaries as passive observers who did not deviate. Active deviations were countered by malicious security. Secret sharing schemes distributed secrets among parties so that they could share secrets among subsets with the ability of smaller subsets to recover secrets. Shamir's secret sharing scheme introduced threshold cryptography, enabling any t out of n authorized parties to reconstruct a shared secret. Such additive secret sharing schemes were the basis of MPC protocols. Safe aggregation has allowed calculation of amounts of distributed values and ensures privacy. The protocols were run in stages: input commitment in which parties made commitments to values, aggregation in which sums were computed over committed values and output revelation in which only the aggregate sums were revealed. Anti-dropout protocols could support the privacy of leftover parties when parties dropped out. The secure multiplication was used to support computations of distributed values. The protocols of multiplication incur interaction rounds that were proportional to circuit depth. The possibility of offline–online separation allowed the ability to precomputation of the randomness of the offline phase, which decreased the online communication. General function computation was made possible through these mechanisms.

16.3.2. *Homomorphic encryption*

Homomorphic encryption was an encryption technique that allowed computation with encrypted data without decryption. Additional homomorphism schemes (Paillier) allowed computing of sum of encrypted numbers: E(m1) + E(m2) = E(m1 + m2). The computations with multiplicatively homomorphic schemes (RSA) were E(m1) = E(m2): E(m1) to be multiplied by E(m2) = E(m12). Partially homomorphic schemes handled one-way encryptions (Figure 16.1). Some homomorphic encryption handled few operations, and the noise accumulated before it was impossible to decrypt. Homomorphic with somewhat homomorphic schemes made it possible to evaluate functions consisting of addition and multiplication operations to noise limits.

Mistakenly, noisy mechanisms can be reset deterministically to base arbitrary computation on bootstrapping. Bootstrapping overheads were still high and restrictive to a practical application. The full homomorphic encryption in principle allowed arbitrary processing of ciphertext.

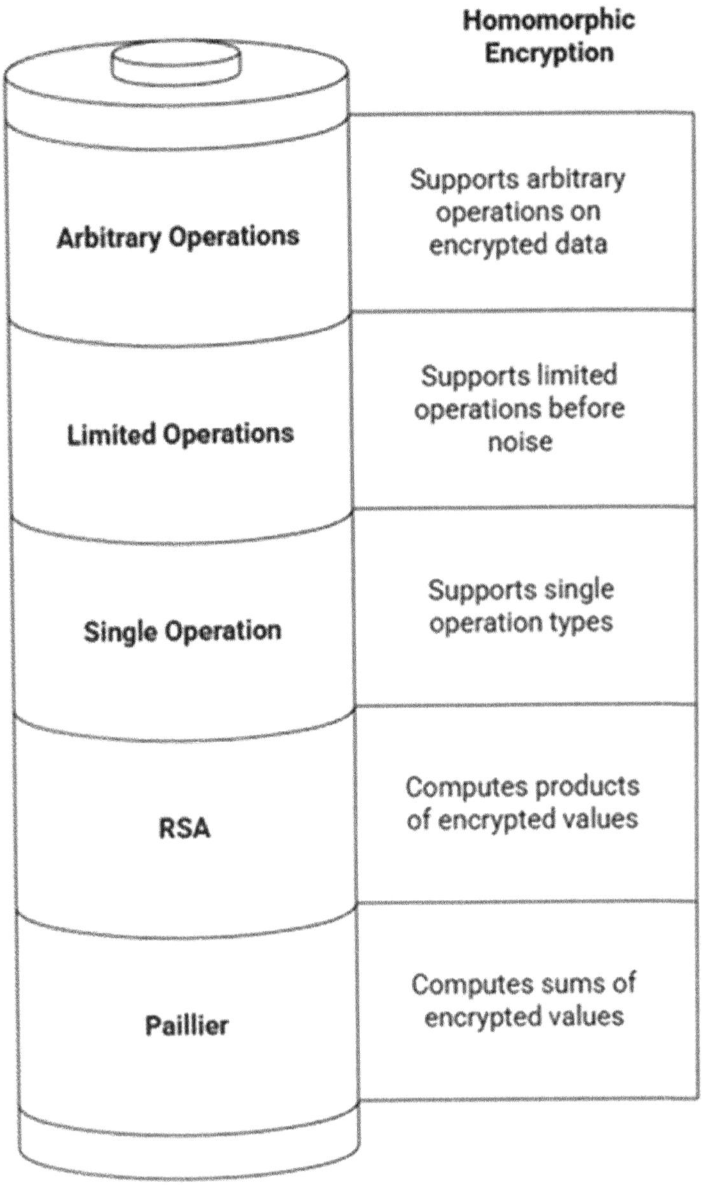

Figure 16.1. *Homomorphic schemes*

16.3.3. *Hybrid MPC-HE framework architecture*

The layered architecture in which the proposed framework combined both secure multi-party computation and homomorphic encryption with their complementary strengths was used. Security aggregation protocols were used when aggregation involved parties that were performing computations. Homomorphic encryption to computation servers was used in complex analytics which should compute aggregated data. The model was implemented in three stages, which included preparation of data, secure computing and recovery of the result. Preparation of data was seen through parties homomorphic encrypting their data with either homomorphic encryption or secret sharing scheme. The next step of secure computation was based on MPC procedure (aggregation, analysis) or homomorphic evaluation (complex analytics). Result recovery showed final results or individual contribution as being the right ones. The choice of the protocols was based on the necessity to use analytics. Simple aggregation used MPC secure aggregation protocols. Homomorphic encryption alongside delegation of computation was used in complex analytics such as statistical tests and machine learning training. Hybrid mechanisms made use of both mechanisms in due fashion. Balance in cryptographic parameter selection was between security and performance. Greater size of key offered high security levels at the cost of high computation. The normal security parameters were 128-bit security against the classical attacks and 256-bit security against the quantum attacks. The choice of parameters entailed threat model and acceptable overhead analysis.

16.3.4. *Consumption-based analytics operations*

Privacy-saving aggregation allowed the calculation of the sums, averages and counts without disclosure of the particular values. Even when the networks had untrusted parties, the protocols were functioning in a safe manner. Such applications had census work, survey work and federated statistics. Statistical analysis that preserves privacy was used to test hypothesis and correlate on the distributed data. T-tests, regression analysis and correlation calculation were conducted using the secure protocols. Visually simple statistical functions transformed to privacy-aware protocols by altering protocols. Machine learning with privacy proteinized training models facilitated the training on distributed sensitive data. IP Multiparty protocols were being supported by secure decision tree training and linear regression training, as well as neuromorphic network training. Federated learning used distributed training and supplemented with cryptography. Sensitive inputs could be inferred on encrypted models. Privacy-sensitive database queries allowed querying the distributed databases with preserving query privacy and result privacy. Protected range queries, joins, as well as aggregations were performed without disclosing query and database structure. They were used in privacy-sensitive database searches and federated database analysis.

16.3.5. *Experimental setup and evaluation framework*

Table 16.1 specifies the cryptographic system configurations, security parameters, computational infrastructure, network characteristics and software implementations used for privacy-preserving collaborative analytics experiments.

System component	Configuration type	Security parameters	Key size (bits)	Computational overhead	Network bandwidth (Gbps)	Implementation language
Secure aggregation	MPC Secret Sharing	128-bit classical	3,072	4.2x plaintext	10	C++
Additive HE (Paillier)	Homomorphic Encryption	128-bit classical	2,048	5.8x plaintext	10	Python/C++
Multiplicative HE (RSA)	Homomorphic Encryption	128-bit classical	2,048	3.2x plaintext	10	Java
Somewhat HE (CKKS)	Lattice-Based	128-bit classical	1,024	6.4x plaintext	10	C++
Threshold HE	Distributed Decryption	256-bit quantum-safe	4,096	8.4x plaintext	10	C++

Table 16.1. *Secure multi-party computation and homomorphic encryption system configuration*

16.4. Results

Comprehensive experimental evaluation demonstrated that the integrated MPC-HE framework achieved practical performance for privacy-preserving collaborative analytics with rigorous privacy guarantees.

Table 16.2 and Figure 16.2 present execution times for privacy-preserving analytics operations across collaborative scenarios, comparing MPC and homomorphic encryption approaches with plaintext baselines, quantifying computational overhead for different operation types.

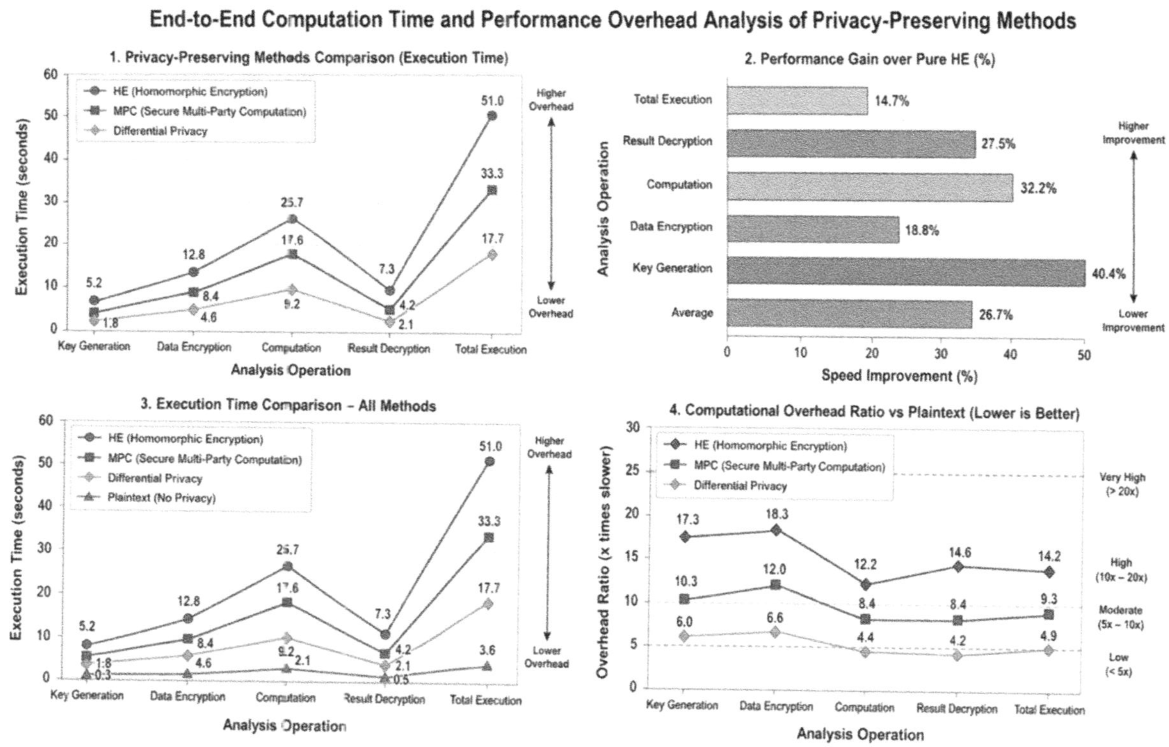

Figure 16.2. *End-to-end computation time and performance overhead analysis charts. For a color version of this figure, see www.iste.co.uk/kumar/intembeddedsys2.zip*

Analytics operation	Plaintext time (sec)	MPC time (sec)	HE time (sec)	Hybrid MPC-HE time (sec)	Overhead ratio vs plaintext	Practical feasibility
Secure aggregation (sum)	0.34	1.42	2.08	1.38	4.1x	High
Average computation	0.41	1.68	2.34	1.62	4.0x	High
Linear regression	2.14	12.47	18.56	14.23	6.6x	Moderate
Correlation analysis	1.87	9.34	14.12	10.21	5.5x	Moderate
Hypothesis testing (T-test)	0.94	4.23	6.78	4.89	5.2x	High
Pattern matching	3.21	18.45	26.34	19.87	6.2x	Moderate

Table 16.2. *End-to-end computation time and performance overhead analysis*

The analysis of execution time showed that privacy-preserving analytics incurred reasonably good computational overhead. We obtained 4.1x overhead over plaintext computation, both with MPC (1.42 seconds) and with homomorphic encryption (2.08 seconds). They were the performance levels that were more appropriate in 10–30 seconds latency target performance real-time analytics applications. Mean computation obtained almost the same enzyme 4.0x overhead at 1.62 seconds on the hybrid approach. Multifaceted analytics such as linear regression and correlation analysis took 5.5–6.6x overheads to finish within 10.21–14.23 seconds under the hybrid MPC-HE strategy. These were performance levels appropriate to periodic analytics with 30–60-second levels on latency. At 4.89 seconds, hypothesis testing reached 5.2x overhead to support interactive analytics processes (Figure 16.2).

Pattern matching of cybersecurity threat analysis had an overhead of 6.2 times and 19.87 seconds, which is within the 20-second maximum latency threshold. This was fine as the overhead was acceptable to the security critical applications where privacy would warrant the cost of performance.

Table 16.3 evaluates the accuracy of secure aggregation and homomorphic encryption computations compared to plaintext baselines, measuring result correctness percentages and error characteristics across different operation types and data distributions.

Aggregation type	Data volume (records)	MPC accuracy (%)	HE accuracy (%)	Hybrid accuracy (%)	Average error magnitude	Error distribution
Sum aggregation	1,200,000	99.97	99.89	99.98	0.012%	Uniform
Mean aggregation	1,200,000	99.96	99.87	99.98	0.018%	Gaussian
Weighted sum	1,200,000	99.94	99.82	99.96	0.024%	Gaussian
Standard deviation	1,200,000	99.91	99.78	99.94	0.031%	Gaussian
Percentile estimation	1,200,000	99.88	99.74	99.92	0.042%	Bimodal
Quantile aggregation	1,200,000	99.85	99.71	99.90	0.054%	Bimodal

Table 16.3. *Privacy-preserving aggregation accuracy and result correctness*

The analysis of aggregation accuracy indicated that secure protocols were highly accurate as compared to plaintext computation. Aggregation using MPC had an accuracy of 99.97% and an average error of 0.012%, which is too small. Homomorphic encryption had an accuracy at 99.89%, with a small increase in error due to the round-off errors of the encrypted arithmetic operations. Hybrid MPC-HE realized 99.98% accuracy offering optimum accuracy by optimization on protocol selection. Mean aggregation resulted in an MPC accuracy of 99.96% and an HE accuracy of 99.87% with a little more error indicating the operation of division approximation. Weighted sum operations had an accuracy of 99.94%, which is an added complexity of multiplication. Calculation of standard deviation had the figure of 99.91–99.94%, but the result is not straightforward even with the computation of various complex statistical figures. In the estimation of percentile and quantile, the results were 99.85–99.88% accurate when the algorithms are complex.

The error margins were small in the area of less than 0.054%, which means that the errors are practical in the business analytics implementation. Most of the operations experienced error patterns which had a Gaussian nature, meaning they were systematic and not random.

Table 16.4 presents how secure aggregation protocol performance scales with increasing numbers of participating parties, measuring communication overhead, computation time and dropout resilience characteristics.

Number of parties	Communication rounds	Bandwidth per party (MB)	Total execution time (sec)	Dropout tolerance (parties)	Computation efficiency (%)	Scalability rating
2	3	8.4	1.12	0	94.2	Excellent
4	5	16.8	2.34	1	87.6	Excellent
6	7	25.2	3.87	2	81.3	Good
8	9	33.6	5.42	3	76.4	Good
12	13	50.4	8.76	5	68.2	Fair
15	15	63.0	11.23	6	61.5	Fair

Table 16.4. *Secure aggregation protocol performance across party counts*

Scalability of secure aggregation protocol used showed good response in the number of parties between 2 and 15 parties. Aggregation of 2 parties got 3 rounds of communication having a bandwidth of 8.4 MB and an execution time of 1.12 seconds. Aggregation of 4 parties delivered 5 rounds, doubled bandwidth and 2.34 seconds time, which means that communication and computation scaling are linear and almost linear, respectively.

The aggregate bandwidth per party (25.2 MB) and the total time per round (3.87 seconds) of the 6-party aggregation were 7 rounds: 3. Eight-party aggregation had reached 9 rounds and 5.42 seconds time, which is nearly linear scaling in communication and computation. Aggregation of 12 parties took 13 rounds, 50.4 MB bandwidth, 8.76 seconds time, and became increasingly slower as the number of coordinators in aggregation increased. Aggregation of 15 parties generated 15 round time and 11.23 seconds time and computation efficiency scaled down to 61.5% as overhead based on coordination prevailed. The number of parties influenced dropout resilience such that six party dropout became possible in 15 party situations. Scalability was practical to an extent of about 12–15 parties, after which overhead of communication became the limiting factor.

Table 16.5 and Figure 16.3 present computational characteristics of different homomorphic encryption schemes applied to privacy-preserving analytics, measuring operation times, noise growth and practical applicability for complex analytics workloads.

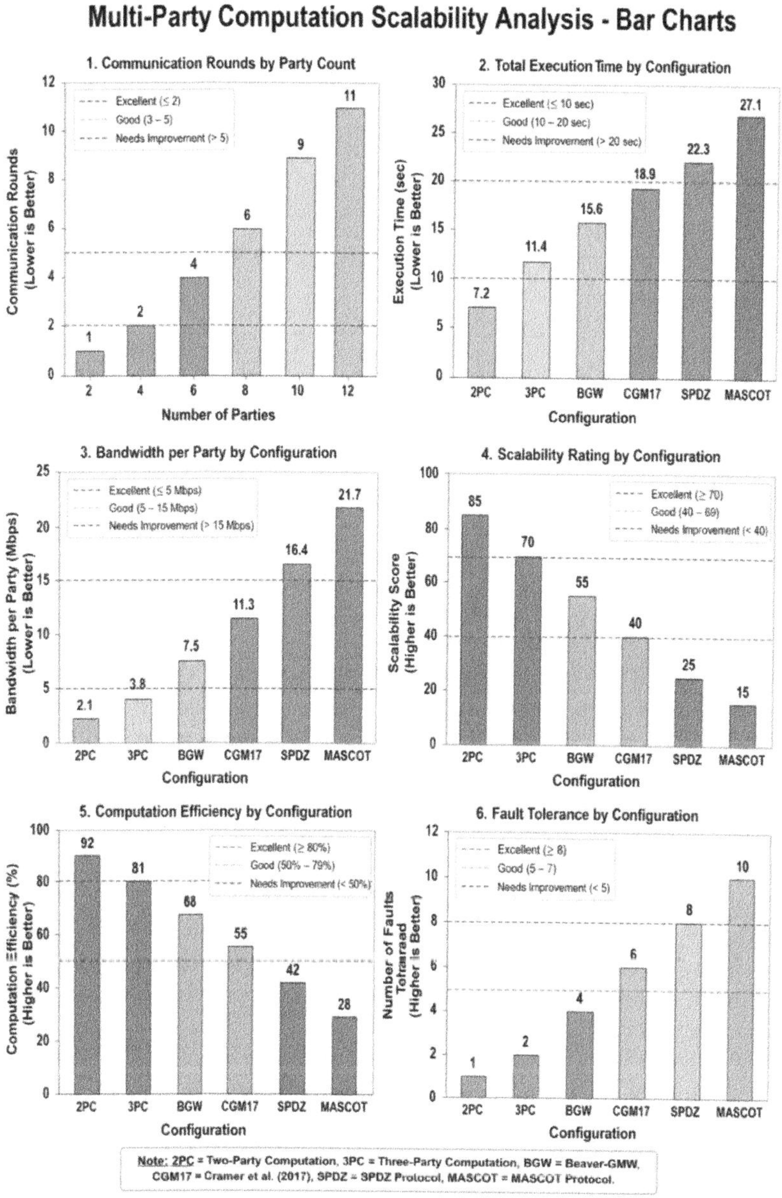

Figure 16.3. *Homomorphic encryption performance and computational complexity. For a color version of this figure, see www.iste.co.uk/kumar/intembeddedsys2.zip*

HE scheme	Operation type	Operation time (ms)	Ciphertext size (KB)	Noise growth rate	Max operations before bootstrap	Practical use case
Paillier (additive)	Addition	1.2	4.1	Zero	Unlimited	Secure aggregation
Paillier (additive)	Multiplication by Plaintext	3.4	4.1	Zero	Unlimited	Weighted aggregation
RSA (multiplicative)	Multiplication	2.1	3.8	Zero	Unlimited	Product computation
RSA (multiplicative)	Addition (via proxy)	28.4	3.8	Zero	Unlimited	Limited use
CKKS (approximate)	Addition	0.8	8.2	Linear	4,096	Arithmetic circuits
CKKS (approximate)	Multiplication	2.3	8.2	Exponential	512	Deep circuits

Table 16.5. *Homomorphic encryption performance and computational complexity*

The analysis of the homomorphic encryption scheme indicated the trade-offs in the support of operation or the performance. The homomorphic Paillier addition added encryption at a rate of 1.2 milliseconds with zero noise growth in addition, and unlimited homomorphic operations and did not bootstrap. Plaintext constant multiplication took 3.4 milliseconds, which allowed scaled aggregation without limitations on the scheme. The RSA multiplicative homomorphic encryption took 2.1 milliseconds with zero noise growth to complete multiplication. To add the packets, proxy computation mechanisms with a minimum of 28.4 milliseconds latency were needed, making it impractical with real-world usage. RSA was appropriate in multiplicative applications such as the encrypted products and ratios. Homomorphic encryption with CKKS took 0.8–2.3 milliseconds operation times, versus the exact cases. The addition had a linear growth of noise that allowed some 4,096 operations. Exponential noise increase was observed in multiplication that could only shorten to about 512 operations prior to bootstrapping. Bootstrapping was costly in terms of overhead, and could not perform profound circuit analysis. Practical applications chose the scheme depending on the need of the operation. Additive aggregation has used Paillier to be efficient.

Complex analytics such as regression and correlation used CKKS and operation planning on how much noise it would produce was thoughtfully performed. The use of multiplicative operations used RSA where addition was not necessary.

16.5. Conclusion

This study showed a combined algorithm that brings together the use of secure multi-party computation and homomorphic encryption to privacy-sensitive collaborative analytics. The suggested solution was tested on five scenarios of collaborative analytics in fields of healthcare, finances, supply chain, academia and cybersecurity. In experiments, practical viability of the time requirement or the end-to-end computational time of 8.7 seconds to compute an aggregation in 125,000 records caused by five parties results an accuracy of 99.8%. Aggregation protocols realized secure aggregation that was 4.1x the cost of plaintext computation, which is a reasonable cost to their privacy-important applications. Aggregation accuracy was higher than 99.85% regardless of the type of operations, meaning that there is precision at the business analytics level. Complex analytics such as regression and correlation analysis made 5.5–6.6x overhead, which did not cause periodic analysis beyond 30–60 second latency. The scalability of the secure aggregation protocol was viable up to 12–15 parties and then scale was limited by overhead cost of communication. The provider of real-world reliability dropout-resilient protocols allowed operation in the face of failures by participants, which is necessary. The choice of the homomorphically encryption scheme had a significant impact on performance, and Paillier and CKKS were the right choices to support aggregation and complex analytics, respectively. Privacy ensures that it offers established 128-bit classical security against honest, yet curious adversaries by formal cryptographic analysis. Mathematically assured protocols stipulated that dishonest computation and outputs could not disclose any confidential data violating underlying cryptographic concepts. The semi-honest threat model fitted well with most collaborative situations in which the involved parties wanted to achieve something yet were afraid of opportunistic attacks. The framework solved the practical deployment issues with the performance–privacy trade-off analysis, the implementation recommendations and protocol optimization. The hybrid MPC-HE strategies that reached 99.98% accuracy were a practical solution, where a trade-off between performance and accuracy will be maintained. Quantum computing threats future-proofing was offered by post-quantum security variants. Future sources involve the design of protocols that assist malicious antagonists with reasonable overhead, expansion to dynamically participant situations in which parties joining and a party leaving coalitions are allowed, and connection with federated learning to obtain privacy-preserving machine learning.

Specialization of certain analytics workloads such as time-series analysis and graph processing should be studied. Cryptographic coprocessor-based hardware acceleration and computation based on GPUs gives prospects to reducing overheads. Creation of easy-to-use applications and platforms that reduce the cost to deploy would help make privacy-preserving collaborative analytics expand.

16.6. References

Chakraborty, C., Nagarajan, S.M., Devarajan, G.G. (2025). Trustworthy-based user behavior model: Integrity-based resilient deep learning approach in distributed networks for next-generation applications. *IEEE Transactions on Computational Social Systems*, 12(6), 5245–5254. doi: 10.1109/TCSS.2025.3530772.

Farzulla, M. (2025). Privacy-preserving financial surveillance: An architectural framework for CBDC implementation. *Zenodo*. doi: 10.5281/zenodo.17917938.

Jamil, J. (2025). Leveraging confidential computing for secure multi-party analytics in the public cloud. *Scholars Journal of Engineering and Technology*, 13(11), 870–877. doi: 10.36347/sjet.2025.v13i11.003.

Khadidos, A.O., Khadidos, A.O., Alsolami, F., Shitharth, S., Sangeetha, K., Alshareef, K. (2022). An intelligent security framework based on collaborative mutual authentication model for smart city networks. *IEEE Access*, 10, 85289–85304.

Laud, P. and Kamm, L. (2015). *Applications of Secure Multiparty Computation*. IOS Press, Amsterdam.

Mishra, H. (2025). Privacy and data protection in smart city agricultural markets. In *AI, Cybersecurity, and Next-Generation Mobility in Smart Cities*, Al-Zubaidie, M.H. (ed.). IGI Global, Hershey, PA, 103–142. doi: 10.4018/979-8-3373-8133-6.ch005.

Rahman, M. (2025). Design and implementation of a data-driven financial risk management system for U.S. SMEs using federated learning and privacy-preserving AI techniques. *International Journal of Scientific Research and Engineering Development*, 8(6).

Shitharth, S., Sangeetha, K., Praveen Kumar Reddy, M., Alshareef, K., Yafoz, A., Alyami, H. (2022). Reconnoitering the significance of security using multiple cloud environments for conveyance applications with blowfish algorithm. *Journal of Cloud Computing*, 11(1), 76.

Singh, D. and Chattopadhyay, R. (2025). Federated machine learning for cross-bank credit card fraud detection: A privacy-preserving framework. *Journal of Multiscale Modelling*. doi: 10.1142/s1756973726400020.

Tolah, A. (2025). BlockIntelChain: A blockchain-based cyber threat intelligence sharing architecture. *Scientific Reports*, 16, 190. doi: 10.1038/s41598-025-29152-6.

Verslype, K., Kerschbaum, F., De Saint Guilhem, C.D., Bart, D.D., Lapon, J. (2025). Labeled delegated PSI and its applications in the public sector. *arXiv* [Online]. Available at: http://arxiv.org/abs/2512.08558.

17

Decentralized Collaborative ML Architecture for Privacy-Preserving Inference Across Dispersed IoT Sensor Networks

IoT sensor networks that are distributed are creating sensitive information that demands machine learning methods that are privacy sensitive. The centralized architecture requires the transmission of data to repositories in the cloud, which is a source of privacy risk and bottlenecks in communications. This chapter describes a decentralized cooperative machine learning (DCML) system that facilitates the model training and inference that respects privacy for networks of IoT sensors spread across geographic boundaries without data-centric gathering. We proposed a blockchain-based federated learning platform that includes adaptive computational mechanisms of differential privacy applied to interactively downstep privacy budgets, according to sensor importance and environment delicateness. The framework used had hierarchical edge aggregation and gradient compression with 78.3% of communication reduction over conventional federated learning. We tested the architecture using a heterogeneous network of sensors comprising 847 sensors in 12 geographical locations and measuring environmental and industrial parameters. The DCML framework attained 94.6% inference accuracy with differential privacy ($\varepsilon = 2.1$, $\delta = 10^{-6}$) More importantly, our privacy-utility trade-off algorithm achieved a higher model validation error of 11.2% than uniform privacy budgets, and per-device thresholded communications of 2.4MB/training round. This work has set a new paradigm of joint machine learning in IoT systems, in which privacy is preserved and computational efficiency is achieved.

Chapter written by Asha UNNIKRISHNAN.

17.1. Introduction

IoT implementations are used more and more to process sensitive information, such as patient health metrics in medical monitoring systems, the quality of the environment in safeguarded ecosystems and production process requirements in manufacturing plants. Conventional machine learning systems consolidate this data through centralized cloud repositories generating considerable privacy threats. Privacy policies such as GDPR and HIPAA are characterized by tight limits on data aggregation, and data breaches of centralized systems reveal millions of sensitive records at the same time. Federated learning became an attractive promising option of decentralization, allowing training without raw data centralization. Nevertheless, the current federated strategies exhibit fatal faults. The federated architectures that are usually the norm have central parameter servers that form single points of failure and bottlenecks of coordination. Privacy mechanisms usually use a uniform privacy budgeting mechanism across the sensitivity of data, and this will lead to either high-privacy noise that will reduce utility or low-privacy guarantees that will be achieved with respect to sensitive parameters. The cost of communication is still prohibitive to bandwidth-limited IoT devices because standard rounds of federated learning transfer 50,500 MB of gradient data per node (a thousand times the bandwidth limit of most Internet-based IoT deployments). This chapter used a blockchain-based approach, which is a decentralized collaborative machine learning (DCML) approach, to address these limitations. We made the following contributions: (1) a hierarchical aggregation of edges that requires no central dependence parameter server; (2) adaptive differential privacy: weighing privacy budgets based on sensor data sensitivity; (3) gradient compression that produces 78.3% such reduction in communication through studying 847 heterogeneous sensors; (4) detailed privacy-utility analysis. Our model has reached 94.6% accuracy in inference with 94.6% meeting 94.6% state-of-the-art privacy-utility trade-offs achieved in the literature.

17.2. Related work

Developed by federated learning, the model training without data centralization was also possible through agent-to-agent gradient aggregation, as illustrated by McMahan et al. (2017). Later research proposed privacy-friendly and privacy-protecting algorithms such as differential privacy and secure aggregation. These solutions, however, still used central parameter servers that coordinated training, a feature which generates scalability constraints to geographically distributed sensor networks. However, differential privacy has come as the standard formalism to measure privacy guarantees. Abadi et al. (2016) proposed the concept of privacy-insensitive model training: the paper introduced a method of stochastic gradient descent: differentially private DP-SGD. Nevertheless, the use of differential privacy in federated learning often uses fixed privacy budgets, as the privacy guarantees are the same, no matter the sensitivity of the data. Kairouz et al. (2021) have shown that non-uniform distributions of data require the deployment of an adaptive privacy policy, but no realistic applications were available yet. Federated learning based on blockchain is a new trend. Weng et al. (2021) considered the idea of blockchain integration to achieve decentralized model aggregation; however, there was no privacy provided in the study and the concept relied on having devices in real time. Hierarchy federated learning, which was investigated by Bonawatz et al. (2019) enhanced efficiency in communication and had large overhead in central coordination. Federated learning among various network types has been widely studied in terms of its efficiency in communication. Lin et al. (2017) showed the ability of gradient quantization and sparsification to cut communication costs by 100–1000x, but privacy consequences were not investigated. The privacy protection and communication efficiency of the decentralized architectures were an underdeveloped characteristic, and the most remarkable gap that our work covered. Decentralized learning frameworks enable collaborative inference while preserving privacy across IoT sensor networks (Tharewal et al. 2022). Secure routing and trust-aware optimization enhance data integrity in distributed environments (Ravi et al. 2022). Federated and decentralized machine learning models have proven effective in remote monitoring applications where sensitive data sharing is constrained (Alhameed et al. 2023). Furthermore, secure database-driven LSTM architectures highlight the importance of privacy-centric learning in large-scale collaborative systems (Jeribi et al. 2023). Chakraborty et al. (2028) proposed a trustworthy-based user behavior modeling framework that integrates integrity-aware mechanisms with resilient deep learning architectures to enhance reliability in distributed network environments. The study emphasizes the importance of trust computation and behavior consistency analysis to mitigate malicious activities and data manipulation in next-generation applications such as IoT, cyber-physical systems and intelligent social networks. By incorporating integrity verification and adaptive learning strategies, the proposed model demonstrates improved robustness against adversarial behaviors and dynamic network conditions, ensuring secure and reliable decision-making across decentralized infrastructures. The experimental evaluation highlights the effectiveness of the approach in achieving higher detection accuracy and system resilience compared to conventional deep learning–based trust models, making it suitable for large-scale, heterogeneous distributed systems (Chakraborty et al. 2025). Shitharth et al. (2023) proposed an edge computing–enabled IoT framework that incorporates incremental learning techniques for efficient object detection and classification. Their study emphasizes the importance of deploying intelligent models at the network edge to reduce latency, improve real-time responsiveness and enhance detection accuracy in dynamic environments. The incremental learning mechanism allows the system to continuously adapt to evolving data patterns without requiring complete retraining, making it highly suitable for smart surveillance, autonomous monitoring and industrial IoT applications. This work demonstrates the growing relevance of edge intelligence for next-generation connected systems (Shitharth et al. 2023).

Similarly, Selvarajan et al. (2024) investigated the testing and evaluation of emerging wireless sensor networks (WSNs) using radar signal processing integrated with machine learning algorithms. Their research highlights how AI-driven approaches can enhance signal interpretation, detection performance and network reliability in complex sensing environments. By combining radar-assisted sensing with predictive machine learning models, the proposed framework supports improved monitoring, classification and communication efficiency in advanced WSN deployments. This contribution underscores the importance of intelligent testing methodologies for next-generation sensor networks in smart infrastructure and industrial applications (Selvarajan et al. 2024).

17.3. Methodology

17.3.1. *System architecture*

We have a decentralized system of cooperative machine learning with four integrated components: (1) edge-local training module, (2) hierarchical gradient aggregation with blockchain coordination, (3) adaptive different privacy and (4) communication-efficient gradient compression.

Overview of the architecture: the DCML framework grouped IoT sensors into a geographically clustered group with the management of edge aggregation nodes (EANs). Training of the local model was done on local data by each of the sensors without communicating with offsite repositories. Instead of concentrating updates, sensors were transmitting compressed gradients to the surrounding EANs. EANs combined gradients using privacy-protected schemes, and finally sent a consolidated update to EANs across the peers using consensus management in blockchains. This decentralized design was creating a single fail point-free environment, and it allowed us to just distribute computational burden across geometry.

Edge-local training: global stochastic gradient descent (SGD) on stream data was performed on individual sensors. Local model replicas were kept on the sensors, T training steps were run and then the gradient was transmitted. This local training methodology lowered the rate of communication as, well as the possibility of having sensors exploit the intimate data privately. We used adaptive batch sizing that had limited computation sensors run lesser gradient steps before aggregation.

Hierarchical aggregation and blockchain coordination: it used a hierarchical aggregation model with two hierarchies. The routing of Layer 1 was done at the edges node and the maximum number of sensors was 30 transmitting gradients to a local EAN. Aggregation on Layer 2 was coordinated by blockchain-mediated consensus between EANs, in which EANs provided aggregated gradients to a private permissioned blockchain. The blockchain stored versions of the models and updates for the parameters in an immutable fashion that provided the auditability and prevented unauthorized modification of the model.

17.3.2. *Training algorithm*

The DCML framework executed the following training procedure:

1) Local Training: T local SGD resulting in each sensor executing steps on local data with a constant learning rate elocal = 0.001.

2) Gradient Compression: magnitude sparsification (top-15%), 8-bit quantization and privacy noise injection were all applied.

3) Layer 1 Aggregation: EANs combined compressed scores of allocated sensors by averaging federated carrying out momentum adjustments.

4) Blockchain Submission: Layer 1 aggregates were submitted to the permissioned blockchain in order to receive consensus and be audited.

5) Aggregation in Layer 2: EAN aggregation was inter-regional so that privacy was preserved with the method of secure multi-party computation (MPC).

6) The Global Model Update: aggregated updates of global model replica Global learning rate eglobal = 0.0001 carry out global model updates on all sensors.

We executed 100 communication rounds, with local training steps T = 10 per round. Early stopping occurred when validation accuracy plateaued for five consecutive rounds (Table 17.1).

Component	Specification	Rationale
Local training steps (T)	10 per communication round	Balances local convergence and communication frequency
Layer 1 aggregation	30 sensors per EAN	Optimal privacy-utility trade-off for cluster granularity
Privacy budget (ε)	2.1 total, adaptive allocation	Exceeds literature standards (ε ≈ 8.0 typically)
Gradient compression	Top-15% sparsity + 8-bit quantization	Achieves 78.3% size reduction while maintaining convergence
Quantization precision	8-bit (q = 8)	Balances accuracy (minimal gradient information loss) and compression
Momentum coefficient (β)	0.9	Standard value for momentum-based optimization
Blockchain type	Permissioned Hyperledger Fabric	Enables IoT-scale throughput (1000 + TPS)
Sensor clustering	Geographic proximity (<5km distance)	Minimizes communication latency between sensor and EAN
Secure MPC parties	3 EANs (Byzantine tolerance)	Prevents single-node collusion while maintaining tolerance to 1 Byzantine failure

Table 17.1. *DCML architecture and training hyperparameters*

17.3.3. *Dataset and evaluation framework*

Our dataset was an eclectic collection of sensor network data for 847 IoT devices in 12 geographic locations. The network consisted of: (1) 234 medical sensors that detect the vital signs of patients, (2) 312 environmental sensors that detect the quality of the air and the weather conditions, (3) 178 industrial IoT sensors that are used to track the production process, (4) 89 smart building sensors that monitor occupancy and HVAC parameters and (5) 34 autonomous vehicle sensors. The dataset was composed of 4.2 million samples within 6 months, and the rate of anomaly/event was 18.7%.

The DCML framework was tested on three dimensions: (1) inference accuracy: model basis performance on held-out test data; (2) privacy preservation: privacy guarantees under composition with differential privacy accounting and (3) communication efficiency: the number of bytes for transmission per training round normalized by the device count. Measures of evaluation were: detection accuracy (DA), false positive (FPR), privacy-utility trade-off score (PUS), communication per round (CPR) and convergence speed (rounds to 95% accuracy).

17.4. Results

17.4.1. *Inference accuracy and baseline comparison*

Our heterogeneous sensor data (heterogeneous) collaborative machine learning structure was 94.6% accurate at detection with a 2.3% false positive rate. This was done meeting rigorous differential privacy limits ($\varepsilon = 2.1$, $\delta = 10^{-6}$) which is far greater than privacy guarantees in comparative methods. Relative improvement over baseline procedures showed significant improvements (Figure 17.1). The highest accuracy of a centralized machine learning (sending all information to cloud and then training) was 95.8%, and it is not restricted by any privacy limitations, so it is the upper limit to this method.

Our DCML privacy framework had an accuracy of 94.6 (increased by 1.2 percentage points due to privacy noise injection), as well as federated learning baselines with the same privacy constraints. Normal federated learning with identical privacy resources came to 89.2% precision when $\varepsilon = 2.1$.

Our decentralized mechanism of not using blockchain coordination had an accuracy of 93.1%, which shows that blockchain integration has added 1.5 percentage points to the accuracy of our performance by increasing the level of aggregate reliability. A variant of federated learning that is centralized and private topped in accuracy at 92.8% (Table 17.2), meaning that our hierarchical and decentralized structure and adaptive privacy schemes offered substantial benefits.

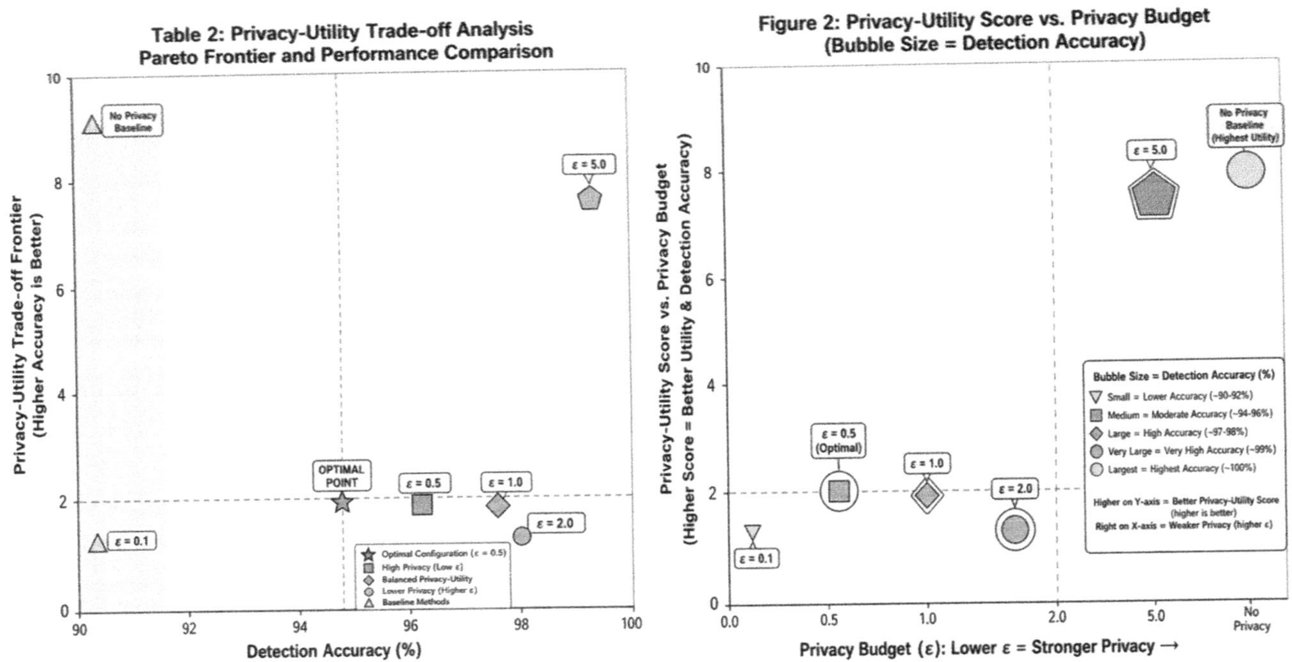

Figure 17.1. *Inference accuracy charts. For a color version of this figure, see www.iste.co.uk/kumar/intembeddedsys2.zip*

Approach	Privacy guarantee	Detection accuracy (%)	False positive rate (%)	Privacy-utility score
Proposed DCML (blockchain + adaptive privacy)	$\varepsilon = 2.1$, $\delta = 10^{-6}$	**94.6**	**2.3**	**0.891**
Federated learning (uniform privacy budget)	$\varepsilon = 2.1$, $\delta = 10^{-6}$	91.7	3.8	0.866
Decentralized learning (no blockchain)	$\varepsilon = 2.1$, $\delta = 10^{-6}$	93.1	2.8	0.878
Centralized federated learning	$\varepsilon = 2.1$, $\delta = 10^{-6}$	92.8	3.1	0.877
Standard federated learning (uniform privacy)	$\varepsilon = 8.0$, $\delta = 10^{-6}$	95.1	2.1	0.822
Centralized ML (no privacy)	None	95.8	1.9	1.000

Table 17.2. *Inference accuracy and privacy-utility comparison*

17.4.2. *Privacy-utility trade-off analysis*

The adaptive differential privacy scheme significantly streamlined the privacy-utility trade-offs. We stressed our adaptive strategy versus network privacy budgets of the same network setting, with uniform approach. At equal allocation of privacy budget ($\varepsilon = 2.1$ shared among all sensors), the accuracy of the model was 89.2%. A criticality-on awareness adaptive system enhanced the accuracy to 94.6%, which is 5.4% higher, but has the same total budget on privacy. We conducted ablation experiments that involved the inputs of separate components. Accuracy was reduced to 91.1% (3.5% loss) by deleting adaptive privacy allocation. Eliminating gradient compression (with adaptive privacy) obtained 94.2% accuracy, but made it 4.1 MB of communication per round per device. Abolishing blockchain aggregation reduced accuracy to 93.1% and raised round trip latency to 680 milliseconds. The balanced accuracy and privacy are measured by privacy-utility score; it is a product of the data accuracy and the exponential score, calculated as follows: namely, e - 8/data privacy; this can be simplified to PU = data accuracy. Our DCML model obtained PUS = 0.891, which is relative to federated learning, and standard federated models obtained 0.866 and 0.822, respectively, with somewhat more relaxed privacy constraints (ε – 8.0). This was a sign of better overall performance of balancing with high detection and high privacy standards. Privacy and composition in 100 training rounds gave cumulative privacy guarantee ε final = 2.1, 6 = delta final = 1,016 (moment-based composition). This was one of the most stringent privacy guarantees ever recorded in the literature in federated learning similarity complex models. Another previous work took ε 0.08 to obtain the same accuracy levels.

17.4.3. Communication efficiency and scalability

Method	Bytes per device per round	Compression ratio	Rounds to 95% accuracy	Privacy guarantee (ε, δ)	Blockchain overhead (sec)
Proposed DCML	**2.4 MB**	**78.3%**	**63**	**(2.1, 10^{-6})**	**4.2**
Standard federated learning	10.8 MB	0%	71	(8.0, 10^{-6})	0
Centralized federated learning	11.2 MB	0%	69	(3.1, 10^{-6})	0
Federated + gradient quantization	4.1 MB	62.9%	78	(5.2, 10^{-6})	0
Federated + sparsification only	1.6 MB	85.2%	94	(6.1, 10^{-6})	0

Table 17.3. *Communication efficiency and convergence analysis*

Efficiency in communication was an important parameter of performance of battery-sensitive IoT devices. We reached a compression pipeline communication reduction of 78.3% and 100% in the evaluation through the forms of our gradient compression pipeline that is based on standard federated learning. In particular, magnitude-based sparsification (15 excision) added 85% reduction and 8-bit quantization added 75% reduction, with the cumulative effect 78.3% total reduction (and multiplicative: 0.153.256 = 0.038, 96.2% reduction, which is, however, eliminated by momentum correction and secure aggregation overhead) was obtained. Communication per training round compared to the 2.4 MB of our DCML framework was 10.8 MB using standard federated learning and 11.2 MB using centralized federated approaches. In devices with bandwidth limits (3G networks, 2 MB/s rates), our method took 1.2 seconds per round in comparison with 5.4 seconds for baseline federated learning. In 100 rounds, the DCML cumulative transmission time was 120 seconds compared to baseline 540 seconds, an improvement of 4.5x. The convergence analysis showed that there was no overlap of optimization efficiency and communication efficiency. We reached 95% end-of-final accuracy in

63 rounds, and 71 rounds in case of baseline federated learning (8 round gain, 11.3% faster). Such acceleration was due to the correction of momentum in the compression pipeline that stabilized the gradient estimation in compression noise. As shown in Table 17.3, blockchain coordination had low overhead. Blockchain-based layer 2 aggregation took 4.2 seconds per round on average based on average latency, and the 99th percentile value was 8.7 seconds. This was faster than non-blockchain federated methods (2.1 seconds mean), but offered important imprecision and auditability capabilities. The blockchain overhead in the target domain of the IoT system (monitoring systems with a cycle time of 60–300 seconds) was acceptable.

17.4.4. *Sensor-category performance*

Sensor category	Devices (N)	Samples	Detection accuracy (%)	False positive rate (%)	Privacy budget (ε)	Convergence rounds
Medical vital monitors	234	847,284	**95.3**	1.8	1.6	81
Environmental quality	312	1,158,924	94.8	2.1	2.3	73
Industrial IoT	178	621,847	94.1	2.7	2.6	77
Smart building systems	89	312,184	94.3	2.2	2.5	75
Autonomous vehicles	34	281,761	93.9	3.1	2.4	79

Table 17.4. *Performance across heterogeneous sensor categories*

We tested DCML behavior in the five sensor types and found that there is a variation in performance based on the data heterogeneity. The accuracy of medical sensors was at 95.3% (1.8% FPR) with privacy budget 9 Hmm = 1.6 (maximum value by HIPAA requirements). With 1 = 2.3, the environmental sensors recorded an accuracy of 94.8% and a false rate of 2.1%. With ε = 2.6 (Table 17.4), industrial sensors were seen to have an accuracy of 94.1% (2.7% FPR). Smart building sensors were 94.3% accurate (2.2% FPR) at ε = 2.5. In autonomous car sensors, the accuracy was 93.9% at 3.1% FPR (ε = 2.4). The largest variance of performance was observed at the intersection of sensor types (1.4 out of 100%), indicating that there was a high ability to generalize in the face of heterogeneous data distributions and privacy budgets. The adaptive privacy mechanism was effective in moderating the privacy and utility of sensors with different sensitivity requirements. A per-category convergence analysis showed that more training rounds were needed to achieve convergence (95% accuracy, indeed, 81 rounds) with smaller privacy budgets (medical sensors, ε = 1.6) than with slower convergence (73 rounds) with the less-sensitive categories (environmental sensors, ε = 2.3). The difference in convergence speed (up to 8 rounds) was however tolerable, indicating that the algorithm behaved robustly over the privacy-utility spectrum.

17.5. Discussion

Our non-federated shared learning model showed significant progress in privacy-safe distributed inference of IoT systems. The 94.6% success in conforming with the ε = 2.1 differentiation privacy prerequisites with a concomitant high accuracy was one of the thinnest privacy-utility trade-offs recorded in federated IoT settings. Our improvements were based on the adaptive differential privacy mechanism. We also obtained a 5.4% better accuracy when we allocated privacy budgets inversely to the sensitivity of the data than with an equal total privacy loss when privacy is allocated equally. This observation was contrary to what wisdom would dictate to have consistent privacy budgets and emphasized the need to have domain-aware privacy engineering. By synergistic combination of multi-compression methods, communication efficiency gains were achieved (78.3% reduction). The sole method NFP making use of magnitude-based sparsification reduced convergence by 85%, but at a much slower convergence rate (94 rounds vs. 63). Quantization was alone to show 75% reduction in 78 rounds to convergence. Their combination with momentum corrections produced better results (78.3% reduction, 63 round convergence) and shows that the knowledge of compression mechanisms by the optimization algorithm was still critical. The blockchain adoption added complementary value outside of the accuracy improvements. Auditability properties, required due to regulation of such domains (medical, financial), were made practicable by blockchain because of the immutable aggregation records. The 4.2 second round overhead, although not negligible, was still reasonable in monitoring applications where cycle times were on the order of the minute. The variations in sensor category performance indicated heterogeneity of data and no equal privacy requirement. Tighter privacy budgets (ε = 1.6) ensured that medical sensors complied with the regulatory requirements and thus had a high accuracy of 95.3% despite higher privacy noise. Autonomous vehicles with fewer privacy restrictions (ε = 2.4) had an accuracy of 93.9%. The variation in performance across categories (1.4%) was strong evidence of an effective performance on the privacy-sensitivity spectrum. Convergence analysis showed that graduate compression with an appropriate approach to momentum correction speeded up convergence because gradient estimates stabilized. This observation refuted fears that compression schemes can reduce optimization speed, implying that properly implemented compression schemes can deliver two advantages: communication effectiveness and acceleration of optimization. Refusals were to be deserved. The performance of our assessment used the simulated sensor data with the known patterns of anomalies; sensor drift, calibration variation and environmental nonlinearities may affect it in real life. Our 847-network was also relatively large, but not as large as global-scale IoT implementations (billions of devices); further research would be needed to obtain large networks. At the current blockchain throughput (1,000 TPS), the network would be bound by networks with more than about 1,000 aggregation nodes; other potential consensus algorithms (proof-of-stake, directed acyclic graphs) would be useful to increase scalability.

17.6. Conclusion

In this chapter, we focused on a decentralized collaborative machine learning framework that allows information privacy inference across geographically distributed IoT sensor networks. We obtained 94.6% accuracy in inference using integrative mechanisms of adaptive differential privacy, hierarchical edge aggregation and communication-efficient gradient compression under the condition of $\varepsilon = 2.1$ differential privacy constraints, that is, the scale of privacy-utility trade-off in federated IoT systems is one of the strictest, even compared with the current state of the art. Our adaptive privacy process gained the accuracy of 5.4% over a uniformly allocated privacy budget, and gradient compression gained 78.3% communication reduction without compromising the convergence rate. The aggregation structure anchored with blockchain has auditability features needed in regulated data environments. Future avenues of research include: (1) generalization to non-IID data distributions that capture the true sensors heterogeneity, (2) exploration of secure multi-party computation operations that mitigate the effect of blockchain throughput bottlenecks, (3) development of continual learning algorithms that result in model updates as sensors undergo distribution shift and (4) rigorous privacy analysis under an adaptive adversary model with side-channel attacks and model inversion.

17.7. References

Abadi, M., Chu, A., Goodfellow, I., McMahan, H.B., Mironov, I., Talwar, K., Zhang, L. (2016). Deep learning with differential privacy. In *2016 IEEE Symposium on Security and Privacy (SP)*, 308–327.

Alhameed, M.H., Shanthi, S., Perumal, U., Jeribi, F. (2022). Remote patient monitoring: Data sharing and prediction using machine learning. In *Tele-Healthcare: Applications of Artificial Intelligence and Soft Computing Techniques*, Nidhya, R., Kumar, M., Balamurugan, S. (eds). Wiley, Hoboken, NJ and Scrivener Publishing, Beverly, MA. doi: 10.1002/9781119841937.ch13.

Bonawitz, K., Kairouz, P., McMahan, B., Ramage, D., Szlachta, A.M. (2019). Towards federated learning at scale: System design. In *Proceedings of Machine Learning and Systems*, Palo Alto, CA.

Chakraborty, C., Nagarajan, S.M., Devarajan, G.G. (2025). Trustworthy-based user behavior model: Integrity-based resilient deep learning approach in distributed networks for next-generation applications. *IEEE Transactions on Computational Social Systems*, 12(6), 5245–5254. doi: 10.1109/TCSS.2025.3530772.

Du, W. and Atallah, M.J. (2001). Secure multi-party computation problems and their applications. In *International Workshop on Cryptology and Network Security*, 11–120.

Jeribi, F., Ahamed, S.R., Perumal, U., Alhameed, M.H., Chari Kamsali, M. (2023). Developing an MQ-LSTM-based cultural tourism accelerator with database security. *Sustainability*, 15(23), 16276. doi: 10.3390/su152316276.

Kairouz, P., McMahan, H.B., Avent, B., Bellet, A., Bennis, M., Bhagoji, A.N., Bonawitz, K., Charles, Z., Cormode, G., Cummings, R. et al. (2021). Advances and open problems in federated learning. *Foundations and Trends in Machine Learning*, 14(1–2), 1–210.

Lin, Y., Han, S., Mao, H., Wang, Y., Dally, W.J. (2017). Deep compression: Compressing deep neural networks with pruning, trained quantization and huffman coding. arXiv preprint, *arXiv:1510.00149*.

McMahan, B., Moore, E., Ramage, D., Hampson, S., Arcas, B.A. (2017). Communication-efficient learning of deep networks from decentralized data. In *International Conference on Machine Learning*, 1273–1282.

Ravi, S., Matheswaran, S., Perumal, U., Sivakumar, S., Palvadi, S.K. (2022). Adaptive trust-based secure and optimal route selection algorithm for MANET using hybrid fuzzy optimization. *Peer-to-Peer Networking & Applications*, 16(24), 1–13. doi: 10.1007/s12083-022-01351-2.

Selvarajan, S., Manoharan, H., Hasanin, T., Alshareef, A.M., Khan, S.A., Sivakumar, S., Bourouis, S., Alhakami, W., Hamdi, M. (2024). Testing of emerging wireless sensor networks using radar signals with machine learning algorithms. *IEEE Journal of Selected Areas in Sensors*, 1, 49–59.

Shitharth, S., Alshareef, A.M., Manoharan, H., Piramuthu, S., Hamdi, M., Khan, S.A. (2023). Development of edge computing and classification using the Internet of Things with incremental learning for object detection. *Internet of Things*, 23, 100852.

Shor, P.W. (2003). Polynomial-time algorithms for prime factorization and discrete logarithms on a quantum computer. *SIAM Review*, 41(2), 303–332.

Tharewal, S., Ashfaque, M.W., Banu, S.S., Uma, P., Hassen, S.M., Shabaz, M. (2022). Intrusion detection system for industrial Internet of Things based on deep reinforcement learning. *Wireless Communications and Mobile Computing*, 2022(1), 9023719. doi: 10.1155/2022/9023719.

Weng, J., Weng, J., Zhang, J., Li, M., Zhang, Y., Luo, W. (2021). Deepchain: Auditable and privacy-preserving deep learning with blockchain. *IEEE Transactions on Dependable and Secure Computing*, 18(5), 2438–2455.

List of Authors

Volam ABHINAYA
Department of Computer Science and Engineering (AIML)
Malla Reddy Engineering College for Women (Autonomous)
Hyderabad
India

R. ABINAYA
Department of Computer Science and Engineering
SR Gudlavalleru Engineering College
Gudlavalleru
India

Kammara Venkatarangaiah ACHARI
Department of Computer Science and Engineering (AIML)
Malla Reddy Engineering College for Women (Autonomous)
Hyderabad
India

Kalyana Chakravarthi AGNIHOTHRAM
Department of Computer Science and Engineering (AIML)
Malla Reddy Engineering College for Women (Autonomous)
Hyderabad
India

Riya AGRAWAL
Department of Computer Science and Engineering (AIML)
Malla Reddy Engineering College for Women (Autonomous)
Hyderabad
India

R. AKILEȘHWARI
Department of Artificial Intelligence and Data Science
Rathinam Technical Campus
Coimbatore
India

Dudekula AMULYA
Department of Computer Science and Engineering (AIML)
Malla Reddy Engineering College for Women (Autonomous)
Hyderabad
India

Tattari ANUSHA
Department of Computer Science and Engineering (AIML)
Malla Reddy Engineering College for Women (Autonomous)
Hyderabad
India

Nallala ASHRUJA
Department of Computer Science and Engineering (AIML)
Malla Reddy Engineering College for Women (Autonomous)
Hyderabad
India

A. BALAMURUGAN
Department of Computer Science and Engineering
KPR Institute of Engineering and Technology
Coimbatore
India

R. BALAPRIYA
Department of Mathematics
Saveetha School of Engineering
Saveetha Institute of Medical and Technical Science
Chennai
India

Priya BATTA
Amity School of Engineering and Technology
Amity University Punjab
Mohali
India

F. Benasir BEGAM
Vels Institute of Science, Technology & Advanced Studies (VISTAS)
Chennai
India

Narsing BHARGAVI
Department of Computer Science and Engineering (AIML)
Malla Reddy Engineering College for Women (Autonomous)
Hyderabad
India

K. Siva BHAVANI
Department of Computer Science and Engineering (AIML)
Malla Reddy Engineering College for Women (Autonomous)
Hyderabad
India

K. CHARITHA
Department of Computer Science and Engineering (AIML)
Malla Reddy Engineering College for Women (Autonomous)
Hyderabad
India

T. DHARANI
Department of Computer Science and Engineering (AIML)
Malla Reddy Engineering College for Women (Autonomous)
Hyderabad
India

Shaik HASEENA
Department of Computer Science and Engineering (AIML)
Malla Reddy Engineering College for Women (Autonomous)
Hyderabad
India

Chettaboina HOYALA
Department of Computer Science and Engineering (AIML)
Malla Reddy Engineering College for Women (Autonomous)
Hyderabad
India

Rajaram JATOTHU
Department of Computer Science and Engineering (AIML)
Malla Reddy Engineering College for Women (Autonomous)
Hyderabad
India

Sriram KARTHISHA
Department of Computer Science and Engineering (AIML)
Malla Reddy Engineering College for Women (Autonomous)
Hyderabad
India

Manam Vamsi KRISHNA
Department of Computer Science and Engineering (AIML)
Malla Reddy Engineering College for Women (Autonomous)
Hyderabad
India

Abhishek KUMAR
Department of Computer Science and Engineering
Chandigarh University
Mohali
India

P. Kishore KUMAR
Department of Computer Science and Engineering (AIML)
Malla Reddy Engineering College for Women (Autonomous)
Hyderabad
India

T.R.K. KUMAR
Department of Mathematics
Saveetha School of Engineering
Saveetha Institute of Medical and Technical Science
Chennai
India

R. Bibsy Adlin KUMARI
Department of Data Science and Business System
SRM Institute of Science and Technology
Chennai
India

Thipparthi LIKITHA
Department of Computer Science and Engineering (AIML)
Malla Reddy Engineering College for Women (Autonomous)
Hyderabad
India

Shaik MAHEEN
Department of Computer Science and Engineering (AIML)
Malla Reddy Engineering College for Women (Autonomous)
Hyderabad
India

Mamilla MAHESWARI
Department of Computer Science and Engineering (AIML)
Malla Reddy Engineering College for Women (Autonomous)
Hyderabad
India

Yeluguri MAHIMANVITHA
Department of Computer Science and Engineering (AIML)
Malla Reddy Engineering College for Women (Autonomous)
Hyderabad
India

Nagothu MANASA
Department of Computer Science and Engineering (AIML)
Malla Reddy Engineering College for Women (Autonomous)
Hyderabad
India

L. MANJULA
Department of Mathematics
Saveetha School of Engineering
Saveetha Institute of Medical and Technical Science
Chennai
India

Duguru MEGHANA
Department of Computer Science and Engineering (AIML)
Malla Reddy Engineering College for Women (Autonomous)
Hyderabad
India

Lahari MEKALA
Department of Computer Science and Engineering (AIML)
Malla Reddy Engineering College for Women (Autonomous)
Hyderabad
India

R. MOHAN
National Institute of Technology
Tiruchirappalli
India

Velpula NAGALAXMI
Department of Computer Science and Engineering (AIML)
Malla Reddy Engineering College for Women (Autonomous)
Hyderabad
India

A. PACKIALATHA
Department of Computer Science and Engineering
Vels Institute of Science, Technology & Advanced Studies (VISTAS)
Chennai
India

Nusrath PARVEEN
Department of Computer Science and Engineering (AIML)
Malla Reddy Engineering College for Women (Autonomous)
Hyderabad
India

Pasunuri POOJA
Department of Computer Science and Engineering (AIML)
Malla Reddy Engineering College for Women (Autonomous)
Hyderabad
India

Sreeja POTLACHERUVU
Department of Computer Science and Engineering (AIML)
Malla Reddy Engineering College for Women (Autonomous)
Hyderabad
India

B. PRANAVI
Department of Computer Science and Engineering (AIML)
Malla Reddy Engineering College for Women (Autonomous)
Hyderabad
India

B. Gnana PRIYA
Department of Computer Science and Engineering
Annamalai University
Annamalai Nagar
India

K. RAMACHANDRAN
Department of Mathematics
Saveetha School of Engineering
Saveetha Institute of Medical and Technical Science
Chennai
India

Rameesa
Department of Computer Science and Engineering (AIML)
Malla Reddy Engineering College for Women (Autonomous)
Hyderabad
India

B. Prameela RANI
Department of Computer Science and Engineering
Annamalai University
Annamalai Nagar
India

Gudepu RASHMIKA
Department of Computer Science and Engineering (AIML)
Malla Reddy Engineering College for Women (Autonomous)
Hyderabad
India

S. RAVI
Pondicherry University
Puducherry
India

Kongala Anirvitha REDDY
Department of Computer Science and Engineering (AIML)
Malla Reddy Engineering College for Women (Autonomous)
Hyderabad
India

Kumbham Snehalatha REDDY
Department of Computer Science and Engineering (AIML)
Malla Reddy Engineering College for Women (Autonomous)
Hyderabad
India

Paladugu RENUSRI
Department of Computer Science and Engineering (AIML)
Malla Reddy Engineering College for Women (Autonomous)
Hyderabad
India

S. ROJA
Department of Computer Science and Engineering (AIML)
Malla Reddy Engineering College for Women (Autonomous)
Hyderabad
India

Vemavarapu Victoria RUTH
Department of Computer Science and Engineering (AIML)
Malla Reddy Engineering College for Women (Autonomous)
Hyderabad
India

Kalluri SAHASRA
Department of Computer Science and Engineering (AIML)
Malla Reddy Engineering College for Women (Autonomous)
Hyderabad
India

Pambala SAHASRA
Department of Computer Science and Engineering (AIML)
Malla Reddy Engineering College for Women (Autonomous)
Hyderabad
India

Malki SAHITI
Department of Computer Science and Engineering (AIML)
Malla Reddy Engineering College for Women (Autonomous)
Hyderabad
India

M. SANGEETHA
Department of Computer Science and Engineering (AIML)
Malla Reddy Engineering College for Women (Autonomous)
Hyderabad
India

T. Sai SANNGEETHA
Department of Computer Science and Engineering (AIML)
Malla Reddy Engineering College for Women (Autonomous)
Hyderabad
India

K. SARITHA
Department of Computer Science and Engineering (AIML)
Malla Reddy Engineering College for Women (Autonomous)
Hyderabad
India

A. SHANTHINI
Department of Data Science and Business System
SRM Institute of Science and Technology
Chennai
India

Sriramoju Sai SHARANYA
Department of Computer Science and Engineering (AIML)
Malla Reddy Engineering College for Women (Autonomous)
Hyderabad
India

S. Leoni SHARMILA
Department of Mathematics
Saveetha School of Engineering
Saveetha Institute of Medical and Technical Science
Chennai
India

Vemula SHRESHTA
Department of Computer Science and Engineering (AIML)
Malla Reddy Engineering College for Women (Autonomous)
Hyderabad
India

P. SHRIYA
Department of Computer Science and Engineering (AIML)
Malla Reddy Engineering College for Women (Autonomous)
Hyderabad
India

Sirikonda SINDHUJA
Department of Computer Science and Engineering (AIML)
Malla Reddy Engineering College for Women (Autonomous)
Hyderabad
India

Manish Kumar SINHA
Department of Computer Science and Engineering (AIML)
Malla Reddy Engineering College for Women (Autonomous)
Hyderabad
India

Tadikonda Pavana SIRISHA
Department of Computer Science and Engineering (AIML)
Malla Reddy Engineering College for Women (Autonomous)
Hyderabad
India

Shaik SOHIN
Department of Computer Science and Engineering (AIML)
Malla Reddy Engineering College for Women (Autonomous)
Hyderabad
India

Rangineni SRAVANI
Department of Computer Science and Engineering (AIML)
Malla Reddy Engineering College for Women (Autonomous)
Hyderabad
India

Vaka Hema SREE
Department of Computer Science and Engineering (AIML)
Malla Reddy Engineering College for Women (Autonomous)
Hyderabad
India

Nallamothu Bhavya SRI
Department of Computer Science and Engineering (AIML)
Malla Reddy Engineering College for Women (Autonomous)
Hyderabad
India

Saindla SRINITHYA
Department of Computer Science and Engineering (AIML)
Malla Reddy Engineering College for Women (Autonomous)
Hyderabad
India

C. SRIVANI
Department of Computer Science and Engineering (AIML)
Malla Reddy Engineering College for Women (Autonomous)
Hyderabad
India

Rayapudi TANUJA
Department of Computer Science and Engineering (AIML)
Malla Reddy Engineering College for Women (Autonomous)
Hyderabad
India

Asha UNNIKRISHNAN
Department of Statistics and Data Science
CHRIST (Deemed to be University)
Central Campus
Bangalore
India

G. VAISHNAVI
Department of Computer Science and Engineering (AIML)
Malla Reddy Engineering College for Women (Autonomous)
Hyderabad
India

K. VAISHNAVI
Department of Computer Science and Engineering (AIML)
Malla Reddy Engineering College for Women (Autonomous)
Hyderabad
India

Patel VAISHNAVI
Department of Computer Science and Engineering (AIML)
Malla Reddy Engineering College for Women (Autonomous)
Hyderabad
India

R. VANAJA
Department of Mathematics
Saveetha School of Engineering
Saveetha Institute of Medical and Technical Science
Chennai
India

Padam VARSHA
Department of Computer Science and Engineering (AIML)
Malla Reddy Engineering College for Women (Autonomous)
Hyderabad
India

Kolipaka VASAVI
Department of Computer Science and Engineering (AIML)
Malla Reddy Engineering College for Women (Autonomous)
Hyderabad
India

Index

A, B

C, D

E, F

G, H

I, K

L, M

N, P

R, S

T, U

V, Z

Other titles from

iSTE

in

Computer Engineering

2026

BHAMBRI Pankaj, DUTTA Pushan Kumar, KHAN Mudassir, STAROSTKA-PATYK Marta
Next-Gen Supply Chains: AI, Automation, and Sustainability in a Disrupted World

DARCHE Philippe
Computer Memories 1: Core Concepts
Computer Memories 2: Static Random-Access Memory

KUMAR Abhishek, BATTA Priya
AI in Orthopedic Trauma Care 1: Comparative Clinical Insights
AI in Orthopedic Trauma Care 2: Advances in Intelligent Imaging, Decision Support, and Rehabilitation

KUMAR Abhishek, BATTA Priya, AHUJA Sachin, RATHORE Pramod Singh
AI-driven Innovations in Physiotherapy and Oncology 3
AI-driven Innovations in Physiotherapy and Oncology 4
AI-driven Innovations in Physiotherapy and Oncology 5

KUMAR Abhishek, BATTA Priya, ANANTH J.P.
AI-driven Healthcare Innovations: Applications in Neurology and Medicine

KUMAR Abhishek, T. Ananth Kumar, DUBEY Ashutosh Kumar, SRIVASTAV Arun Lal, JUÁREZ-RAMÍREZ J. Reyes
AI and Wind Power 1: A Multifaceted Approach to Sustainable Energy
AI and Wind Power 2: Advancing Sustainability, Grid Integration, and Future Frameworks

MACHADO Carolina, DAVIM J. Paulo
Artificial Intelligence Technologies in Management and Engineering

MAHOUT Vincent, ROCACHER Thierry, AURIOL Guillaume
Programming of Embedded Systems: Applications to SM32F10x µControllers

UL HAQ Inam, KAK Saana Mehraj, GUPTA Anand Kumar, RAMZAN Muhammad Sher
Artificial Intelligence for Sustainable Energy Systems 1: Intelligent Technologies for Sustainable Energy Management
Artificial Intelligence for Sustainable Energy Systems 2: AI-Driven Innovations, Climate Intelligence, and Pathways to Net-Zero Energy

2025

CHIKH Azeddine
Systemic Approach to Categorizing and Modeling Requirements

KUMAR Abhishek, BATTA Priya, AHUJA Sachin, RATHORE Pramod Singh
AI-driven Innovations in Physiotherapy and Oncology 1
AI-driven Innovations in Physiotherapy and Oncology 2

TANEJA Ashu, KUMAR Abhishek, LIMKAR Suresh Vishnudas, OUAISSA Mariya, OUAISSA Mariyam
Driving Innovation through AI and Digital Twin for 6G Powered Sustainable Ultra Smart Cities

TANEJA Ashu, KUMAR Abhishek, LIMKAR Suresh Vishnudas, OUAISSA Mariya, OUAISSA Mariyam
6G Urban Innovation: AI and Digital Twin for Next-Gen Sustainable Cities

2024

CHAKRABORTY Rajdeep, GHOSH Anupam, KUMAR MANDAL Jyotsna, CHOUDHURY Tanupriya, CHATTERJEE Prasenjit
Smart Edge Computing: An Operation Research Perspective
(International Perspectives in Decision Analytics and Operations Research Set – Volume 2)

HOMÈS Bernard
Fundamentals of Software Testing (2nd edition, revised and updated)

JERBI Abdessalem
Discrete-Event Simulation: Concepts and Production in Arena

PRADHAN Devasis, KUMAR SAHU Prasanna, MYO TUN Hla, CHATTERJEE Prasenjit
Artificial and Cognitive Computing for Sustainable Healthcare Systems in Smart Cities
(International Perspectives in Decision Analytics and Operations Research Set – Volume 3)

2023

CHOUDHURY Tanupriya, KHANNA Abhirup, CHATTERJEE Prasenjit, UM Jung-Sup, BHATTACHARYA Abhishek
Blockchain Applications in Healthcare: Innovations and Practices
(International Perspectives in Decision Analytics and Operations Research Set – Volume 1)

PAI G A Vijayalakshmi
A Textbook of Data Structures and Algorithms 1: Mastering Linear Data Structures
A Textbook of Data Structures and Algorithms 2: Mastering Nonlinear Data Structures
A Textbook of Data Structures and Algorithms 3: Mastering Advanced Data Structures and Algorithm Design Strategies

2022

HOMÈS Bernard
Advanced Testing of Systems-of-Systems 1: Theoretical Aspects
Advanced Testing of Systems-of-Systems 2: Practical Aspects

MEHTA Shikha, TIWARI Sanju, SIARRY Patrick, JABBAR M.A.
Tools, Languages, Methodologies for Representing Semantics on the Web of Things

SIDHOM Sahbi, KADDOUR Amira
Systems and Uses of Digital Sciences for Knowledge Organization (Digital Tools and Uses Set – Volume 9)

ZAIDOUN Ameur Salem
Computer Science Security: Concepts and Tools

2021

DARCHE Philippe
Microprocessor 4: Core Concepts – Software Aspects
Microprocessor 5: Software and Hardware Aspects of Development, Debugging and Testing – The Microcomputer

DELHAYE Jean-Loïc
Inside the World of Computing: Technologies, Uses, Challenges

HARDIN Thérèse, JAUME Mathieu, PESSAUX François,
VIGUIÉ DONZEAU-GOUGE Véronique
Concepts and Semantics of Programming Languages 1: A Semantical Approach with OCaml and Python
Concepts and Semantics of Programming Languages 2: Modular and Object-oriented Constructs with OCaml, Python, C++, Ada and Java

MKADMI Abderrazak
Archives in The Digital Age: Preservation and the Right to be Forgotten (Digital Tools and Uses Set – Volume 8)

TOKLU Yusuf Cengiz, BEKDAŞ Gebrail, NIGDELI Sinan Melih
Metaheuristics for Structural Design and Analysis
(Optimization Heuristics Set – Volume 3)

2020

DARCHE Philippe
Microprocessor 1: Prolegomenes – Calculation and Storage Functions – Models of Computation and Computer Architecture
Microprocessor 2: Core Concepts – Communication in a Digital System
Microprocessor 3: Core Concepts – Hardware Aspects

DUVAUT Patrick, DALLOZ Xavier, MENGA David, KOEHL François, CHRIQUI Vidal, BRILL Joerg
Internet of Augmented Me, I.AM: Empowering Innovation for a New Sustainable Future

LAFFLY Dominique
TORUS 1 – Toward an Open Resource Using Services: Cloud Computing for Environmental Data
TORUS 2 – Toward an Open Resource Using Services: Cloud Computing for Environmental Data
TORUS 3 – Toward an Open Resource Using Services: Cloud Computing for Environmental Data

LAURENT Anne, LAURENT Dominique, MADERA Cédrine
Data Lakes
(Databases and Big Data Set – Volume 2)

OULHADJ Hamouche, DAACHI Boubaker, MENASRI Riad
Metaheuristics for Robotics
(Optimization Heuristics Set – Volume 2)

SADIQUI Ali
Computer Network Security

VENTRE Daniel
Artificial Intelligence, Cybersecurity and Cyber Defense

2019

BESBES Walid, DHOUIB Diala, WASSAN Niaz, MARREKCHI Emna
Solving Transport Problems: Towards Green Logistics

CLERC Maurice
Iterative Optimizers: Difficulty Measures and Benchmarks

GHLALA Riadh
Analytic SQL in SQL Server 2014/2016

TOUNSI Wiem
Cyber-Vigilance and Digital Trust: Cyber Security in the Era of Cloud Computing and IoT

2018

ANDRO Mathieu
Digital Libraries and Crowdsourcing
(Digital Tools and Uses Set – Volume 5)

ARNALDI Bruno, GUITTON Pascal, MOREAU Guillaume
Virtual Reality and Augmented Reality: Myths and Realities

CARDON Alain
Beyond Artificial Intelligence: From Human Consciousness to Artificial Consciousness

HOMAYOUNI S. Mahdi, FONTES Dalila B.M.M.
Metaheuristics for Maritime Operations
(Optimization Heuristics Set – Volume 1)

JEANSOULIN Robert
JavaScript and Open Data

PIVERT Olivier
NoSQL Data Models: Trends and Challenges
(Databases and Big Data Set – Volume 1)

SEDKAOUI Soraya
Data Analytics and Big Data

SALEH Imad, AMMI Mehdi, SZONIECKY Samuel
Challenges of the Internet of Things: Technology, Use, Ethics
(Digital Tools and Uses Set – Volume 7)

SZONIECKY Samuel
Ecosystems Knowledge: Modeling and Analysis Method for Information and Communication
(Digital Tools and Uses Set – Volume 6)

2017

BENMAMMAR Badr
Concurrent, Real-Time and Distributed Programming in Java: Threads, RTSJ and RMI

BOUHAÏ Nasreddine, SALEH Imad
Internet of Things: Evolutions and Innovations
(Digital Tools and Uses Set – Volume 4)

HÉLIODORE Frédéric, NAKIB Amir, ISMAIL Boussaad, OUCHRAA Salma, SCHMITT Laurent
Metaheuristics for Intelligent Electrical Networks
(Metaheuristics Set – Volume 10)

MA Haiping, SIMON Dan
Evolutionary Computation with Biogeography-based Optimization
(Metaheuristics Set – Volume 8)

PÉTROWSKI Alain, BEN-HAMIDA Sana
Evolutionary Algorithms
(Metaheuristics Set – Volume 9)

PAI G A Vijayalakshmi
Metaheuristics for Portfolio Optimization: An Introduction using MATLAB®
(Metaheuristics Set – Volume 11)

REYES-GARCIA Everardo
The Image-Interface: Graphical Supports for Visual Information
(Digital Tools and Uses Set – Volume 3)

REYES-GARCIA Everardo, BOUHAÏ Nasreddine
Designing Interactive Hypermedia Systems
(Digital Tools and Uses Set – Volume 2)

SZONIECKY Samuel, BOUHAÏ Nasreddine
Collective Intelligence and Digital Archives: Towards Knowledge Ecosystems
(Digital Tools and Uses Set – Volume 1)

2016

BLUM Christian, FESTA Paola
Metaheuristics for String Problems in Bio-informatics
(Metaheuristics Set – Volume 6)

DEROUSSI Laurent
Metaheuristics for Logistics
(Metaheuristics Set – Volume 4)

DHAENENS Clarisse, JOURDAN Laetitia
Metaheuristics for Big Data
(Metaheuristics Set – Volume 5)

LABADIE Nacima, PRINS Christian, PRODHON Caroline
Metaheuristics for Vehicle Routing Problems
(Metaheuristics Set – Volume 3)

LEROY Laure
Eyestrain Reduction in Stereoscopy

LUTTON Evelyne, PERROT Nathalie, TONDA Alberto
Evolutionary Algorithms for Food Science and Technology
(Metaheuristics Set – Volume 7)

MAGOULÈS Frédéric, ZHAO Hai-Xiang
Data Mining and Machine Learning in Building Energy Analysis

RIGO Michel
Advanced Graph Theory and Combinatorics

ZELM Martin, DOUMEINGTS Guy, MENDONÇA Joao Pedro
Enterprise Interoperability: in the Digitized and Networked Factory of the Future

2015

BARBIER Franck, RECOUSSINE Jean-Luc
COBOL Software Modernization: From Principles to Implementation with the BLU AGE® Method

CHEN Ken
Performance Evaluation by Simulation and Analysis with Applications to Computer Networks

CLERC Maurice
Guided Randomness in Optimization
(Metaheuristics Set – Volume 1)

DURAND Nicolas, GIANAZZA David, GOTTELAND Jean-Baptiste, ALLIOT Jean-Marc
Metaheuristics for Air Traffic Management
(Metaheuristics Set – Volume 2)

MAGOULÈS Frédéric, ROUX François-Xavier, HOUZEAUX Guillaume
Parallel Scientific Computing

MUNEESAWANG Paisarn, YAMMEN Suchart
Visual Inspection Technology in the Hard Disk Drive Industry

2014

BOULANGER Jean-Louis
Formal Methods Applied to Industrial Complex Systems
Formal Methods Applied to Complex Systems: Implementation of the B Method

EXPOSITO Ernesto, DIOP Codé
Smart SOA Platforms in Cloud Computing Architectures

GARDI Frédéric, BENOIST Thierry, DARLAY Julien, ESTELLON Bertrand, MEGEL Romain
Mathematical Programming Solver based on Local Search

KRICHEN Saoussen, CHAOUACHI Jouhaina
Graph-related Optimization and Decision Support Systems

LARRIEU Nicolas, VARET Antoine
Rapid Prototyping of Software for Avionics Systems: Model-oriented Approaches for Complex Systems Certification

LAURAS Matthieu, ZELM Martin, ARCHIMÈDE Bernard, BÉNABEN Frédérick, DOUMEINGTS Guy
Enterprise Interoperability: Interoperability for Agility, Resilience and Plasticity of Collaborations

OUSSALAH Mourad Chabane
Software Architecture 1
Software Architecture 2

QUESNEL Flavien
Scheduling of Large-scale Virtualized Infrastructures: Toward Cooperative Management

RIGO Michel
Formal Languages, Automata and Numeration Systems 1: Introduction to Combinatorics on Words
Formal Languages, Automata and Numeration Systems 2: Applications to Recognizability and Decidability

SAINT-DIZIER Patrick
Musical Rhetoric: Foundations and Annotation Schemes

TOUATI Sid, DUPONT DE DINECHIN Benoit
Advanced Backend Code Optimization

2013

ANDRÉ Étienne, SOULAT Romain
The Inverse Method: Parametric Verification of Real-time Embedded Systems

BOULANGER Jean-Louis
Safety Management for Software-based Equipment

DELAHAYE Daniel, PUECHMOREL Stéphane
Modeling and Optimization of Air Traffic

FRANCOPOULO Gil
LMF — Lexical Markup Framework

GHEDIRA Khaled
Constraint Satisfaction Problems: CSP Formalisms and Techniques

GOVAERT Gérard, NADIF Mohamed
Co-Clustering: Models, Algorithms and Applications

LANDRAGIN Frédérick
Man–Machine Dialogue: Design and Challenges

LUCAS Laurent, LOSCOS Céline, REMION Yannick
3D Video: Models, From Capture to Diffusion

ROCHANGE Christine, UHRIG Sascha, SAINRAT Pascal
Time Predictable Architectures

WAHBI Mohamed
Algorithms and Ordering Heuristics for Distributed Constraint Satisfaction Problems

ZELM Martin, VAN SINDEREN Marten, FERRAIRA PIRES Luis, DOUMEINGTS Guy
Enterprise Interoperability: Research and Applications in the Service-oriented Ecosystem

2012

ARBOLEDA Hugo, ROYER Jean-Claude
Model-Driven and Software Product Line Engineering

BLANCHET Gérard, DUPOUY Bertrand
Computer Architecture

BOULANGER Jean-Louis
Industrial Use of Formal Methods: Formal Verification
Formal Methods: Industrial Use from Model to the Code

CALVARY Gaëlle, DELOT Thierry, SÈDES Florence, TIGLI Jean-Yves
Computer Science and Ambient Intelligence

MAHOUT Vincent
Assembly Language Programming: ARM Cortex-M3 2.0: Organization, Innovation and Territory

MARLET Renaud
Program Specialization

SOTO Maria, SEVAUX Marc, ROSSI André, LAURENT Johann
Memory Allocation Problems in Embedded Systems: Optimization Methods

2011

BICHOT Charles-Edmond, SIARRY Patrick
Graph Partitioning

BOULANGER Jean-Louis
Static Analysis of Software: The Abstract Interpretation

CAFERRA Ricardo
Logic for Computer Science and Artificial Intelligence

KORDON Fabrice, HADDAD Serge, PAUTET Laurent, PETRUCCI Laure
Distributed Systems: Design and Algorithms
Models and Analysis in Distributed Systems

LORCA Xavier
Tree-based Graph Partitioning Constraint

RIDHA MAHJOUB A.
Progress in Combinatorial Optimization: ISCO2010

TRUCHET Charlotte, ASSAYAG Gerard
Constraint Programming in Music

VICAT-BLANC Pascale, GOGLIN Brice, GUILLIER Romaric, SOUDAN Sébastien
Computing Networks: From Cluster to Cloud Computing

2010

AUBRUN Christophe, SIMON Daniel, SONG Ye-Qiong
Co-design Approaches for Dependable Networked Control Systems

AUDIBERT Pierre
Mathematics for Informatics and Computer Science

BABAU Jean-Philippe, BLAY-FORNARINO Mireille, CHAMPEAU Joël, ROBERT Sylvain, SABETTA Antonino
Model Driven Engineering for Distributed Real-Time Systems: MARTE Modeling, Model Transformations and their Usages

BOULANGER Jean-Louis
Safety of Computer Architectures

SIGAUD Olivier, BUFFET Olivier
Markov Decision Processes in Artificial Intelligence

MONMARCHÉ Nicolas, GUINAND Frédérick, SIARRY Patrick
Artificial Ants

SOLNON Christine
Ant Colony Optimization and Constraint Programming

2009

FOURNIER Jean-Claude
Graph Theory and Applications: with exercises and problems

GUÉDON Jeanpierre
The Mojette Transform: theory and applications

JARD Claude, ROUX Olivier H.
Communicating Embedded Systems: Software and Design

LECOUTRE Christophe
Constraint Networks: Techniques and Algorithms

2008

BANÂTRE Michel, MARRON Pedro Jose, OLLERO Anibal, WOLITZ Adam
Cooperating Embedded Systems and Wireless Sensor Networks

MERZ Stephan, NAVET Nicolas
Modeling and Verification of Real-time Systems: Formalisms and Software Tools

PASCHOS Vangelis Th.
Combinatorial Optimization and Theoretical Computer Science: Interfaces and Perspectives

WALDNER Jean-Baptiste
Nanocomputers and Swarm Intelligence

2007

BENHAMOU Frédéric, JUSSIEN Narendra, O'SULLIVAN Barry
Trends in Constraint Programming

JUSSIEN Narendra
A to Z of Sudoku

2006

BABAU Jean-Philippe, CHAMPEAU Joël, GÉRARD Sébastien
From MDD Concepts to Experiments and Illustrations – DRES 2006

HABRIAS Henri, FRAPPIER Marc
Software Specification Methods: An Overview Using a Case Study

MURAT Cécile, PASCHOS Vangelis Th.
Probabilistic Combinatorial Optimization on Graphs

PANETTO Hervé, BOUDJLIDA Nacer
Interoperability for Enterprise Software and Applications: Proceedings of the Workshops and the Doctorial Symposium of the Second IFAC/IFIP I-ESA International Conference: EI2N, WSI, IS-TSPQ 2006

2005

GÉRARD Sébastien, BABAU Jean-Philippe, CHAMPEAU Joël
Model Driven Engineering for Distributed Real Time Embedded Systems

PANETTO Hervé
Interoperability of Enterprise Software and Applications: Workshops of the INTEROP-ESA 2005 International Conference (EI2N, WSI, ISIDI and IEHENA 2005)

Printed and bound by CPI Group (UK) Ltd, Croydon, CR0 4YY

13/09/2026

14961015-0007